As Long as the Rivers Run

As Long as the Rivers Run: Hydroelectric Development and Native Communities in Western Canada

JAMES B. WALDRAM

THE UNIVERSITY OF MANITOBA PRESS

© The University of Manitoba Press 1988
Winnipeg, Manitoba R3T 2N2
Printed in Canada

Design and maps by Norman Schmidt

Jacket photographs:
Greg McCullough, Canada Department of
Fisheries and Oceans (shoreline);
Western Canadian Pictorial
Index, 1324–39560 (aerial view of dam).

Treaty No. 5 (Appendix 1)
reproduced with permission
of the Minister of Supply and
Services Canada.

Cataloguing in Publication Data

Waldram, James B. (James Burgess)

    As long as the rivers run

    Bibliography: p.
    Includes index.
    ISBN 0-88755-143-2

1. Indians of North America - Prairie Provinces -
Social conditions. 2. Métis - Prairie Provinces -
Social conditions.* 3. Hydroelectric power plants -
Social aspects - Prairie Provinces. 4. Hydroelectric
power plants - Political aspects - Prairie Provinces.
5. Hydroelectric power plants - Environmental aspects -
Prairie Provinces. I. Title.
E78.M25W34 1988   305.8'97'0712   C88-098050-8

For Linda, Kaitlin and Amara

Contents

Maps

Preface

This book is about the politics of hydroelectric dam construction as it concerns the Native communities which are inevitably located in the vast hinterland areas where such development takes place. The emphasis is on historic continuity. The process of hydro development in this century, and particularly the manner in which Indian and Métis people have been removed physically and bureaucratically from their water resources, is paralleled by the treaty and scrip processes of the late nineteenth and early twentieth centuries. These early processes had the effect of removing the Native people from most of their land to facilitate non-Native settlement and resource exploitation. What little land they officially retained was augmented by their utilization of relatively large tracts of other land for hunting and trapping, and the use of waterways for fishing and transportation. But hydro developments after 1950 have resulted in a steady erosion of these opportunities. Reserve land has been flooded. Some lakes and rivers have been impounded, and others have dried up. The social, cultural and economic consequences of hydro dam construction, while little known to the general public, have been devastating to the people who happened to be located along the prime rivers and lakes. Furthermore, in their struggle to protect their rights, to have mitigative measures undertaken, and to receive proper compensation for damages, they have been frustrated by both provincial and federal governments, and by hydro utilities and industries. We might all wonder why such frustration should exist. Surely development projects which cost in the hundreds of millions of dollars would include the provision of mitigation and compensation measures. Surely the people to be affected would receive the benefits of a development designed to benefit all. Surely these people would be better off after construction of the dams than they were before. Unfortunately, such is not the case.

That I have come to write this book is, in many ways, fortuitous. Before I became a graduate student in applied anthropology at the University of Manitoba, I knew little of hydro projects and Native communities. Searching for a thesis topic, I was carefully guided toward the hydro issue in northern Manitoba by my two advisors, John Matthiasson and William (Skip) Koolage. Both of them had been active in supporting the struggle of Native people in the North vis-a-vis hydro projects, and though having shared the loss of the political battle to stop such development they retained an active interest in investigating the effects these had had on the people. Hence, my interests came to mirror theirs: I was concerned primarily with the social and economic consequences of hydro projects on Native communities. My first investigation took place at Easterville.

Easterville had already been studied by anthropologist Michael Landa, and I proposed to continue the study of the long-term consequences of the Grand Rapids Dam on that community. While there, I met extensively with former and current members of the band council, and began to see how complex the political story of dam building had been. And the story was continuing; negotiations were under way to try to convince the Manitoba government and Manitoba Hydro to fulfill the provisions of an agreement they had signed with the people some fifteen years earlier. The agreement, I thought at the time, looked surprisingly like a treaty.

While working in Manitoba, I became increasingly aware of the Churchill River Diversion Project further to the north, and the community of South Indian Lake. Feeling that I was only now beginning to develop an expertise in socioeconomic impact assessment, I decided to initiate a new study in South Indian Lake as part of my doctoral studies at the University of Connecticut. My advisors there, Pertti Pelto, Robert Bee and Norman Chance, were very supportive of the research. Again, my primary concerns were the socioeconomic effects of the project, but it soon became clear that for the people of South Indian Lake, as for the residents of Easterville, the political story was just as important. I proceeded to gather all information I could on the politics of the Churchill River Diversion, in conjunction with my impact study. The South Indian Lake story had direct parallels with that of Easterville, but at this point the notion of a common process had yet to emerge in my mind.

Upon moving to Saskatchewan, I was alerted through the media to the predicament of the community of Cumberland House, which had apparently experienced negative effects resulting from the construction of the Squaw Rapids Dam, upstream on the Saskatchewan River. I thought that much could be learned through an investigation of the politics of this development, and buried myself in the offices of the Saskatchewan Archives Board. When I emerged, the parallels between the Cumberland House saga and that of Easterville and South Indian Lake became clear. The processes of hydro project planning and negotiations with the Native people in the hinterland regions were almost identical. And the parallels were more than mere coincidence: many of the role players seemed to surface in more than one community's story. Furthermore, the processes by which these people had come to be victimized by hydro dam construction were so similar to the processes by which they had lost their lands through treaty making and scrip allocation that I knew I had found the link. The story had to be told.

Researching the topic of the politics of hydroelectric development and Native communities has necessitated the utilization of a wide variety of archival and interview material, and especially material generally unavailable from archival sources. Unfortunately, the period under consideration in this book, 1957 to 1988, is one in which there were severe archival restrictions. I have been able to access important materials only through much hard work, and in some cases only with much luck.

While working in Easterville, Manitoba, in 1978 and 1979, I was informed by the band chief that there was a large number of boxes filled with paper and other materials in the back rooms of the band office. No one recalled exactly what was in them, but he suggested I might like to have a look. Mixed in with reams of government reports and miscellaneous band council documents, I found an enormous volume of papers, memoranda and letters dealing with the construction of the Grand Rapids Dam and the relocation of the Indian band. Many of these were copies that had been forwarded to the band and subsequently forgotten. A copying machine was made available to me to reproduce these documents for my own purposes, but its repeated failures meant that handwritten notes of many documents had to be taken. These data form the backbone of the chapter on Easterville.

Good fortune also followed me to South Indian Lake, Manitoba. One day during research there in 1982, I happened by the community council office. The council clerk was in the process of cleaning out a back room, and in effect throwing out everything therein. Noticing the large volume of papers awaiting disposal, and recalling my experiences at Easterville, I requested a reprieve, and was able to comb through the materials, selecting whatever I wished. To my surprise, I found valuable documents pertaining to the early period of the construction of the Churchill River Diversion, and the involvement of the community in political and legal action.

At Cumberland House, Saskatchewan, my luck ran out. Arriving there in 1984, I learnt to my horror that, a few years previous, an overzealous council clerk had cleaned out the back rooms and had destroyed a large volume of paper. It is believed that whatever records the community had that pertained to the construction of the Squaw Rapids Dam were lost at that time. As a result, I have had to resort to the public archival holdings to detail the Cumberland House story, with the result that the chapter on Cumberland House is not as comprehensive as are the others.

Other avenues of research have been made available to me as well. I obtained much written material from lawyers and various government sources, and from private groups and individuals, many of whom were intimately involved in the issues and who agree with me that the story needs to be told. In keeping with sound social science research principles, all archival material, and hence material generally available to the public, is so indicated in the end notes to each chapter. Other written materials, or notes made from written materials, which are not as yet in the public domain, are in my possession.

In all three communities, I have conducted both formal and informal interviews with local residents and politicians. I have also interviewed lawyers and other individuals who have played, or continue to play, a role in the political story of these communities. But many of the most important events took place many years ago, in some cases almost thirty, and memories fade over time. The oral tradition of the communities retains only the general themes, and specific details are lost. This was proven true not only of the local people who were role players in the political arena, but also of the lawyers who defended their interests. For this reason, the most important details have been derived from written sources, and these invariably have been authored by non-Natives and non-residents of the communities. In many ways, this book is as much about the lawyers and governments involved as it is about the communities and the Native people who lived in them.

This book, then, is the end product of a period of research which spans eight years. It is intended for a wide audience, though it adheres to the rigours of social science methodology and documentation. First and foremost, the book is intended for the Native communities themselves, and the people who gave so much of their time to the research. They have a genuine interest in having their story documented, and with the passage of time many of the specific details of that story have become blurred. I hope that the book stands the true test of research and publishing and is accepted by them as a faithful rendering of a significant part of their history.

The book is intended for others as well. Academics interested in Native history in Canada or in the Canadian political process should find some valuable information contained herein. Lawyers who currently are representing or will in the future represent Native communities will see the trials and tribulations of their colleagues whose attempts to defend the interests and rights of Native people were frequently frustrated and thwarted. Elected representatives of government, and government bureaucrats too, will be able to see the lessons of the past and, I would hope, come to realize that as this country's first citizens, the Native peoples deserved fairer treatment. It is not too late to redress past wrongs.

It has been a century or more since most Native people in western Canada signed treaties or were given scrip to simultaneously acknowledge their aboriginal rights and surrender many of those rights. The treaties were to have lasted "as long as the rivers run." The hydroelectric era seems to represent both the symbolic termination of these agreements and the re-emergence of the treaty and scrip processes which once again have allowed governments to exploit Native resources for the "common good." New agreements have been signed. But the rivers no longer run.

My analysis begins in Chapter 1 with an introduction to the central issues addressed in this book, and an overview of hydroelectric development in Canada. Chapter 2 contains an analysis of the treaties and of scrip, the two mechanisms by which the Canadian government secured the unfettered title to most of western Canada. I discuss the processes of negotiation and implementation in order to establish the continuity of arguments which I present in subsequent chapters. In Chapter 3, I present individual community case studies, beginning with the story of Cumberland House and the Squaw Rapids Dam. This is followed in Chapter 4 with the story of Easterville and the Grand Rapids Dam, and in Chapter 5 with the story of South Indian Lake and the Churchill River Diversion Project. In Chapter 6 I discuss the parallels between the treaty and scrip processes and negotiations during the hydro era, particularly within the context of the philosophy of the "common good," and of the likely future of Native communities in the new era of hydro dam building in Canada.

Acknowledgements

After eight years of researching the topic of hydroelectric development, I have found the development of a comprehensive list of people who have assisted me a formidable task. Since I owe so many favours, I will seek now to begin repayment; I apologize in advance for those whom I have most certainly neglected to mention.

I am, first of all, indebted to my former academic advisors, who guided me through the years and provided the necessary training and understanding with which to tackle a very complex issue. They are: John S. Matthiasson and William W. Koolage, Jr., at the University of Manitoba; and Pertti J. Pelto, Robert L. Bee and Norman A. Chance at the University of Connecticut.

I would like to acknowledge the assistance of Percy Mink, Riley Easter, Alpheus Brass, Percy George, Marcel Ledoux, and John and Chris Andrews in Easterville; and in The Pas, Henry Wilson and Oscar Lathlin of the Swampy Cree Tribal Council, and Rick Hay of the Freshwater Fish Marketing Board. I would also like to acknowledge the assistance of Noah Soulier, Willie Moose, Hubert Moose, Alfred Dumas, Paul Thomas, Steve Ducharme, Fred Moose, Louis and Dora Dysart, Riley Moose, David Moose, Robert B. Dysart, Graham Montgomery, Peter Fulton and Brian Murray in South Indian Lake. I also appreciate the assistance given to me by Victor John Martin of the Manitoba Keewatinowi Okimakinak in Thompson. I am indebted to Bill Carrière, Moise Dussion and John Carrière in Cumberland House. In Winnipeg, the following have been of great assistance to me: Joe Keeper and Ken Young, Northern Flood Committee; Ralph Abramson and Murray Wagner, Treaty and Aboriginal Rights Research

Centre; Robert Newbury, Drew Bodaly and Bob Hecky of the Freshwater Institute; Harvey Pollock; Harold Buchwald; Yude Henteleff; Patti Rennick; and Ron Harder.

Some of the data gathered during the first phase of this research was initially published in the *Canadian Journal of Native Studies*, vol. 4, no. 2, 1984.

A variety of agencies and organizations have provided funds to support my research, some of which has resulted in the production of data for this book. These include: the Northern Studies Committee, the University of Manitoba; the University of Connecticut Research Foundation; the National Science Foundation, Doctoral Dissertation Improvement Grant No. BNS-8203066; the Wenner-Gren Foundation for Anthropological Research Grant No. 4141; Sigma Xi, the Scientific Society; the Treaty and Aboriginal Rights Research Centre, and the First Nations Confederacy; and the Social Sciences and Humanities Research Council of Canada, Doctoral Fellowship. A time-release research grant from the University of Saskatchewan allowed me to commit more time to the writing of this book than otherwise would have been available.

I would like to thank Laurie Barron and two anonymous reviewers for the Social Science Federation of Canada for reading and commenting on a draft of this manuscript. I would also like to thank Carol Dahlstrom of the University of Manitoba Press for her careful editing of the manuscript.

Finally, I would like to acknowledge the assistance of my wife, Linda Jaine, who not only encouraged me throughout much of the research and writing of this book, but who also contributed her extensive knowledge of the Native political scene and her considerable editorial skills.

This book has been published with the help of a grant from the Social Science Federation of Canada, using funds provided by the Social Sciences and Humanities Research Council of Canada.

This book expresses the views of the author alone and not necessarily those of any individual and agency acknowledged here. I remain solely responsible for errors of fact or interpretation.

As Long as the Rivers Run

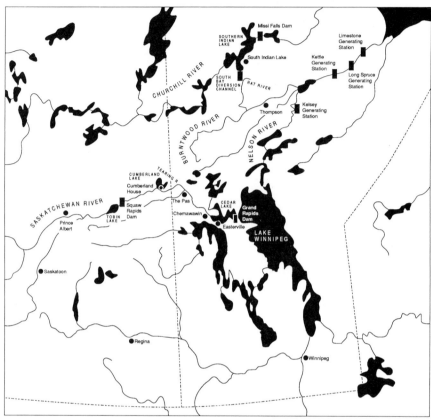

Map 1. The Study Region

Hydroelectric Development and Native People in Canada

1

We want to tell a story, our story, of what can happen to Indian people when their land is flooded by a hydro project and their way of life is forced to change. . . . It is only ten years since we left the home we had chosen about one hundred years ago when the white men first came into our country and told us that we must give up our land and settle down to live on a reserve which we chose at that time. We were told that this reserve would be our home as long as the sun shines, the rivers flow, and the grasses grow. [1]

The treaty-making era between the Canadian government and the Indians of western Canada began in 1871, with the signing of Treaties One and Two in what is now southern Manitoba and Saskatchewan. The purpose of these treaties, as with most others, was to obtain title to the land and thereby free it for settlement by eastern Canadians and immigrants from European countries. Subsequent "numbered" treaties had the same purpose, and had the same consequences for the Indians of the West. Indeed, it is hard to believe that the Indians would have so readily surrendered their land had they been informed of the curtailment of their rights that would follow.

For the Métis of western Canada, the process of land alienation both parallels and contrasts that of the Indians. The Manitoba Act of 1870, the legislation which formed the Province of Manitoba after Louis Riel's Provisional Government voluntarily relinquished its authority, acknowledged the Métis' rights to the land as a result of their Indian heritage. But rather than signing treaties, the federal government decided to issue scrip, administered on an individual basis, which served the dual purpose of getting the Métis to surrender their interest in the land, and of freeing the land for settlement. Perhaps even more quickly than the Indians, the Métis realized the extent to which their heritage, the land, had been taken from them.

The comment offered by the Indian person at the beginning of this chapter poignantly describes the fact that Native people have been asked to accommodate non-Natives since the days of first contact. If indeed the Indian people were told that the treaties and their reserves would last for "as long as . . . the rivers flow," then what can be made of the fact that, as one northern Métis explained in 1984, "the rivers are no longer rivers."[2] What has happened in the one hundred or so years since the treaties were signed that, at least symbolically, appears to violate the spirit and intent of the treaties? Quite simply, what has happened is the dawning of the era of the hydroelectric megaproject. This book is about that era.

If it is true that the Indians of western Canada were promised that the treaties would remain in force for "as long as the rivers run," then what can be made of the fact that hydroelectric developments have dammed or diverted many of those rivers? When the water levels in lakes and rivers downstream from hydro dams become bone dry as water backs up in huge reservoirs, has there been a violation of the treaties? When Indian reserve land has been flooded, has the spirit of the treaties been broken? In the middle of winter, when a Métis hunter on a skidoo breaks through the thin ice downstream of a dam, has his heritage been sacrificed?

It is my argument that the philosophies and procedures operating during the nineteenth-century treaty-making and scrip commissions are once again evident in the efforts of the hydroelectric developers in dealing with existing Native[3] claims, legal or moral, to these water resources. The attitude of the treaty makers has remained intact through the years; and the processes whereby governments and public and private electrical power utilities have secured the right to construct hydro facilities, and thereby alter and frequently destroy the livelihood of many Indian and Métis peoples, represents a continuity with the past. The processes are similar: a resource is identified as valuable to the general society, and the Natives who are using that resource must be convinced that they should surrender it for the "common good." Negotiations frequently, though not always, ensue, and agreements are occasionally signed. Native communities may even be relocated to make room for the development. Once the resource has been secured and the Native people have been appeased, they are largely ignored. Poverty and hardship frequently result, as the people discover that they can no longer make a living from the resources, and particularly the waterways, of their traditional territories. Disagreements and arguments develop over what was promised at pre-development meetings, and over the interpretation and implementation of the signed agreements. Legal action or mediation frequently is employed by Natives to seek redress, but generally their interest is made subservient to that of Canadian society.

There comes to mind a profound sixteenth-century Franciscan proverb: "Where there are no Indians, there is no wealth."[4] The early Spanish explorers and conquistadors were aware that the Indians of the New World had already identified the "wealth" of their lands, though it may have been in a different form or used for a different purpose. Simply put, if there were no Indians in a given territory, there could be no resources of value to the Europeans. Such a view is as appropriate to Canada as it is to the Latin American context in which the proverb was coined. In Canada, the treaty-making process was designed to remove, and had the effect of removing, the Indian people from valuable resources; the scrip process had the same effect for the Métis. The land was made available for agricultural settlement, and resources such as the forests and minerals fueled the newly developing economy of the Canadian West. The small parcels of land reserved for the Indians were generally not designed to contain resources of value to Canadian society. It seemed that the Native people had lost control of every conceivable source of wealth as identified by non-Natives. Once the land had been secured, the Native inhabitants became a non-issue, at least for a time. But eventually, with changes in technology, a new source of wealth was targeted. The powerful rivers of the North, utilized by the Native people both in precontact and post-contact times, were identified as sources of electricity that would supply the increasing demand for energy by industry and private consumers.

The rivers, like the land a century earlier, were not unoccupied or unused. They were used by the Native people, and they represented a resource of immense value. In fact, it could be easily argued that the true backbone of the northern Native economy was not, and is not, the land, but rather the lakes, rivers and streams. Their service as transportation corridors was evident; but perhaps less evident was the interrelationship among the waterways, the Natives, and the animals they hunted. As one Indian analyst described it: "Water is life. The rivers are the veins of Mother Earth for Indians."[5] However, as the Franciscan proverb would seem to predict, the Native people, largely forgotten by the national society once their resources had been obtained, would, by their use of the water resources, once again point the way to renewed development.

Native people, of course, do not "own" the water resources in a private-property sense, and no mention of ownership was made in the treaties. However, Natives have utilized the waterways "since time immemorial" and believe that these resources, like the land, vegetation and animals, were given to them by the Creator for their use and benefit. Some compelling legal issues have developed in recent years surrounding the extent to which Natives have riparian rights.[6] Nonetheless, it has been the view of the provincial governments and their utilities that Native people have no special rights to the waterways, and hydro developments have proceeded accordingly. The basis of the argument presented by government is that the waterways are a common property resource, and that development should be undertaken in the public interest, for the "common good."

My purpose, then, is to detail the processes whereby Native interest in the use of the water resources was sacrificed for the "common good." I investigate this issue through micro-level analyses, by examining the political process in the context of hydro development as it pertains to three Native communities and to three different hydro projects.

The three communities to be discussed, Easterville and South Indian Lake in Manitoba, and Cumberland House in Saskatchewan, are excellent subjects for such an analysis. All three are Cree and Cree-Métis communities in the Treaty Five area; all are located on major river systems; and all experienced hydro development within a decade of each other. Yet the differences among the communities are also noteworthy, particularly in the way they differ in significant legal and cultural contexts. The story of Easterville is one of a predominantly status- and treaty-Indian reserve community; that of South Indian Lake, a status- and treaty-Indian non-reserve community; and that of Cumberland House, a predominantly Métis community. In all three, a minority population of Natives, either Métis or non-status Indian, in the cases of Easterville and South Indian Lake, and status-treaty Indians in the case of Cumberland House, compounds the stories. As I shall demonstrate, while their geographical location and inclusion in the Treaty-Five area accounts for some of the parallels in the treatment of the three communities by various governments and hydro utilities, the differing cultural and, more important, the legal statuses of the three communities explains in large part both the political tactics adopted by the relevant governments to execute their development plans and the tactics of the particular Native communities to defend their interests.

HYDROELECTRIC DEVELOPMENT
FROM COAST TO COAST

For many Canadians, the extent to which the country is dependent upon hydroelectricity would probably be surprising. We tend not to think about the source of our heat and lighting. Other sources of energy seem to attract more attention, especially in the media; for example, the world-wide oil crisis in the late 1970s, and the nuclear reactor accidents at Three Mile Island and Chernobyl more recently. For many Native communities these issues have been relatively remote. But living in the shadow of major hydroelectric dams, and experiencing daily the environmental disruptions they cause, northern Native people have developed an acute awareness of the dangers of this "safe" source of energy.[7]

Hydroelectric development has for many years been seen as highly desirable by provincial utilities. Canada is blessed with enormous hydro potential from the many massive rivers that cut through the land. Small-scale water power projects have been common throughout the country for many years, providing relatively inexpensive, pollution-free and renewable electricity. It is only in the last few decades that engineering developments have produced a dramatic change in the focus of hydro development. Sophisticated new technology has allowed for the harnessing of rivers on an unprecedented scale. The small, local power projects became much less prominent as the era of the hydro megaproject was ushered in. Enormous dams and control structures have been designed to provide power on a regional, national and even international scale. While previously the small local projects had had an insignificant effect on the environment, these new monolithic structures have drastically altered environmental conditions by inundating thousands of square kilometres of territory, and occasionally forcing the relocation of entire communities.[8] The damage to fragile ecosystems has been significant, yet the developers, both industrial corporations and provincial and federal governments have tenaciously clung to the common misconception that hydro power is relatively problem free. The Government of Manitoba, for instance, has advertised its "awesome energy reserves" from hydro power as a way of attracting industry to the province.[9] Manitoba has produced public relations materials that declare hydroelectricity a "nonpolluting energy source" which "will never run out" and which gives Manitoba "relative freedom from environmental problems."[10] There are many environmentalists and northern Native people in that province who would dispute such assertions.

It is the southern-based industries and consumers who have reaped the benefits of the development of relatively inexpensive power; and it is the northern residents, who are mostly Native people, who have suffered to attain it, since the truly massive hydro projects in Canada are located in the northern regions on the major river systems, and not in the south or near cities. The ironies of such development abound, but nowhere are they more evident than in the fact that Native communities located near, or otherwise affected by, hydro dams do not obtain free power as a matter of policy. Electricity rates may be even higher in such communities than in the south![11] And it is not an uncommon occurrence for Native householders in these areas to have their electricity disconnected for non-payment of bills, even in the middle of winter. It is brutally ironic that the very construction of the hydro dams has been a primary contributor to the poverty of these people through the destruction of local resources and economic opportunities.

The actual extent to which Native communities in the north have experienced hydro development and have been affected by it is generally not known by analysts of northern development. There has been a tendency among them to concentrate on pipelines, mercury pollution, and comprehensive Native land claims, especially by the media. In order to grasp the exent to which hydro dams have become a fact of life for many northern Native communities, it would be fruitful to detail, province by province and for the Yukon Territory, the major hydro projects and the Natives' reactions to them. By necessity, such a review can be only cursory.

1 Quebec: The most famous hydro project in Canada, and known throughout the world, is the James Bay Project in northern Quebec. Actually a series of large dams on the La Grande River, this project has remained in the public eye for many years, and has recently attracted new attention with the return of Robert Bourassa as Quebec's Premier. A great deal has been written about this project, and about the Indian and Inuit reactions to it, by both Natives and non-Natives. Indeed, despite extensive hydro development in other parts of Canada, James Bay has attained the paramount position among hydro projects whenever Native rights are considered.

In 1912, when northern Quebec was transferred from Canada to

Quebec, statutes were passed requiring Quebec to both recognize the Natives' aboriginal rights and obtain the surrender of these rights.[12] However, in the absence of any urgent need for the northern lands, Quebec was lax in executing its part of the agreement. And since no treaties were actually signed, the Native people claimed ownership of the land when the James Bay Project was announced in 1971. In the words of Billy Diamond, ex-Chief of the Grand Council of the Crees (of Quebec), "The issue for us was not merely a land claim settlement: it was a fight for our survival as a people and the survival of our way of life."[13] They took this argument to court and, in a brief but monumental judgement, Mr. Justice Albert Malouf of the Quebec Superior Court agreed. An interlocutory injunction to stop construction was awarded. However, one week later, the Quebec Court of Appeal suspended the Malouf judgement. The three judges said: "It is, then, the general and public interest of the people of Quebec which is opposed to the interests of about 2,000 of its inhabitants. We believe that these two interests cannot be compared at this stage of the proceedings."[14]

Even though the Malouf judgement was quickly overturned, however, the Native people in Quebec had gained an important bargaining lever: the Court of Appeal made no reference to the question of aboriginal rights, and hence this aspect of Malouf's ruling in favour of the Indians remained unchallenged. The effect was to force the Quebec government to the bargaining table to negotiate the surrender of the traditional lands of the Cree and Inuit. The result of the bargaining process was the James Bay and Northern Quebec Agreement, signed in 1975. This massive document, some 450 pages in length, was hailed as a landmark and a model for all outstanding Native claims settlements. While nevertheless flawed, the agreement did secure for the Native people a measure of legislated control over some of their traditional lands, and a capital base from which to finance new self-governing institutions.[15]

The James Bay Project has overshadowed other hydro developments in Quebec just as it has done to those in other parts of the country. The hunting territories of the Montagnais Indians, to the east of the James Bay Cree, have been seriously threatened since 1940, when the Aluminum Company of Canada (ALCAN) began construction of relatively small hydro dams to provide power for their mining and smelting operations. Hydro-Quebec has also been constructing dams in Montagnais territory. At present, there are thirteen large power plants and five hydro reservoirs in Montagnais territory, as well as a number of smaller, local power production facilities. The Montagnais themselves have, until recently, voiced little opposition to these projects. However, like the Cree to the west of them prior to the James Bay and Northern Quebec Agreement, the Montagnais feel that they have aboriginal rights to the land. Only in the last few years have they begun to mobilize politically, having just created the Conseil Attikamek-Montagnais. While the direction that the group will take has not yet been clearly formulated, it has indicated that it will not follow the model of the James Bay settlement.[16]

2 Ontario: Despite enormous potential, Ontario has actually built very few hydroelectric dams. The energy debate in Ontario seems to have concentrated more on the province's nuclear generating program, particularly the need for and safety of large nuclear plants at Pickering and Darlington, near Toronto. Nonetheless, Ontario has developed plans for the development of the hydro potential of many of its northern rivers.

The northern Ontario Ojibwa communities of Grassy Narrows and White Dog are infamous in Canada, and to some extent internationally, because of the mercury pollution that was discovered in the English–Wabigoon river system in 1970. The consequences of that pollution were devastating and forced a fundamental re-evaluation of human-environment relationships and the plight of northern Native people.[17] Little known, however, is that prior to the mercury pollution the two communities experienced the negative effects of hydro dam construction. Other Native communities in the region were also affected.

As early as the 1920s, hydro projects were completed on Lac Seul, including a diversion of the Ogoki River. This project caused flooding of graveyards belonging to the Lac Seul Indian Band.[18] In 1958, Ontario Hydro completed construction of the White Dog Falls Dam on the Winnipeg River, and the Caribou Falls Dam on the English River. Some fifteen Ojibwa families living at the settlement of One Man Lake were forced to relocate to the White Dog Reserve.[19] Both the Grassy Narrows and Islington (White Dog) bands suffered as a result of these developments, especially in lost fur production.[20] In 1978, Ontario approved plans for a new phase of hydro development, this time with respect to the Little Jackfish, Mattagami, and Moose rivers.[21] Native residents from nearby communities utilize these rivers and surrounding territories extensively, and negative effects are likely.

3 Manitoba: Hydroelectric development in Manitoba has involved

four river systems: the Winnipeg, the Saskatchewan, the Nelson and the Churchill. Development of the latter three especially has caused a variety of problems for the Native residents of the northern parts of the province.

The first major hydro project to affect Native people was the Grand Rapids Dam, completed in 1964 on the Saskatchewan River near the community of Grand Rapids. The Indian bands at Grand Rapids, Moose Lake, Chemawawin, and to a lesser extent The Pas, experienced a variety of problems as a result of the construction of a reservoir or forebay behind the dam on Cedar Lake. Virtually no political opposition was offered at the time, as these communities were relatively isolated from the general Canadian society, and were largely unaware of the extent to which they might resist. However, after construction of the dam, the Native residents began to investigate the circumstances surrounding the construction of the dam, and began to hire lawyers and to initiate legal action for compensation.[22]

In 1974, another hydro project was completed on the Churchill and Nelson rivers to the north. The Churchill–Nelson River Hydro Project entailed the diversion of water from the Churchill River south into the Nelson, where the generating facilities were constructed. The project also called for the regulation of Lake Winnipeg, to further increase flow to the Nelson.

The Native community of South Indian Lake was seriously affected by the Churchill–Nelson River Hydro Project, and to a lesser extent so were Nelson House, Cross Lake, Split Lake, York Factory and Norway House. Through independent and collective legal and political action on the part of Natives, a variety of compensation agreements has been achieved, and a comprehensive and binding agreement was developed with the Manitoba government. The latter agreement, known as the Northern Flood Agreement, has a number of elements which parallel the James Bay and Northern Quebec Agreement, although it is much more limited in scope.[23]

At present, the huge Limestone Generating Station is under construction on the Nelson River. The tenth largest dam in Canada, it is scheduled to go into operation by the beginning of the next decade. The original plan for Limestone dates back to the days of New Democratic Party (NDP) Premier Edward Schreyer, who began the preliminary phases of construction in the mid-1970s. However, when the Progressive Conservative government of Sterling Lyon came to power in 1977, the project was shelved, only to be re-introduced by the NDP government of Howard Pawley in 1985.[24] Much opposition by Natives seems to have been silenced, at least for the moment, by a comprehensive plan to hire Native people for the dam's construction.[25]

4 Saskatchewan: As Manitoba and Saskatchewan share river systems, it is not surprising that there exists some overlap in hydro development and its effects. The first Saskatchewan dam to significantly affect Native northerners was the Island Falls Dam, constructed near the community of Sandy Bay on the Churchill River. In fact, Sandy Bay was constructed primarily to provide a labour camp for Native workers both in construction of the dam and in its operation.[26] Located just inside the Saskatchewan border, the power station was designed to service the Hudson Bay Mining and Smelting Company copper and zinc mine near Flin Flon, Manitoba. When, in 1968, the generating station was automated, the non-Native employees were transferred to Flin Flon. The Native employees, who were also offered employment in the Manitoba town, generally declined to move, choosing rather to remain at Sandy Bay. However, with the automation of the plant, the economic base of the community was destroyed, and the people lapsed into a spiral of increasing poverty.[27] In 1983, an *ad hoc* committee known as the Sandy Bay Task Force was created to negotiate a compensation deal with the Saskatchewan Power Corporation, which had purchased the Island Falls plant from the Hudson Bay Mining and Smelting Company. While some houses have been acquired from the abandoned non-Native community at Island Falls, the Sandy Bay leaders have yet to conclude to their satisfaction the compensation negotiations.[28]

In 1942, the Whitesand Dam was completed on the Reindeer River near Reindeer Lake. This was done primarily to provide a more regulated water flow to the Island Falls Dam, but resulted in an increase in the level of Reindeer Lake of some one and a half metres. Saskatchewan Native communities such as Southend, and Manitoba communities such as Brochet, which used the lake and adjacent rivers and streams, have complained for many years of the disruptions the project has caused. Commercial and domestic production of fish and fur has declined, and transportation has been made more difficult.[29] The Island Falls and Whitesand dams were both sold by the Hudson Bay Mining and Smelting Company to the Saskatchewan Power Corporation in 1983. The Peter Ballantyne Band on behalf of the residents of Southend and other Native communities in northern Saskatchewan, and the Treaty and Aboriginal Rights Research Centre of Manitoba on behalf of the community of Brochet, are currently investigating the legality of the construction of these facilities and the related flooding of Indian lands.

The Saskatchewan River upstream from Grand Rapids has proven to be suitable for other hydro projects. Saskatchewan completed the Squaw Rapids Dam there in 1964, and in the process created a large forebay out of the river, which is now known as Tobin Lake. Downstream from the Squaw Rapids Dam lies the Native community of Cumberland House, perhaps the oldest permanent settlement in the province. The dam has had a negative effect on this community, particularly as a result of the periodic releases of water from the floodgates, which result in rapid downstream fluctuations in the water level of the various rivers, streams and channels in the Cumberland Delta region. The Native residents of Cumberland House initially offered no resistance to the dam during construction; but in the post-project period they have initiated extensive political and legal action in pursuit of both mitigative measures and compensation.

In 1973, the Saskatchewan government announced its intention to proceed with another northern hydro project, this time on the Churchill River in the territory occupied by the communities of the Peter Ballantyne Indian Band. As proposed, the new Wintego Dam would flood some 267 square kilometres of territory and produce three hundred megawatts of power.[30] But an enormous furor greeted the announcement, resulting eventually in the formation of the Churchill River Board of Inquiry to examine all the social, economic and environmental issues surrounding the project. Spearheaded by the Federation of Saskatchewan Indians, the opposition succeeded in detailing the pitfalls of the proposal, and by the time the Churchill River Board of Inquiry submitted its final report arguing against the project, the Saskatchewan government had already decided it was no longer feasible.[31] However, in 1986 Saskatchewan once again announced its intention to pursue hydro development on the Churchill River by 1993.[32] It is quite likely that opposition will once again develop.

A new hydro dam has recently been completed in the province at Nipawin, upstream from the Squaw Rapids Dam on the Saskatchewan River. Once again it is the community of Cumberland House which has expressed the greatest concern about the future effects of the project. In 1984 an attempt to obtain an injunction halting the dam's construction was unsuccessful. It is too early to determine whether the fears of the Cumberland House community will be realized.

5 Alberta: The Bighorn Dam, located on the South Saskatchewan

River near the British Columbia border, was constructed in the early 1970s, and caused flooding of Indian graveyards and other sacred places.[33] The Indian people of the area, especially the Stoney Band at Morley, have argued that the dam has had a serious effect on the wildlife and other resources of the area. Describing the politics of the dam's construction, one observer noted:

The purpose of this dam is somewhat vague, and the procedures the government used to investigate the benefits of such a dam are certainly suspect. Even more significant, perhaps, is that hearings which were held to discuss the pros and cons of the dam's construction were not undertaken until the forest clearing for the reservoir had already begun, and the clearing was not discontinued while the hearings were conducted. Obviously, the government had its mind made up, which might explain in part why witnesses against the dam were insulted and harassed during the hearings and asked to supply detailed proof for just those details about which the government should have provided proof.[34]

The Stoney Indian Band has also recently threatened legal action against the federal government and one of Alberta's two energy companies, TransAlta Utilities, over agreements made between them which allowed for the construction of three dams on the Stoney Reserve some seventy-five years ago. The three dams, the Horseshoe, the Kananaskis and the Ghost River, were constructed with the consent of the Department of Indian Affairs, which the band alleges failed to protect their interests. Omitted from the agreements were clauses which the band argued for at the time: that the band would retain mineral rights to surrendered land; and that the land would revert to the band if not needed by the utility.[35]

Currently, the Alberta government is developing plans for a hydroelectric project on the Slave River in the northern part of the province. Two Indian bands, one Cree and the other Chipewyan, both located at Fort Chipewyan, have expressed concern over the anticipated effect of the dam on the water regime downstream, and particularly on Great Slave Lake. A great deal of opposition met the announcement of the project; some noted that the primary reason for its advancement by Peter Lougheed's Progressive Conservative government was for the employment it would create, and not for the power. Described as a "vote-getter," the project led to the formation of the Slave River Coalition, which consisted of a variety of environmental and Native groups united in opposition to the project.[36]

6 British Columbia: The Kemano I Dam was completed in 1956 by ALCAN on the Kemano River in central British Columbia. Designed to provide power to its mining and smelting operations, ALCAN's complex project involved the diversion of one river and the flooding of seven lakes to create a huge reservoir of some 890 square kilometres; the town of Kitimat was also constructed as part of the project.[37]

The Kemano I Project caused widespread environmental damage and significant human dislocation. The Indians of the Haisla Reserve feel that they did not receive adequate advice from the Department of Indian Affairs officials at the time, and that the one-time-only payment of fifty thousand dollars that Indian Affairs encouraged them to accept represents insufficient compensation for damages caused to them.

The Haisla Band currently has a specific land claim filed with the federal government on this issue. The Carrier–Sekani Tribal Council has also submitted a specific claim regarding the dam, and these two claims have been joined by a third, that of the Cheslatta Indian Band.[38]

The Cheslatta Indian Band suffered the greatest negative effect of the Kemano I Project. In 1952, on short notice (reports differ, ranging from "hours" to "two weeks"), the band was forced to relocate as the waters on adjacent Murray Lake began to rise some nine metres. Poor weather conditions, which turned the dirt roads into quagmires, prevented the band from quickly moving out much personal property and livestock, and a great deal was lost as the people quickly evacuated their homes and community.[39] In April 1984, the band submitted its claim to the federal government, detailing their grievances and emphasizing, "It is a horrible thing to lose your land, resources, burial grounds, gathering areas, fishing stations, trapping cabins, trails, etc. in order to make way for someone else's progress."[40] Feeling the financial pressures of prosecuting the claim, in 1985 the band advertised shares in the eventual settlement, in which any money loaned to the band would be repaid at nine percent interest upon its resolution.[41]

B.C. Hydro and ALCAN have recently announced their intention of commencing the Kemano II Project, which will use the remaining power potential of the Kemano River. Opposition has already surfaced, notably from the Cheslatta Band and the Gitk'san-We'tsewu'tan Tribal Council.

The W.A.C. Bennett Dam, part of B.C. Hydro's Peace River Hydroelectric Project, was completed in 1968. Flooding behind the dam created one of the world's largest artificial lakes, known as Williston Lake, covering some sixteen hundred square kilometres.[42] The project has caused serious environmental disruptions downstream, particularly in the Peace-Athabasca Delta, leading to vigorous protests by Native groups and environmentalists in British Columbia, Alberta and Saskatchewan.

The potential effects of the Bennett Dam were of little concern to B.C. Hydro when the project was planned, and few provisions were made for those who would be forced out of their traditional territories by the rising waters. The major impact report detailing the likely downstream effects concentrated on the non-Native people and the value of the resources to them. As Hugh Brody states, the report's only reference to Natives in the affected area was a comment by one Indian, who said, "By the time the water comes, I find some other place." The Native residents were "expected to move along, make do, or somehow disappear."[43]

Native communities all along the Peace River have suffered because of the Bennett Dam. Several Sekani Indian bands in the interior of British Columbia have experienced increased economic hardships resulting from the flooding of their traditional hunting, fishing and trapping areas behind the dam.[44] Downstream, particularly in the Peace-Athabasca Delta area, reduced river flows have led to the drying of valuable resource territories utilized by the Cree and Chipewyan of Fort Chipewyan, Alberta.[45] A lawsuit against B.C. Hydro was launched in 1970 by the Cree and Chipewyan bands, and by the Métis Association of Alberta on behalf of the community's Métis residents, but the action never made it to court.[46] Currently, the Cree Indian Band of Fort Chipewyan is negotiating with the federal government for a land settlement, hoping to replace lands destroyed by the dam.[47]

7 Yukon Territory: Although there are several small hydro dams in the Yukon, which exist primarily to supply power to resource industries, it is the Aishihik Project which has attracted the most attention. Small by comparison to the other projects so far discussed, this dam raised the level of Aishihik Lake about 1.2 metres, and substantially decreased the flow downstream along the Aishihik River.[48] At the time of the hearings into the project, Native groups argued that the effects on Native communities could be significant, and they requested that the project not be implemented until their land claims were settled. The federal government, particularly Minister of Indian Affairs and Northern Development Jean Chrétien, decided to go ahead with

the project.[49] In 1976, the Yukon Native Brotherhood filed a claim against the federal government, seeking almost five million dollars in compensation for damages done to the Native village of Aishihik as a result of the unnaturally high water levels.[50]

Treaties, Scrip and the Alienation of Native Lands in Western Canada

2

I want you to think of my words, I want to tell you that what we talk about is very important. What I trust and hope we will do is not for to-day or to-morrow only; what I will promise, and what I believe and hope you will take, is to last as long as the sun shines and yonder river flows.[1]

Prior to the arrival of Europeans in North America, the various Indian groups that inhabited the continent were truly the masters in their own homeland. They exercised full rights to the occupation and use of the land, the subsurface minerals, the wildlife and the fishes, and the waterways. Insofar as these rights were limited or curtailed in the pre-contact period, it was done primarily in the context of band and tribal political and military relations. It appears that all Indian groups had some concept of prior right to land and resource use, and perhaps even collective land ownership, and in the absence of military conflict these rights were normally respected by other Indian groups. An equilibrium of land use and occupancy was achieved. The arrival of Europeans in North America upset this equilibrium as they superimposed their own concepts of property rights and rules of property acquisition on the Indian inhabitants. After 1763, as a result of the Royal Proclamation, English jurisprudence governed land acquisition in British North America, and for the most part European settlers and the colonial and subsequent Canadian governments were required to follow an established procedure. This procedure entailed the official surrender to the Crown of Indian title to the land, usually in return for a variety of Crown promises and undertakings. In western Canada, this surrender was effected through the signing of treaties with the Indian people, and through the issuance of scrip to the Métis.

POLITICS AND LEADERSHIP IN
THE PRE-TREATY PERIOD

Before examining the treaty and scrip processes, it is necessary to provide the ethnographic context for the discussion by describing the political system of the northern Cree Indians as it existed in the pre-treaty
period, and the changes to that system wrought by contact with the
Europeans.

All three communities under discussion are located in the Subarctic
ethnographic area. Although various ethnologists have drawn somewhat different boundaries for this region, a recent authoritative
account has described the Subarctic area as essentially that of the
boreal forest region which stretches in a massive band across much
of Canada and Alaska. In general terms, we might say that the Subarctic area is located between the plains in the west and the eastern woodlands in the east, which demarcates the southern boundary, and the
tundra, which demarcates the northern boundary. In much of Canada,
this region corresponds to the Canadian Shield, although it also
includes the Hudson Bay lowlands, the Mackenzie borderlands, the
Cordillera, the Alaska Plateau, and the territory south of the Alaska
Range.[2] In all, some 3,218,600 square kilometres, from the Atlantic
to the Pacific, are included. It is an enormous area.

Despite its size, the Subarctic region in pre-contact times was not
heavily populated. It has been estimated that only some 60,000 Indians
occupied this territory, existing primarily in small bands and extended
family units.[3] Indeed, while rich in resources, the region did not yield
those resources easily to its first human occupants, and this had a significant effect on group size, mobility and indeed the cultures themselves. In most areas, the boreal forest is dense, black-and-white spruce
and jack pine being most prevalent. It is a cold region, characterized
by long winters during which even large water bodies freeze solid, and
complemented by short, hot summers. Major food sources for the northern Indians included: large mammals such as woodland caribou (*Rangifer tarandus caribou*), barren ground caribou (*Rangifer tarandus
groenlandicus*), and moose (*Alces alces*); and small mammals, such as
snowshoe hare (*Lepus americanus*), beaver (*Castor canadensis*) and
muskrat (*Ondatra zibethicus*). In coastal areas, the harbor seal (*Phoca
vitulina*), the beluga whale (*Delphinapterus leucas*), the harp seal
(*Phoca groenlandica*) and the ringed seal (*Phoca hispida*) were important sources. Waterfowl species of significance were the snow goose
(*Chen caerulescens*), the Canada goose (*Branta canadensis*) and vari-

ous duck species. In addition, a wide variety of fish species were caught, particularly lake sturgeon (*Acipenser fulvescens*), various suckers, northern pike *(Esox lucius)*, goldeye *(Hiodon alosoides)*, lake trout (*Salmo gairdnerii*) and walleye or pickerel (*Stizostedion vitreum vitreum*).[4] A detailed list of all animal species hunted by the Subarctic Indians would be exhausting; suffice it to say here that there was no shortage of species to hunt.

The similarities in environment and resources from one end of the Subarctic to the other are paralleled by the similarities in cultures found there. The Subarctic peoples were hunters and fishermen, and for much of the territory the resources were rarely plentiful enough to allow large congregations of people for anything but seasonal or short-term activities. But the cultures were not identical, and many important differences have been detailed. What we might refer to as "tribes" existed in the region, in the sense that certain cultural commonalities have allowed some aggregation of groups by ethnologists. Linguistic parameters have been used to group these peoples into two major categories – the Algonquian speakers and the Athapaskan speakers. Among the former have been identified the Northern Ojibwa, the Cree, the Montagnais and the Naskapi.[5] Among the latter are the Chipewyan, Hare, Slave, Locheaux and Dogrib, all of whom are sometimes referred to as Dene. Dialect differences are also evident, particularly with the large Algonquian language groups. In the pre-contact context, there existed little evidence of political, economic or other activity on the part of these Indian groups. Language and kinship ties were used to maintain links among those who were similar, but there exists no evidence of unified "tribal" actions. Personal affiliation was usually expressed in terms of one's kin group or band rather than one's "tribe."

The Indian residents of all three communities under discussion can be referred to in ethnographic terms as Western Wood Cree.[6] The available evidence suggests that, prior to European contact, there existed three major divisions of Western Woods Cree: the Rocky or Northern Cree, the Swampy Cree and the Strongwoods Cree. The cultural heritage of the people of both Easterville and Cumberland House would be that of the Swampy Cree, while the people of South Indian Lake might be properly referred to as Rocky Cree.

The smallest social unit among these Cree was the nuclear family, consisting of a husband, a wife and their children.[7] However, extended families were also common, in which a parent might join the unit, or perhaps even a brother and his family. These units were, by and large, self-contained economic entities; within each were embodied most, if not all, of the skills essential to survival in the boreal forest environment. Indeed, it was the exigencies of that very environment that occasionally forced the Cree to fission down to these small units in order to survive. Wherever possible, larger units were formed, which have been called local bands. Consisting of several related families, the local bands ranged from ten to thirty individuals. These bands were formed whenever the resources allowed, and usually in association with fall, winter and spring fishing and hunting activities. Periodically, particularly in summer, a number of local bands would come together to form the regional band, the largest and most complex of the Cree sociopolitical groups. Excellent hunting and fishing opportunities, especially the consistent return of migrating animals and fowl or the spawning of fish, which resulted in a relatively stable though short-term food supply, led to regional band formation, and these units often comprised more than one hundred persons.

The Cree, as a hunting people, were of course strongly influenced by the natural environment. The plant-and-animal subsistence base was not wholly dependable, and the uncertainty of the subarctic environment permeated Cree social organization. The ordering of social relations at all levels of Cree sociopolitical existence was based primarily on kinship. The Cree kinship system was bilateral, meaning that any given individual recognized relatives on both his father's and his mother's sides of the family. This system provided for the maximum possible number of relatives. Kin were expected to support and assist each other, to share food and other possessions; a bilateral kinship system was in practice extremely flexible and adaptive. The Cree were egalitarian to a great extent; there were no social classes, and distribution of resources was equal. But this adaptiveness also encompassed a very loose form of leadership and political organization which, functional in the pre-contact period, became less so after contact.

There was no formal or institutionalized system of leadership in pre-contact Cree society. This, of course, is not to say that the Cree were leaderless, for in fact there were many potential leaders. One ethnologist has referred to leadership among the Cree as "polycephalous," literally "many heads."[8] Their adaptation to a hunting way of life meant that, in times of scarcity or hardship, the larger group could divide into smaller entities, each one retaining all of the skills to survive. Hence many individuals developed these necessary skills and were capable of being leaders. But leadership was largely defined by the existence of followers, and followers could in no way be coerced into associating themselves with a particular individual who wished to be a leader. An individual who excelled at a variety of tasks might find himself with followers, at least for the duration of a task for which he had a particular gift. Hence, a renowned hunter would attract followers. But he would have no power of control over them. A leader could only hope to influence his followers, and followers were free to leave at any time and join another group. The flexible kinship system ensured that a variety of options would be available to everyone.

During the winter, when Cree social organization likely existed at its smallest and most basic level, that is, the level of the family, leadership primarily rested with the eldest male, at least for activities within the male domain, such as hunting and camp movements. Therefore, the local band would be necessarily composed of a number of potential leaders, and various individuals might assume such a role for particular tasks. The existence of a single camp leader has occasionally been described in the ethnographic literature, although this was probably less common than the polycephalic pattern.[9]

Decision-making was a group process and involved the eventual achievement of consensus through discussion. Recognized leaders were obviously influential in the making of particular decisions, but they had no more power to enact decisions than did anyone else. Decision by consensus served to reduce tensions among band members by minimizing factional disputes and allowing all members to have their say. In the context of a subarctic hunting society, such a system of decision-making was likely adaptive.

Some significant changes in Cree sociopolitical organization occurred with European contact and expansion into the subarctic area. A number of more formalized and even institutionalized leadership positions were created by the European immigrants to mold the Indians in their own image. For instance, the appointment of fur-trade "captains" by the traders became commonplace. Frequently provided with a uniform to enhance his authority, and joined by a number of similarly appointed "lieutenants," the captain was charged with the responsibility of leading a fur party to the trading post, acting as a liaison with the traders, and generally maintaining order while business was conducted. He was accorded special treatment by the traders, including receiving extra presents, as a means of further enhancing his authority.[10] The captain was not always a prominent leader in a band; as well, only one captain per band was likely appointed, and this had a disruptive effect on the traditional patterns of leadership. However, it is questionable whether, outside of the fur-trade context, the captains by virtue of their status were able to attain positions of enhanced authority among their people. The people, it seems, may have been content to play the game of the fur traders to promote their own interests.

Cree leadership also underwent a significant change with the introduction of the treaty process. The treaty commissioners desired that each band have a formally elected "chief" to sign the treaty on behalf of his "people," and proved to be quite high-handed in achieving such. It is important here to point out that, among other things, Cree culture and sociopolitics did not give any single individual the power to sign such an agreement on behalf of others. Once elected or appointed by the treaty commissioners, the chief received clothing, medals, and even a larger annuity than did the other band members. Subsequently, all dealings with the Indians, at least theoretically, began to operate through the office of the chief, as a pseudo-democratic system was developed for them by the traders. The process of formal elections to select chiefs and band councillors was introduced, but these individuals were given little actual power by the federal government. Frequently, such people as non-Native traders, nurses and teachers developed as the *de facto* leadership in Indian communities, and their power to access resources largely unavailable to the Indians supported their enhanced status. Government bodies whose mandates were to deal with the chief and council frequently circumvented these individuals and worked through the non-Native brokers.[11] Hence, a new form of leadership was foisted upon the people which, while formalized and institutionalized, was in fact quite impotent.

As the hydro era dawned on the Cree territory in Manitoba and Saskatchewan, leadership and political organization existed in a form which represented its dual heritage: part Indian, and part European. However, the legacy of this dual heritage did not benefit the Cree. Unfortunately for the Indians, non-Natives, through their federal government, had felt it necessary to undertake the control of and responsibility for many of the day-to-day concerns of the Cree people. In effect, the Cree, like the other Native people in western Canada, lost control of their lives. There was an atrophy in the effectiveness of their own traditional political organization, an organization which in its pristine form would nevertheless not likely have been particularly effective when opposition to the dams surfaced. However, it would not have deluded them in the way that the imposed formal democratic system did, since they were led to believe that through proper representation and the democratic process their rights and interests would be protected. Of course, by this time there also existed a large body of mixed-blood peoples, and their political position was even more ambiguous than that of the Indians. To be succinct, when first approached by the hydro utilities concerning their development plans, effective political organization did not exist in these communities, and the people were largely unfamiliar with the English language and had virtually no understanding of the Canadian legal system or of lawyers. The last major decision of similar magnitude which the Cree had to make concerned the signing of Treaty Five, in which little opportunity for actual negotiation had been provided. Learning the machinations of the Canadian political system and the techniques of local-level organizing proved very much to be learning "on the job."

PRELUDE TO THE WESTERN CANADIAN TREATY ERA

It is estimated that, between 1781 and 1902, 483 treaties, adhesions to treaties, and other forms of land surrenders were signed in Canada.[12] Adding to this the treaties and adhesions in western and northern Canada in the post-1920 period, we estimate at least 492 agreements. Specifically defining a *treaty* is problematic, and while in much of Canada a signed document is the hallmark, verbal agreements were not uncommon. Quite likely a large number of oral agreements were made between Indians and Europeans, particularly in the early post-contact period, of which we have no record.

The earliest treaties, signed in eastern Canada, were "peace and friendship" agreements, whereby both sides undertook not to launch military campaigns against the other, and sometimes even to form alliances against a third group.[13] There was very little substance to these agreements and, at least prior to 1763, they were undertaken not as a result of a moral or legal obligation on the part of the Europeans, but rather in the interests of the preservation of their fledgling colonies and nascent capitalist enterprises.

The Royal Proclamation of 1763 has frequently been referred to as the Indian "charter of rights,"[14] and despite possible arguments concerning its implications for Indians in Canada, it is nevertheless true that it set the stage for the signing of treaties with Indians on a larger and more formal scale. The proclamation was issued by King George III after Britain had acquired most of France's colonial possessions. The major purpose of the proclamation concerned the mode of governing British North America, including the new territories. But a small part of the proclamation dealt with the Indians' prior occupa-

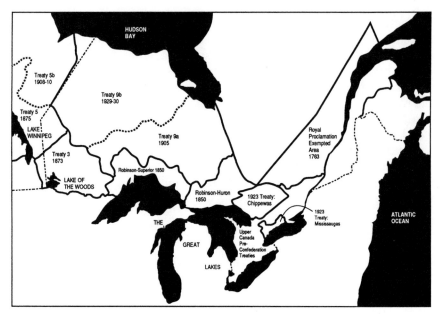

Map 2. The Eastern Canadian Treaties

tion of the territory: "And whereas it is just and reasonable, and essential to our Interest, and the security of our Colonies, that the several Nations or Tribes of Indians with whom We are connected, and who live under our protection, should not be molested or disturbed in the Possession of such Parts of Our Dominions and Territories as, not having been ceded to or purchased by Us, are reserved to them or any of them, as their Hunting Grounds."[15] It was proclaimed that the acquisition of such Indian lands could only be made through a "purchase" by the Crown, and not by individuals. Such a provision was designed to prevent the "Great Frauds and Abuses [which] have been committed in purchasing Lands of the Indians" in the years preceding the proclamation.[16]

Hence, the Royal Proclamation established both a precedent in recognizing some Indian right (if ill-defined) to the lands they occupied, and the procedure whereby such lands could be acquired by the Crown and subsequently made available to non-Native settlers. Certain lands were specifically omitted from the proclamation, most notably the vast terrritory of Rupert's Land which had been under the control of the Hudson's Bay Company since the royal charter was first granted to the Company of Adventurers in 1670. This effectively excluded most of western Canada, and left the company to deal with the Indians as it saw fit. However, when the Hudson's Bay Company surrendered its charter to Canada in 1870, it became clear that in law the Indian and Métis inhabitants retained aboriginal title to Rupert's Land.[17] In accordance with the principles established by the Royal Proclamation of 1763, it was incumbent upon the new Canadian government to properly secure the surrender of these lands. This it did by signing treaties in the case of Indians, and issuing scrip in the case of Métis.

Between 1871 and 1929, most of western and northern Canada west of the Ontario-Quebec border was surrendered through treaties. These treaties, known as the "numbered" treaties (ranging from Treaty One to Treaty Eleven) were in fact a continuation of a process established by the Royal Proclamation and entrenched in the Robinson-Huron and Robinson-Superior treaties, both signed in 1850 (see Map 2).

The Robinson treaties are important because they set the tone as well as the method for the subsequent numbered treaties, though it is apparent that they did not establish a set formula for providing various provisions in exchange for the surrender of land.[18] Furthermore, like many of the treaties to follow, the Robinson treaties were signed at the request of the Indian inhabitants of the northern shores of the two great lakes, who feared that recent mineral discoveries in the region would result in an influx of settlers and an erosion of their land rights.[19] Despite the potential wealth of the region, however, the Indians did not receive a bountiful settlement since the lands were considered by the government to be "notoriously barren and sterile."[20] The Robinson treaties broke with previous traditions in that, for the first time, provisions for annuities, reserves, and the right to hunt and fish on unsurrendered tracts of land were included. The claims of the "half-breeds" to the land were also recognized at the urging of the Indians with whom they lived, and some two hundred of them were allowed to sign the treaties.[21]

No further treaty activity occurred in western Canada until 1871, four years after the Dominion of Canada was formed. Under Section 91(24) of the British North America Act (now the Constitution Act, 1982), "Indians, and Lands reserved for Indians" became the responsibility of the Canadian federal government.[22] But the concern of the new government for the acquisition of Indian lands was not paramount in the very early years of its mandate. Indeed, at least one author has argued that the federal government had no policy or plan whatsoever for dealing with the Indians and the growing number of Métis in the North-West.[23] It was the threat of imminent settlement of their lands which prompted the Ojibwa Indians in the North-West Angle in northwestern Ontario and the Saulteaux of southern Manitoba to request treaties. Even still, it was quite likely a combination of historic events which prompted the federal government to recommence the treaty-signing process.

In 1867, when Canada was formed, the vast North-West was still under the domain of the Hudson's Bay Company. The new Canadian government quickly moved to acquire Rupert's Land from the company in order to further the interests of its National Policy. Under this policy, Prime Minister John A. Macdonald's government saw the integration of the western hinterlands within the realm of Ontario, in a relationship that, as formulated, was clearly exploitive.[24] Settlement of the agricultural lands by eastern immigrants, and the construction of a transcontinental railway, were two key components in this policy. But the acquisition of Rupert's Land in order to facilitate the National Policy was not a simple matter. Many Native residents in the North-West were alarmed that Canada and the Hudson's Bay Company would negotiate without them. The land, to their minds, was Indian and Métis land. In fact, this very issue was an important spark in the so-called Red River Rebellion, in which the Métis under Louis Riel established a provisional government and negotiated the entry of

Manitoba into confederation as a province, not as a colony as the National Policy dictated.[25] Grievances surrounding the land sale existed for many years. As late as 1876, at the signing of Treaty Six in Saskatchewan, Sweet Grass, a prominent Plains Cree Chief, remarked: "We heard our lands were sold and we did not like it; we don't want to sell our lands; it is our property, and no one has a right to sell them."[26] When the land transfer was finally approved in 1870, it was not without conditions. The deed of the company's land surrender to Queen Victoria stated: "Any claims of Indians to compensation for lands required for purposes of settlement shall be disposed of by the Canadian Government in communication with the Imperial Government; and the Company shall be relieved of all responsibility in respect of them."[27] Hence, the federal government became responsible for settling with the Indians and Métis for the acquisition of the lands formerly held by the Hudson's Bay Company.

THE TREATY-MAKING PROCESS

The treaty-making process in western Canada proved to be a relatively easy one for the federal government. For the most part, the Indians were willing, even anxious, to sign, and in some cases had even requested treaties. While some negotiations took place, they were in many respects just formalities which preceded the signing of a document prepared in advance by the government. It is true that some Indian groups managed to have additional clauses included in the treaties, for example the "famine and pestilence" and "medicine chest" provisions in Treaty Six, but clearly the Indians were negotiating from a disadvantaged position. As Cumming and Mickenberg have written, "Despite the insight and skill exhibited by their negotiators, it is clear that the Indians were not in an equal bargaining position with the Government. The Indians were a non-literate people and the concept of a treaty was foreign to their culture. Their negotiators apparently relied upon the advice of missionaries and the North-West Mounted Police, neither of whom could be called disinterested parties."[28] Such a view has its critics, particularly because it appears that the Indians were innocent (and some might say ignorant), and were easily duped into surrendering their land for a few loose promises. A belief in the shrewdness of the Indian negotiators is not incompatible with the fact that they received a miniscule fraction of the value of the land they were surrendering. Given the attitude of the federal government at

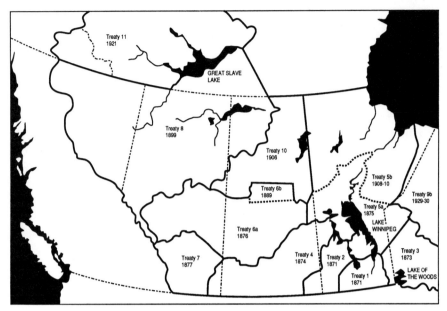

Map 3. The Numbered Treaties in Western Canada

that time, the fact that any additional promises were secured is quite remarkable.

Map 3, showing the treaty areas, clearly demonstrates the existence of two general treaty-making processes. Between 1870 and 1877, the first seven treaties were signed in an area which corresponds to the western fertile belt that was essential to western settlement. In fact, the signing dates of each of these treaties demonstrates a westward pattern which reflects the process of settlement. Despite this, at least one investigation has concluded that "the expedience with which treaty activities were conducted between 1871 and 1877 merely reflects the haste with which the Dominion was stitched together and should not be taken to imply that government's motive was to steal Indian land or to obtain it by trick or fraud."[29] *Steal, trick* and *fraud* may be gratuitously harsh terms, since none of these devious tactics was necessary. In fact, the federal government was not anxious to sign treaties with the Indians, even in the face of imminent and increasing settlement, and despite the existence of precedents in recognizing Indian title. After Treaties One and Two were signed, the federal government actually decided not to obtain the land surrender of other Indians until absolutely necessary, which meant until the land or resources were required.[30] Once again it was the Indians who petitioned for treaties and, through a real or perceived threat of force, convinced the government to treat with them. However, although the Indians played a significant role in initiating, and maintaining, the treaty-making process in the fertile belt, it is quite likely that the government would soon have begun the process anyway. Discoveries of the vast resource wealth of the west occurred quickly in the final quarter of the nineteenth century.

The second treaty-making process began in 1889, with the adhesion of the Montreal Lake Indians to Treaty Six in Saskatchewan, followed by Treaty Eight (1899), Treaty Nine (1905), Treaty Ten (1906), adhesion to Treaty Five (1908 to 1910), Treaty Eleven (1921), and finally adhesion to Treaty Nine (1929). These treaties have been referred to as "northern resource development" treaties,[31] and were designed to obtain Indian title to lands which, largely unsuitable for agriculture and settlement, nevertheless possessed great value as a result of mineral discoveries and other natural resources. In comparison to the treaties signed during the earlier treaty-making process, the northern treaties were done more expeditiously and allowed for even less negotiation on the part of the Indians.

The first treaties negotiated, Treaties One, Two and Three, were logically the forerunners of the subsequent numbered treaties. At the outset of negotiations, it was clear that there would be little room for negotiating the terms of the treaty. The Indians were told that, "whether they wished it or not, immigrants would come in and fill up the country, . . . and in a little while would spread all over it." They were also told that "they must make up their minds; if there was to be a treaty, it must be on a basis like that offered."[32] Faced with such an ultimatum, the Indians relented.

The terms were very basic, and included a three-dollar-per-capita annuity (subsequently increased to five dollars) and the provision of reserves based on 160 acres per family of five. No mention was made of Indian retention of hunting, fishing or trapping rights on ceded lands in the treaty itself. However, the Lieutenant-Governor of Manitoba and the North-West Territories, Adams Archibald, negotiating on behalf of the federal government, did promise orally that the Indians would "still be free to hunt over much of the land included in the treaty," at least until non-Natives required it for farming or other purposes.[33] Thus, from the beginning of the treaty-making process, oral and written understandings can be seen to be diverging. Treaties One and Two are unique in that some of the oral promises made during negotiations were acknowledged subsequently by the government, who officially added them to the treaty through amendment. Significantly, the right of Indians to hunt, fish and trap was not included in the amendment.[34]

While the signing of Treaties One and Two occurred fairly expeditiously (in both cases, less than a week was required), Treaty Three proved to be extremely difficult, perhaps more so than any subsequent treaties. Initial contact with the Indians was made in 1871, and a return visit in 1872 found the Indians "not to be ready for the making of a treaty."[35] The new Lieutenant-Governor, Alexander Morris, returned in 1873 and was forced into "protracted and difficult" negotiations with the Indians.[36] The Indians told Morris, "We think where we are is our property,"[37] and requested annuities and other payments greatly in excess of that which Morris was authorized to pay. The Lieutenant-Governor was unmoved, insisting that what he had offered was "just, kind and fair," and threatening to leave if the Indians refused to accept the treaty.[38] A report of the negotiations quoted Morris's comments to the Indians as follows: "I am very sorry; you know it takes two to make a bargain. . . . I have to go away and report that I have to go without making terms with you. I doubt if the [Treaty] Commissioners will be sent again to assemble this nation."[39] The Indians' response to Morris was perceptive, yet hollow insofar as they were clearly in a disadvantaged position. Stated one Chief: "My terms I am going to lay down before you; the decision of our Chiefs; ever since we came to a decision you push it back. *The sound of the rustling of the gold is under my feet where I stand;* we have a rich country; it is the Great Spirit who gave us this; where we stand upon is the Indians' property, and belongs to them. If you grant us our requests you will not go back without making the treaty [emphasis original]."[40] Morris was not persuaded, despite the accuracy of the words which the Chief spoke. When he indicated his willingness to sign the treaty with separate bands, setting aside his preference for unanimity, one by one the bands consented. Recent analysts have referred to this as the "domino" effect, common to the signing of many treaties, in which the obvious immediate benefits of a treaty, particularly the food, clothing and cash payouts, would break the opposition of specific bands or chiefs who were reluctant to sign. The key was to get that first signature.[41]

Treaty Four was signed in the Fort Qu'Appelle area of southern Saskatchewan in 1874 and 1875. The treaty with the Plains Cree and Saulteaux is unique in that for the first time trapping rights on surrendered land were specifically guaranteed to the Indians, in addition to hunting and fishing rights. Otherwise, the terms of the treaty were similar to those of Treaty Three, and included the provision of annuities (five dollars per capita) and reserves (one square mile per family of five).

The Indians, while desiring the treaty, were not prepared to sign immediately. They objected to the fact that the Hudson's Bay Company had been paid by the Canadian government for the land; the Indians felt they should have received payment as the rightful owners. Lieutenant-Governor Morris was not prepared to discuss this issue, and informed the Indians "that the [treaty] proposals of the Commissioners were final, and could not be changed." Furthermore, the Indians had heard of the terms of Treaty Three and demanded the same terms, particularly the provision of "presents" for five successive years as compared to Morris's proposal of one year only. But Morris made it clear that the lands of the Indians in the North-West were not as valuable as those in the Treaty Three area: "You must know that the steamboats had been running through their waters, and our soldiers had been marching through their country, and for that reason we offered the Ojibbeway [sic] a larger sum than we offered you." The

Indians relented and signed the treaty, less than a week after Morris had arrived.[42]

In 1875, another expedition was undertaken to the Qu'Appelle region to obtain the adhesion to Treaty Four of Indians not present the previous year. The Saulteaux Indians whom they encountered were not satisfied with the terms of the treaty, and specifically asked for an increase in the annuity to twelve dollars. Their request was denied. Even though these Indians were not present the previous year and had therefore not signed any treaty, the commissioners adopted the view that the terms of Treaty Four represented a "covenant between them and the Government." Furthermore, the Indians were told "that all further discussion on the subject was useless, that if they declined to accept the terms of the treaty we must return and report to the Government that they had broken the promise made last year."[43] Of course, these particular Indians had not made any promise the previous year. Regardless, faced with both moral condemnation and the treaty ultimatum, they too relented and signed.

Treaty Five, initially signed in 1875, with adhesions in 1908, 1909 and 1910, encompassed the three Indian and Métis communities of Cumberland House, Easterville and South Indian Lake. Treaty Six was initially signed with the Plains and Wood or northern Cree Indians in 1876, with an adhesion in 1889. The surrendered territory in what is now central Saskatchewan and Alberta was very fertile, and in addition was becoming extremely important because of the thriving commercial centres of Prince Albert and Fort Edmonton. The terms of the treaty were similar to those in the previous ones, except that the Indians were able to have two additional clauses inserted into the document. The first concerned provision of a "medicine chest" for the Indians, and the second concerned a promise of government assistance in the event of "any pestilence . . . or famine."[44]

The treaty commission, again led by Alexander Morris, found the Indians interested in concluding a treaty but by no means ready simply to sign the pre-written document. Some of the Saulteaux and Cree Indians even tried to convince the other Cree and "French half-breeds" to assist them in preventing Morris from entering the territory.[45] According to Morris's description, one pro-treaty chief made the following prophetic reply to the request: "One of them at length arose, and pointing to the River Saskatchewan, said, 'Can you stop the flow of that river?' The answer was, 'No,' and the rejoinder was, 'No more can you stop the progress of the Queen's Chief.' "[46] Morris was not prevented from entering the territory, and found the Indians very concerned with their future in the face of dwindling buffalo herds and increasing non-Native settlement. Morris presented a contradictory message, however, emphasizing the willingness of the government to assist the Indians in a transformation to settled, agrarian life while simultaneously stressing that the government "did not wish to interfere with their present mode of living."[47] To the Indians, it may have appeared to be the best of both worlds. As Ermineskin Band elder Lazarus Roan once reflected, "That is why they were agreeable to treaty, because the promises were so good."[48] In a little over a week the first Indian names were attached to the treaty.

The adhesion to Treaty Six took place in the Montreal Lake–Lac la Ronge area in 1889. The exact terms of the treaty of 1876 were presented, and little opportunity was afforded to the Indians to negotiate. In fact, the request of one chief to have a day to consider the offer was so strongly discouraged by the treaty commissioner that the treaty was signed that very day.[49]

Treaty Seven in southern Alberta completed the sweep of the southern fertile belt, securing this territory for the expansion of eastern Canadian and European immigrants. Signed in 1877 with the Blackfoot, Blood, Peigan, Sarcee and Stoney Indians, the treaty obtained control for the Canadian government of territory which now includes the cities of Calgary and Lethbridge, and the recreational centre of Banff. In return the Indians received essentially the same as in Treaties Four and Six.

These Indians had heard of the treaties that had been signed to the east of them, and were anxious to settle their claims with the government. With the buffalo herds all but extinct in their region, and the people reeling from the devastating effects of a smallpox epidemic in 1870, the Indians desperately needed assistance. For its part, the government was concerned that the "warlike" and "intractable" Indians might create problems for settlers.[50] Consequently, the new Lieutenant-Governor of the North-West Territories, David Laird, was commissioned to sign a treaty with them.

Treaty negotiations lasted only a few days. The Indians were assured that "their liberty of hunting over the open prairie would not be interfered with,"[51] and were promised the necessary tools and animals to commence farming and herding. Little opposition to the terms of the treaty was expressed, and the treaty was promptly signed.

Having obtained the Indians' title to the land in the southern fertile belt, the federal government imposed a hiatus in treaty-making. It was not until resource development became imminent in the regions north of those surrendered by treaty that the government was prepared to continue the process. Even then, it did so with great reluctance.

The first northern treaty was Treaty Eight, covering what is now northern Alberta, northern British Columbia, and small sections of northern Saskatchewan and the Northwest Territories. By 1899, when the treaty was signed, the Indians inhabiting these northern regions were impoverished and destitute. The collapse of the fur trade had had serious repercussions, and the people saw the provisions of the treaties, however meagre, as essential to their survival. Their continued petitions fell on deaf ears, however; the federal government was not prepared to mount another expensive treaty commission until the land, or the resources on or underneath it, was required.[52] By 1891 the vast mineral potential of the region was becoming apparent, and a Privy Council report recommended the creation of a treaty commission. The reasons were clear; the report stated "that immense quantities of petroleum exist within certain areas of those regions, as well as the belief that other minerals and substances of economic value, . . . the development of which may add materially to the public wealth, . . . appear to render it advisable that a treaty or treaties should be made with the Indians who claim those regions as their hunting grounds, with a view to the extinguishment of the Indian title in such portions of the same, as it may be considered in the interest of the public to open up for settlement."[53] The Indians to be dealt with were the northern Cree, Chipewyan and Beaver, who inhabited the territory identified as rich in resources. Destitution and requests for treaty were insufficient reasons to be included in the treaty.[54]

The Indians expressed concerns that their hunting, fishing and trapping rights not be interfered with as a result of the treaty, and were assured that they would be "just as free to hunt and fish all over" as before the treaty.[55] Such a promise was exactly what the Indians wanted to hear, as Richard Daniel has described. "This picture of a post-treaty life in which Indians would remain free and independent, but with government assistance to fall back on and the prospect of greater opportunities in the fur trade, seems to have been responsible for removing many of the Indian's doubts."[56] However, the treaty as written indicated that such freedom would be "subject to such regulations as may from time to time be made by the Government."[57] The Métis interpreter employed by the commission stated in 1939 that no such proviso was included in the copy of the treaty which he read to the Indians.[58]

The treaty commissioners, in executing their mandate, were clearly not prepared to negotiate additional treaty items, nor did they want to spend a great deal of time obtaining signatures to Treaty Eight. In fact, they were rather cavalier about the whole process, telling the Indians, "The Treaty is a free offer; take it or not, just as you please,"[59] while emphasizing that federal laws would be applied to them regardless. Furthermore, the Indians were requested to decide quickly, as "others are now waiting for our arrival, and you, by deciding quickly, will assist us to get to them."[60] Under these pressures, the Indians did sign quickly, and with relatively little argument. At Lesser Slave Lake and Fort Chipewyan, they signed the day after the treaty commission arrived.[61]

The terms of Treaty Eight were very similar to those in previous treaties, especially Treaty Seven. The Indians were granted five-dollar-per-capita annuities and reserves on the basis of one square mile per family of five.

Treaty Nine was signed in 1905, with adhesions in 1929 and 1930; it involved the Northern Ojibwa and Cree Indians inhabiting the territory in northwestern Ontario to the north of the boundaries of the Robinson treaties and Treaty Three. While increasing settlement in the area was putting some pressure on the Indians, the federal government, and its Ontario counterpart, were primarily concerned with securing the unfettered title to the vast mineral resources of the region. This treaty was unusual in that the Ontario government was allowed input into determining the terms of the treaty and were able to have a representative appointed to the treaty commission.[62]

The "negotiations" of the treaty were rather mechanical. Like the previous treaties, its terms had been drawn up in advance, and the commissioners explicitly instructed that no provisions were to be added or altered in any way.[63] Yet, the Indians were invited to discuss the provisions and request explanations. They expressed their concern that their hunting, fishing and trapping rights would be limited by the treaty, but were told that "their present manner of making their livelihood would in no way be interfered with."[64] Some Indians also expressed their dissatisfaction that the terms of the treaty were not as favourable as those of Treaty Three to the south. For instance, while Treaty Three provided a per-capita annuity of five dollars, Treaty Nine called for only four dollars. Their concerns were not that significant, however, and in each community the treaty was signed very quickly, usually within a day of the arrival of the treaty commission.

Treaty Nine is also unusual in that it is the only treaty in which provincial access to potential water power was an issue. An agreement signed between the Ontario and federal governments in 1905 stipulated that, in the allocation of reserves for the Indians, "no site suitable for the development of water-power exceeding 500 horsepower shall be included." The letter of transmittal by the treaty commissioners described a process in which all resources of value were to be purposefully excluded from the reserves: "They have been selected in situations which are especially advantageous to their owners, and where they will not in any way interfere with railway development or the future commercial interests of the country . . . no valuable water-powers are included within the allotments. . . . When the vast quantity of waste and, at present, unproductive land surrendered is considered, these allotments must, we think, be pronounced most reasonable."[65]

Treaty Ten, signed in 1906, obtained for the federal government the surrender of most of what is now northern Saskatchewan. The primary reason for this treaty with the northern Cree and Chipewyan Indians seems to be related to the fact that Saskatchewan entered confederation as a province the year before, and there was an expressed need to tidy up the Indian title question in the area north of the Treaty Six boundary.

The Indians requested better terms than those offered to them by J. McKenna, the treaty commissioner, but their requests were denied. Their paramount concern, like that of other northern Indians, was that their hunting, fishing and trapping rights be protected. They were also assured "that the same means of earning a livelihood would continue after the treaty was made as existed before it." In fact, McKenna "guaranteed that the treaty would not lead to any forced interference with their mode of life."[66] The Indians were convinced, and signed onto the treaty with little pressure from the commissioner. In most cases, treaty "negotiations" took no more than a day. The terms of Treaty Ten, especially those pertaining to annuities and reserve allotments, were essentially the same as in Treaty Eight.

The final numbered treaty in Canada was Treaty Eleven, signed in 1921. This treaty with the Slave, Dogrib, Loucheux and Hare Indians essentially secured for Canada the resource-rich belt contiguous to the Mackenzie River in the Northwest Territories. In fact, as with Treaty Eight, the federal government was not anxious to sign a treaty in this region until potential resource development warranted. In the case of Treaty Eight, it was the discovery of gold; in the case of Treaty Eleven, it was an oil strike at Norman Wells. For the government, the destitution of the northern Indians was not an issue. As René

Fumoleau has written, "profit and economics . . . exerted their influence where philanthropy . . . failed."[67]

As they were with all the other northern treaties, the Indians were particularly concerned with their hunting, fishing and trapping rights, but their fears that these would be curtailed were alleviated by Commissioner H.A. Conroy.[68] In fact, the Indians were informed that the government expected them to support themselves through these activities, and that twine and ammunition in excess of that granted under other treaties would be provided for just this reason. Other than this issue, the Indians expressed very little disagreement with the terms of the treaty, and the commissioner was able to secure signatures within a day or so of contacting the various bands. As Fumoleau has aptly described it, "treaty negotiations were brief, initial opposition was overcome, specific demands were made by the Indians, promises were given, and agreement was reached."[69] To the government, the process was, in Fumoleau's terms, "a mere formality."[70] The terms of the treaty included a five-dollar-per-capita annuity and reserves based on the formula of one square mile for every family of five.

TREATY FIVE: A BRIEF CASE STUDY

The various numbered treaties are similar in many ways, not only in substance, but also in terms of the process of negotiation that ensued between the Indians and the government agents. As all three communities – Cumberland House, Easterville and South Indian Lake – are within the Treaty Five area, a more detailed examination of this treaty will help to illuminate the parallels between it and the subsequent hydro negotiations.

Treaty Five, signed in 1875, and its adhesions, signed in 1908, 1909 and 1910, was established according to the two treaty-making processes outlined earlier in this chapter. The initial treaty process was related to the need to secure land for settlement as well as important transportation corridors; the adhesions were more related to natural-resource use. The ancestors of the Indian residents of modern-day Easterville (Chemawawin) and Cumberland House were brought into the treaty during the initial process in 1875, while those of South Indian Lake were brought into adhesion with the Nelson House band in 1908.

Unlike the other treaties designed to obtain federal government title to the fertile belt, Treaty Five was not negotiated out of any recognition of agricultural potential in the region to the north of Treaties

One and Two. While it is true that certain parts of this region, particularly the Interlake, had agricultural potential, such potential was largely seen as limited, especially in the more northerly regions. Lieutenant-Governor Alexander Morris made this fact clear in 1873 when he wrote, "The country lying adjacent to Norway House is not adapted for agricultural purposes and . . . there is therefore no present necessity for the negotiation of any treaty with the Indians."[71] A treaty was not to be negotiated with the Indians on this basis, and in fact no treaty was to be negotiated at all until such time as something else of value was associated with the region. Sufficient reasons began to emerge only a few years after the signing of Treaties One, Two and Three in the southern parts of Manitoba, Saskatchewan and northwestern Ontario, and just after Morris wrote his letter of August 1873. At first an adhesion to one of these existing treaties was considered, but Morris argued persuasively for a separate treaty. The reasons for the treaty, and the manner in which the region had now been identified as being of value to non-Natives, was clearly outlined by Morris: "The progress of navigation by steam on Lake Winnipeg, the establishment of Missions and of saw milling enterprises, the discovery of minerals on the shores and vicinity of the Lake as well as migration of the Norway House Indians, all point to the necessity of the Treaty being made without delay."[72] In fact, it was necessary for the government to clear the title to the southwest shore of Lake Winnipeg to allow for intensive settlement of Icelandic immigrants. The Norway House Indians were destitute and had requested resettlement in the Interlake area where they could take up farming. And the enormous potential of the Saskatchewan River as a transportation route, especially in light of the technological advancement toward steam engines, was acknowledged. Indian title to the region was to be secured partly to allow non-Native access to and use of Lake Winnipeg, "its waters, shores, islands, inlets and tributary streams,"[73] including the Saskatchewan River, although there is no indication that the government perceived a necessity to obtain a surrender of the Indian title to these waterways.

The initial treaty-making process was to be done as quickly as possible, since development of the region was seen as imminent. Like the other numbered treaties, Treaty Five was prepared in advance, and taken to the Indians to get their consent. However, unlike the process in many of the other treaties, in Treaty Five reserves were to be allocated at the time of treaty signing to further expedite the removal of the Indians from valuable territory.[74] Only token negotiations would be allowed, as Coates and Morrison have described: "The treaty commissioners would go through an elaborate procedure of explaining the terms, asking for Native suggestions, and securing their acceptance of the package. But there were, in fact, few substantive negotiations."[75] Furthermore, the terms of the treaty were not to be as generous as in other treaties, especially in the amount of land to be allocated for reserves. An incident at Grand Rapids and The Pas in 1876 highlights this fact. When Treaty Commissioner Thomas Howard tried to secure the signatures of Indians missed during the previous year's work, the Indians requested terms similar to those in Treaty Six, which had just been signed to the west of them, and whose terms they knew. The Indians proposed a new treaty along these lines, a proposal which was rejected by Howard. Although the Commissioner was well aware of the value of the land to Canada, he was not prepared to admit it in his reply to the Indians. He told them "that the land they would surrender would be useless to the Queen, while what the Plains Indians would give up [in Treaty Six] would be of value to her for homes for her white children."[76] Why the Queen wanted the Indians' "useless" land was never explained, nor did the Indians apparently enquire.

The first treaty-making expedition in 1875 was relatively successful, securing with ease the surrender of the Berens River, Norway House and Grand Rapids Indians. When the party arrived at Grand Rapids, Morris, leader of the expedition, decided to convince the Indians to relocate to the other side of the Saskatchewan River, since their current location was clearly the most suitable for the development of a new townsite at the foot of the rapids.[77] After exacting a small payment as compensation, the Indians agreed, and the treaty was signed. It took Morris less than a full day at Grand Rapids to complete the treaty, just as it had at Norway House and Berens River the preceding week.

The next year's excursion, under the direction of Thomas Howard, met with a little more difficulty. At Grand Rapids, Howard was informed that the Indians did not believe they had signed the treaty the previous year, but that they had "had only a talk with the Governor preliminary to making the treaty." As Howard notes, "It was only after a great deal of talking on their part, during which they made the most unreasonable demands, and many explanations on my part, that the Indians were satisfied that a treaty had been made."[78] If the Indians were sincere in their belief that no treaty had been made, then the incident highlights the pitfalls of the rapid-fire treaty-making process associated with Treaty Five. Could they have possibly understood the terms of the treaty if they were unaware that they had even signed one?

A few days later, on his way to The Pas, Howard encountered a small settlement of Swampy Cree Indians at "the Che-ma-wa-win," or "Seining Place," where the Saskatchewan River flowed into Cedar Lake. These Indians were a splinter group from Moose Lake, and though they wished to be treated as a separate band, Howard was opposed.[79] After forcing them to travel to The Pas to sign the treaty, Howard decided to treat with them and the Moose Lake Indians as a single band, with only one chief and set of headmen, and hence only one set of treaty payments for these officials. Treaty Five was to be inexpensive as well as quick. Howard's attempts to actually have the Chemawawin Indians relocate to Moose Lake were unsuccessful.

Howard also foresaw a need to have the Indians of the The Pas Band relocated. They were situated close to the small non-Native community, which was likely to grow, and were also occupying lands needed as a railway right-of-way. However, the Indians resisted, and the relocation plan was eventually dropped. These nineteenth-century attempts demonstrate, in the words of Coates and Morrison, the government's "willingness to relocate the Native with minimal consultation if such a move conformed to some larger official purpose."[80] The partially successful attempts to relocate the Indians at Grand Rapids, Chemawawin and The Pas foreshadowed the manner in which the Manitoba government would deal with the problem of the location of these communities when the hydro dam at Grand Rapids was constructed in the mid-twentieth century.

Despite some opposition, Howard achieved the surrender of the Chemawawin, Moose Lake, The Pas and Cumberland House Indians in two days.

The allocation of reserves was another issue, however. Although some lands had been determined at the time the treaty was signed, establishing the actual boundaries would prove to be more difficult. The best example of this is the case of Cumberland House. When the surveyor arrived in 1883, he was informed that the Indians did not want a reserve in the Cumberland area. They did not consider the land suitable for farming, and informed the surveyor that they had been promised land in the more fertile region around the Hudson's Bay Company post at Fort-à-la-Corne, further upstream on the Saskatchewan River. But this area had been surrendered under Treaty Six, and the government did not wish to assign reserve lands in one treaty area to Indians from another. Such a barrier was, of course, entirely the artificial creation of the government. When the surveyor discovered the marginality of the lands about Cumberland House, the government relented and it was decided to allocate some reserve land for the band outside the Treaty Five area.[81]

After the signing of Treaty Five in 1875 and 1876, the federal government demonstrated little concern with obtaining the adhesion of those Indians living north of the treaty boundary. These Indians had fallen upon harsh times, in light of the collapse of the fur trade, and requested treaties as one way of alleviating their plight.[82] The government was not responsive, however, until new non-Native developments became imminent. Then the Indian people discovered how quickly the government could move. In this case, it was the development of a railway line to the port of Churchill which sparked a new round of treaty adhesions.[83]

The first adhesions to the treaty were to be secured in 1908. These were to be adhesions in the true sense of the word; that is, there were to be no negotiations. The treaty commissioners were specifically instructed as to the importance of not making any "outside promises" during the "negotiation" of the treaty. In fact, they were even authorized to attempt to achieve the least expensive terms possible. When the Nelson House Indian Band signed the adhesion in 1908, they accepted, under protest, a three-dollar annuity. The Indians at Split Lake insisted upon, and received, the maximum five-dollar annuity. In 1909, when the commissioners once again passed through the Nelson House area, they were confronted by the band regarding this inequity, and the commissioners agreed to increase the payment to five dollars.[84]

For the most part, the Indians were anxious to sign the treaty adhesion and presented little opposition to the commissioners. While the imminent threat of the railway was certainly a factor, it seems it was not nearly as large a factor in the Indians' willingness to sign as was their general poverty. As Frank Tough has described it, "Indians were prepared to give up aboriginal title under the duress created by decades of the mercantile fur trade."[85] As was the case elsewhere, the treaties were viewed by the Indians as a means of making the transition to a new economic system. Their poverty did not provide a strong position from which to enter serious negotiations with the government. By and large, they were grateful to receive the treaty as it was pre-formulated.

Adhesions to Treaty Five were made in 1908 by the Nelson House and Split Lake bands; in 1909 by those of Oxford House, God's Lake and Island Lake; and in 1910 by the Deer Lake, Churchill and York

Factory bands. In all, these adhesions surrendered 214,680 square kilometres of territory, for a combined Treaty Five total of some 375,610 square kilometres.

In many ways, the text of Treaty Five is very similar to that of the other numbered treaties both in language and in terms. The entire text of the treaty with its representative adhesions is reproduced in Appendix 1. A close reading of the treaty is essential to an understanding of the process of negotiations, and the agreements signed, in the context of twentieth-century hydro projects in this region. In the treaty, the Indian signators agreed to "hereby cede, release, surrender and yield up to the Government of the Dominion of Canada, for Her Majesty the Queen and Her successors for ever, all their rights, titles and privileges whatsoever to the lands included within the following limits."[86] Approximately two-thirds of Manitoba was thus surrendered, under terms that are remarkable for their comprehensiveness and finality, at least from a government perspective. In return, the Indians received reserve allotments based on 160 acres per family of five, a five-dollar annuity for band members, and the "right to pursue their avocations of hunting and fishing throughout the tract surrendered as hereinbefore described, subject to such regulations as may from time to time be made by Her Government of Her Dominion of Canada, and saving and excepting such tracts as may from time to time be required or taken up for settlement, mining, lumbering or other purposes, by Her said Government of the Dominion of Canada, or by any of the subjects thereof duly authorized therefor by the said Government."[87] Hence, the Indians secured the right to continue their hunting and fishing activities, subject to future government regulations and non-Native desires for the land. In effect as soon as the government could identify a manner in which these and other resources could be of value (such as the rivers and lakes for water power), new regulations would be passed which could prevent the Indians from hunting and fishing.

The boundaries of the treaty area were demarcated to a large extent by the various lakes and waterways, and the treaty stipulated that "where lakes form the treaty limits, ten miles from the shore of the lake should be included in the treaty." This would seem to imply that the water in the lake, or more likely the water bed, was owned by the Indians and therefore required inclusion as formally surrendered territory. Other boundaries of the treaty were drawn at certain waterways, not in them, implying that the water itself was not consciously included within the boundaries. The treaty does not discuss any surrender of water directly, however, but reserves the right of the government to "the free navigation of all lakes and rivers, and free access to the shores thereof."[88]

Did the Indians of Treaty Five understand the treaty and its implications? Did they understand the nature of the surrender proposed, and that many of their future rights would be subject to "regulations" made by the government? These are difficult questions, and the relative lack of research on Treaty Five, in particular the Indian view of the treaty, renders an answer difficult. One researcher has emphasized that the Indians were indeed aware of the extent of their aboriginal title in northern Manitoba, and were only prepared to surrender it because of severe economic hardship.[89] Yet, other researchers have argued that the problems encountered at Grand Rapids in 1876 demonstrate that these Indians at least were confused about the intent of the treaty, if not about the treaty itself.[90]

More research has been done on the Indian view of the treaties in Saskatchewan and Alberta than in Manitoba, and some of the findings there are of interest, especially in light of the similarities in treaty texts, treaty "negotiations" and even treaty commission personnel. In the case of Treaty Six, for instance, a research report published by the Federation of Saskatchewan Indians, based in part on the contemporary oral tradition, has argued that the Indians believed they were surrendering only the land, and to be more specific the topsoil, to be used in farming. As Peter Ballantyne Band elder Tom Jobb put it, "What I heard from the stories was that they only gave up the land, not the animals or the rivers or the lakes."[91] This perspective has also been forwarded in the case of Treaty Seven, jointly with the view that the Indians there saw the treaty more as a peace agreement than as a land surrender.[92] Research into Treaty Eight has demonstrated that the treaty commissioners there actually spent very little time explaining the crucial, "cede, release, and surrender" clause of the treaty to the Indians.[93] And as cited earlier there is evidence that the version of the treaty read to the Indians at the Treaty Eight signing made no reference to the powers of the government to curtail through regulations the Indians' hunting and fishing activities.[94] In fact, it is quite likely that in few if any of the treaties this clause was adequately explained.[95] Hence, we are faced with a difficult question: Would the Indians have so readily signed the treaties had they fully understood the texts and their implications? It is clear from the reports of the negotiations that the Indians were very concerned with protecting their traditional activities, in some cases almost to the exclusion of other aspects of the treaties. As well, it has been persuasively argued that, rather than viewing the treaties as sacred and inviolable, the original treaty signators saw the agreements as flexible instruments to be altered as necessary to ensure the economic well-being of the Indians, both in traditional and modern pursuits.[96] The Federation of Saskatchewan Indians' report places this whole question in perspective. It states, in part: "The oral history of the present generation of Churchill River Basin Cree makes it clear that the treaty's signators were explicitly attempting to protect their economy by assuring unbroken and unimpeded access to the very resources from which they drew the entire economic subsistence of their lifestyle. From their point of view, it would have been irresponsible to insist upon anything less than complete control of the resources."[97] But this view is counterbalanced by the general theme that many Indian groups were forced to sign treaties due to serious economic problems, and saw these agreements as one means of adapting to the economic changes occurring in the West, including a decline in the viability of traditional economic pursuits.

THE MÉTIS AND THE SCRIP COMMISSIONS

While the reasons for and method of obtaining the surrender of the Indians' title to the land was fairly straightforward, the case of the Métis and other mixed-bloods proved to be more problematic. They were the offspring of unions between Europeans and Indians, and the federal government never seemed able to develop a definite policy to deal with them. Were they Indians? Were they "white men"? Or were they something else altogether, a separate people with a separate identity? In fact, they were all three, which at least partially explains the government's difficulties in dealing with them.

At the time of the signing of Treaty One, there were at least three identifiable groups of mixed-blood individuals in western Canada. There were the English-oriented *half-breeds,* also sometimes known as the *country born.* Speaking primarily English, their culture was dominated by English and Scottish elements, and they did not readily recognize their Indian ancestry. There were the French-oriented *Métis,* whose culture was in many ways a blend of French and Indian elements, and who spoke mostly French or a French-Cree hybrid language known as *Michif.* While emphasizing their distinctiveness, the Métis acknowledged with pride their Indian ancestry. And there were those mixed-blood individuals who identified with their Indian ancestry to the virtual exclusion of their non-Indian heritage. These people were culturally *Indians.*[98]

The issue of the mixed-blood peoples was first addressed during the negotiations for the Robinson-Superior and Robinson-Huron Treaties in 1850. In these cases, the mixed-blood population was found to be living with the Indians *as Indians,* and it was at the insistence of the Indians that the mixed-bloods be added to the treaty list. The commissioner agreed, based on the fact of their prior occupation of the land and of their obvious relationship with the Indians.[99] No specific lands were set aside for these people. In fact, the government disclaimed any responsibility for the mixed-bloods, leaving the issue in the hands of the Indians.[100]

The handling of the mixed-blood issue in the Robinson treaties set a precedent in the treatment of these people in the subsequent numbered treaties. Generally, where they lived with the Indians, or lived as Indians, they were included in the treaty if they wished, and if the Indians agreed. Hence, they became treaty Indians. Other mixed-blood people, particularly the French-speaking Métis, did not desire to be treated as Indians, a feeling with which the federal government concurred. The federal government was not in the business of creating new Indians, particularly due to the expense of annuity payments. But their handling of the aboriginal title of the Métis by virtue of their Indian ancestry and their prior occupation of the land would prove sloppy, and even deceitful, and have serious repercussions for the Métis for over a century.

The federal government was not particularly concerned with the Métis and their claims in the Red River area of Assiniboia (now Manitoba), and it was this attitude which led ultimately to the "Red River Rebellion."[101] In 1869, as the Hudson's Bay Company was about to sell Rupert's Land to the new Dominion of Canada, it became clear that the Indians were not the only ones who were disgruntled. The Métis, too, saw the land as theirs, and petitioned the federal government to be included in the negotiations that surrounded the sale. The petitions fell upon deaf ears, and when it became apparent that their land would be sold without their approval, they formed a provisional government headed by Louis Riel, seized control of the district, and, as the legal government, initiated negotiations with Canada for the entry of Assiniboia into the Canadian union, not as a crown colony as Canada had planned, but as a province. The List of Rights which Riel and the Métis drafted, designed to protect their language, culture and land in the face of eastern immigration, was accepted by the federal government and transformed into the Manitoba Act of 1870.

The history of the development of the Manitoba Act, and its aftermath, is both complex and controversial. The act set aside 1,400,000 acres of "ungranted" land for the Métis "towards the extinguishment of the Indian Title to the lands in the Province."[102] However, it dictated that the land be allotted to "the children of the half-breed heads of families," and not the heads of families themselves. The real confusion developed as a series of orders-in-council was passed to explain, or alter, this provision, along with three different censuses to ascertain who were eligible Métis. It took a full ten years before the land allocation was completed, but by then many Métis had left the province, and many of those who had remained had lost the title to their allotments.[103] Of the 10,000 Métis determined eligible to receive scrip, by 1886 less than one thousand still retained land.[104]

How the Métis came to be a largely landless class in Manitoba needs some explanation. While the federal government was busy amending the Manitoba Act (which was illegal[105]) and passing orders-in-council, eastern immigrants were moving into Manitoba and settling on lands claimed by the Métis. Resulting conflicts were usually settled in favour of the immigrants.[106] Indeed, it was an integral part of the National Policy that settlement be facilitated, and the federal government was committed to the policy. In 1873, as it became apparent that Métis family heads would not obtain land, it was announced that the family-head descendants of the Selkirk settlers would receive land title in recognition of their pioneering occupation of the soil.[107] The federal government then proposed to deal with the Métis hostility to this plan by issuing scrip to Métis family heads. Scrip in this case consisted of a certificate of entitlement to be issued to the Métis in one of two forms. In the first, land scrip, the certificate stated that the person named on it could buy any unclaimed quarter section of land (160 acres), and the certificate constituted full payment. In the second, money scrip, the certificate was worth $160, and was negotiable by the bearer as payment for crown lands at the going rate of one dollar per acre. A variety of circumstances quickly ensued that ensured that many Métis would not receive their land allotments. Speculation in Métis scrip became rampant, and despite expressions of concern by the government that some Métis were selling their scrip to whomever was available, little was done to prevent it (the passage of legislation notwithstanding). The actual issuance of scrip, and the subsequent allocation of land, was a long process and was fraught with many difficulties. The poverty-stricken Métis simply could not afford to wait for their land, and sold to speculators. Land was allotted by a form of lottery, and the chances of any individual obtaining a desired parcel of land was unlikely. Furthermore, only unoccupied land was allocated, and eastern settlers were quickly taking up the best land in the region. Frequently when a Métis received his allotment, he found his land to be unsuitable, and was sometimes unable to locate the land at all.[108] Viewed as ordinary citizens by the federal government, the Métis, unlike the Indians, had no special legislation to protect them and their lands.[109] Their lands and their allotments were their private property, and hence were subject to alienation. And much of their land was alienated.

Some analysts have argued that the federal government deliberately failed to ensure the land allocations of the Métis, because to do so would interfere with the National Policy. As P.R. Mailhot and D.N. Sprague have written, "The reality, of course, was that the Government of Canada had no intention of creating an autonomous 'half-breed' province. The intention – before, during, and after the passage of the Manitoba Act – was speedy confirmation of grants by the HBC and a land policy that would encourage large-scale immigration from Ontario and the British Isles before settling any other native land claims."[110]

It is believed that Minister of the Interior David Laird "feared that indiscriminate recognition of [Métis] rights under section 32 [of the Manitoba Act] would lead to too great a concentration of half-breeds in the settlement belt."[111] The Métis, he believed, should be displaced in hopes that they would drift north to become fishermen and labourers. John A. Macdonald even went so far as to refer to the provision of land to the Métis under the Manitoba Act on the basis of their "Indian title" as having been incorrect, for the Métis "did not allow themselves to be Indians."[112] But the federal government was caught: the Manitoba Act had clearly identified a Métis aboriginal title to the land, a title which had to be extinguished. Through fraudulence and impropriety, the Métis never obtained much of the land reserved for them under the Manitoba Act. While some were improvident, and others were not interested in land due to their buffalo-hunting traditions, the fact remains that most Métis in Manitoba were farmers, understood the need for land, and would not have readily squandered it away.[113]

During the ten years of fraudulent land allocation and scrip use in Manitoba, many Métis packed up their belongings and left for the

Saskatchewan district and other parts of the North-West. Subsequently, a scrip commission was established to journey throughout the North-West in search of those Manitoba Métis who had not bothered even to claim their scrip. But generally the federal government was not prepared to acknowledge Métis land claims in the North-West until, once again, the threat of serious trouble became imminent. The Métis "Rebellion" in Saskatchewan in 1885 proved to be the necessary spark.

Between 1870 and 1877, the federal government was expeditiously obtaining the surrender of the Indian title to the fertile belt through treaties. Inevitably, the claims of the Métis and other mixed-bloods simultaneously surfaced, and were frequently raised as a matter of concern by the Indians. In the case of Treaty Three, the federal government, no doubt nervous after the Riel episode in Manitoba, readily admitted into the treaty those mixed-bloods willing to declare themselves *Indians.* The others, by exclusion, were considered *Whites,* and not deserving of special treatment. But in 1875, the Métis of Rainy River and Rainy Lake were allowed to sign a memorandum of agreement that provided them with reserves and other treaty benefits as Métis, in return for the surrender of their rights to the land "by virtue of their Indian blood."[114] This proved to be an anomaly however; the federal government never authorized the agreement, the Métis were bureaucratically transformed into treaty Indians, and no other similar agreements were ever signed.

Expedience became the key word in settling Métis claims in much of the North-West. It became policy to deal with Métis claims simultaneously with those of the Indians wherever possible; it was the most inexpensive way to proceed. For instance, when the Métis of the Green Lake area of Saskatchewan petitioned for scrip in 1887, they were denied it because that area had not yet been surrendered by the Indian adhesion to Treaty Six (initiated in 1889).[115] Further, it became evident that, as the treaty and scrip commissions travelled together throughout the North-West (and sometimes the same individuals acted in similar capacities simultaneously for both), the resolution of Métis claims was contingent upon prior resolution of the Indian claims.[116] It is not surprising, then, that the Métis exerted whatever influence they had on the Indians to sign the treaties.

Even though the Dominion Lands Act of 1879 extended the issuance of scrip to Métis in the fertile belt of the North-West, it was not until the Métis appeared ready to rebel against the Canadian government that a scrip commission to settle their claims was despatched.

Unfortunately, the commission arrived too late for the Métis of Duck Lake, Batoche and the surrounding territory, as government inaction precipitated the North-West Rebellion. Yet, even for those who did not participate in this action (the majority of the Métis in the North-West), the issuance of scrip proved not to be a saviour of their land rights. Over ninety percent of the scrip issued was taken as money scrip, which was easily alienable.[117] And many Métis sold their scrip to speculators, as had been done in Manitoba, and would be done in other parts of the territory. The travelling scrip commissions were accompanied by speculators, and a federal banking service to facilitate the buying and selling of scrip was frequently attached as well. Collusion among scrip buyers avoided a costly bidding war; fixed prices were to be offered to the Métis, prices which in no way reflected the true value of their scrip.[118]

Scrip commissions were attached to the treaty commissions negotiating Treaties Five, Eight, Ten and Eleven, as well as to the Montreal Lake adhesion to Treaty Six. "Half-breeds" were usually given the option of taking treaty or scrip. Generally, those who lived as Indians opted for treaty, while the others took scrip. An important factor in the decision to take scrip appears to have been a fear of being placed on reserves.[119] Later, after 1879, the federal government attempted to convince Métis who had taken treaty to withdraw and take scrip, a process which would reduce the overall cost to the government.[120] In the The Pas agency district of Treaty Five, some one hundred families withdrew from the treaty in 1886, including the entire band at Birch River.[121] Just as economic hardship had been a factor in convincing them to sign the treaties, so was their subsequent economic hardship under treaty an encouragement to accept the offer of scrip. As late as 1944, the federal government continued to pursue its policy of de-Indianizing the Métis who had taken treaty when they attempted to remove some seven hundred Métis from the Treaty Eight list in the Slave Lake area. Their attempt was ultimately unsuccessful.[122]

In all, the issuance of scrip as both an acknowledgement and an extinguishment of the aboriginal title of the Métis and other mixed-bloods was nothing short of a scandal. A good comparison of the treaty process and scrip commissions has been provided by Taylor:

The procedure adopted for dealing with the Métis was unilateral. It proceeded by legislation and order-in-council. It did not even have the appearance of a negotiated settlement which the treaties had. Métis commissions did not negotiate terms, but simply examined the status of claimants to determine their eligibility to participate in the compensation offered. Indian title was extinguished, in theory at least, from the bottom upwards, while the Métis title was extinguished from the top down.[123]

Hence, while the treaties have afforded the Indians a special status and some protection, not to mention grounds for contemporary legal action, scrip simply acknowledged Métis special status and then simply removed it. There were no terms, no promises and nothing to negotiate. Furthermore, those Métis who did not receive scrip, and hence did not surrender their Indian title, were nonetheless treated as if they had taken scrip, in the same manner that Indians who did not sign on to the treaties were considered nevertheless to have surrendered their rights in treaty areas. The Métis became like all non-Natives in the country, and were largely forgotten by the federal government.

The Indians and Métis surrendered their aboriginal title to Canada under dubious circumstances. Indeed, it is clear that in virtually every instance the government planned to proceed with development of Native lands with or without a land surrender, and most Natives were made aware of this fact. The Royal Proclamation of 1763 notwithstanding, Indian title was to be secured within the strictest terms possible; if it was not to be secured on terms favourable to the government, it was not to be secured at all. Non-Native development would occur just the same.

Some similarities in the treaty-making and scrip-commission process warrant attention. Where possible, in communicating with Indian bands, the government undervalued the land to be surrendered by describing it as "barren" or "useless" to them, in order to secure the best possible terms for the Dominion. This was done despite the fact that, in most cases, the valuable resource potential of the land was the prime reason for the commencement of the treaty process. The terms of the treaties, even in historic context, can only be described as blatantly inequitable. It is a paradox that, while the resource value of surrendered land has increased over the years with inflation and new resource discoveries, the annuities granted to the Indians have remained fixed at their nineteenth-century levels.

The treaties were always formulated in advance, and the treaty commissioners were at pains to ensure that no "outside" promises were uttered, no terms altered, and that the least expensive avenues were pursued. Granted, some Indian bands were able to negotiate additional promises, but these instances were rare and still represented a bonanza for the government. It is not likely that, for instance, the medicine chest clause included in Treaty Six by the Plains Cree Indians has had any real effect: the federal government undertook to provide medical assistance to all Indians as a matter of policy. Treaty Six Indians have obtained no special benefits because of this clause. Furthermore, where absolutely necessary to facilitate treaty signing, oral promises were made but rarely included in the written version of the treaty. A careful reading of Alexander Morris's work, *The Treaties of Canada with the Indians,* would suggest that the emphasis to conclude a treaty, and hence the looseness with which commissioners offered oral promises, was due primarily to the overbearing desire of commissioners to complete their tasks, to appear efficient and competent in the eyes of their superiors. While the shrewdness of the various Indian negotiators may be rightly emphasized, their negotiating victories were hollow. One need only compare the economic value of the land surrendered to the economic value of the promises extracted to see this clearly. The Indians were forced to bargain from a very weak position, the perceived threat of violence (usually unfounded) being one of their most persuasive tools. Faced with a rapidly declining economy, they saw the treaties as essential to reconstructing their lives. And they knew well that, as settlers and other developments entered their territory, any bargaining position that they did have would quickly erode.

Hence, there was little real negotiation in the treaty discussions. In the case of adhesions, this fact is even more evident. Furthermore, bands absent at the time of a treaty making were subsequently denied the opportunity to make a new treaty or "negotiate" different terms. They were forced to simply sign on to the existing treaty as if the signatures of the leaders of other bands were binding on them.

Insofar as the Indians received token promises under the treaties, which many argue today have yet to be fulfilled, the Métis seem to have ended up with virtually nothing as a product of their "Indian" title to the land. The government's bungling of the Métis issue, especially through the scrip commissions, may in fact have been part of a conspiracy to obtain their lands for other purposes, as Donald McLean suggests, although the evidence for this is still inconclusive.[124] At any rate, many Métis ended up with no land at all, leaving them with the ignominious distinction as "forgotten people." The federal government largely washed its hands of these people after the scrip commissions had completed their work, and neither the federal government nor the provinces have yet to develop any coherent policies to deal with the

Métis as "aboriginal peoples," our new constitution notwithstanding.[125]

In the end, the Native people surrendered about two-thirds of Canada through the treaty and scrip processes. In so doing, they believed their rights had been secured and that they would participate in the development of the western Canadian economy, but that such development would not be at the expense of their culture and traditional economic activities. The promises made were to last as long as the sun shone and the rivers flowed. But, less than one hundred years after the Manitoba Act and the signing of Treaty One, many of the rivers would cease to flow.

Cumberland House and the Squaw Rapids Dam

3

They don't give a damn what happens to the people here.[1]

Cumberland House is primarily a Métis community, and this fact alone does much to explain the manner in which its concerns were and continue to be dealt with in the construction of the Squaw Rapids Dam. Little information on the dam was provided to the community, and hence we have no record of protests concerning the dam prior to or during its construction. Similarly, there is little indication that the Saskatchewan government or the Saskatchewan Power Corporation (SPC) demonstrated any concern for the community or the environmental zone downstream of the dam. Since the construction of the dam, the people of Cumberland House have struggled first to make the government and SPC acknowledge the negative downstream effects of the dam, second to have them acknowledge their liability for these effects, and third to obtain proper compensation and mitigation.

THE COMMUNITY OF CUMBERLAND HOUSE

Cumberland House is a Swampy Cree Indian and Métis community located in the Saskatchewan River Delta on the northeastern edge of the Province of Saskatchewan. It lies just north of the province's Northern Administration District and is situated on an island surrounded by the Saskatchewan, Bigstone and Tearing rivers and the south shore of Cumberland Lake. It is accessible in summer by ferry across the Saskatchewan River at Pemmican Portage, and in winter by an ice road across the river. It is accessible also by airplane.

The area is an environmental region transitional between the parkland and boreal forest, lying on the southern fringe of the Subarctic ethnographic region.[2] It shares many of the physical characteristics of the subarctic, including numerous lakes, streams and rivers, with muskeg and willows in low-lying areas and spruce and pine on the high bluffs. The agricultural potential of the region has also been recognized for many years. The Saskatchewan River Delta as a whole is renowned for its wildlife, especially large game and waterfowl.

Cumberland House consists of an Indian reserve occupied by members of the Cumberland House Indian Band, with a population in 1984 of approximately 244, and a Métis community (including non-status Indians) with a population in 1984 of approximately 1,100. The reserve and the community are located about three kilometres apart, and each has its own administrative bodies. Politically, each operates as a separate community, although in most other spheres (e.g., economics, religion, social life) virtually no distinction can be made between the two groups. The political struggle of the people of Cumberland House has been spearheaded by the Local Community Authority (LCA), which represents the Métis and non-status residents. The Indian band has just recently begun acting separately from the LCA.

The contemporary economy of Cumberland House is diverse, combining components of the "traditional" economy of fishing, trapping (both domestic and commercial) and hunting, with wage-labour activities. In addition, Cumberland House residents are involved in outfitting in a number of hunting camps scattered throughout the region. Although the community has a long history of involvement in wage-labour activities, a significant proportion of their income and, perhaps more important, a significant amount of their economic time is related to harvesting the resources in the Saskatchewan River Delta area.

COMMUNITY HISTORY

Cumberland House is considered to be the oldest community in Saskatchewan, dating back to 1774 when Samuel Hearne established a Hudson's Bay Company post, the first such post in the interior of Rupert's Land. The site was selected by Hearne because there was an excellent network of waterways around the junction of three rivers: the Saskatchewan River, providing access east and west; the Sturgeon River, providing access to the Churchill and Athabasca regions in the north; and the Grass River, providing access to the northeast. Indeed, the history of Cumberland House is intimately intertwined with the history of the rivers and lakes in the region. The community never served as a major fur-trading post, but performed a vital function in the inland fur-trading network as a depot and distribution centre.[3] Further, as the administrative centre for the Hudson's Bay Company's inland trade, the community was at the very heart of the company's attempts to compete successfully with the rival North West Company and free traders that had preceded it into the interior.[4] Throughout its history, Cumberland House saw the bark canoes of the Indians, the large freighting canoes of the voyageurs, the York boats, the stern-wheel steamboats, and finally the outboard-motor boats in the nearby waters. The waterways were, in the past and remain so today, the lifeblood of the community.

In 1821, with the amalgamation of the Hudson's Bay Company and the North West Company, the intense period of competition came to an end, and Cumberland House began to decline in importance.[5] However, its strategic location ensured the viability of the community. In the 1880s, when steamboats were introduced into the Saskatchewan River system, Cumberland House became an important depot for refitting the boats and replenishing supplies, as well as a gateway to the smaller posts of the North.

The Indian population became extensively involved in the fur trade in and around Cumberland House after the post was established in 1774, and with the proliferation of mixed-blood children the permanent population of the community grew. By 1840 the Native population was large enough to justify the establishment of an Anglican Church mission, and in 1870 a Roman Catholic Church mission. Although many of the mixed-blood individuals had been born and raised in the Cumberland House region, following the Red River "Rebellion" in Manitoba in 1870, a number of Métis moved north into the area to escape the onslaught of eastern-Canadian settlers. In 1876, the Indians in the Cumberland House region signed Treaty Five (and in so doing became the only Indians residing in Saskatchewan to be members of Treaty Five).[6] Although they were to be granted a reserve under the treaty, they did not actually receive title until 1930. Between 1876 and 1930, both the Indians and the Métis believed that reserve status had been granted at the time the treaty was signed, and the Métis were living on what they believed to be Indian land. The Métis requested that part of the reserve be surrendered and granted to them. This was done in 1906, even though the land was not yet a legal Indian reserve.[7] By the middle of the twentieth century, most of the Indians had moved away from Cumberland House to a parcel of reserve land at Pinebluff, some forty kilometres to the northwest. However, in the mid-1960s the Indians were relocated back to Cumberland House, likely because of the closure of their school by the Department of Indian Affairs.

As the community moved into the twentieth century, its importance to the fur and transport economy declined. However, the waterways remained important to the Cumberland House residents as access routes to the rich hunting, fishing and trapping that the region offered. By 1950, the Government of Saskatchewan had begun a northern housing program, and Cumberland House saw the replacement of log and mud shanties with wood houses. Airplane and radio service was established to connect the community with the "outside world," an all-weather road from Nipawin was constructed, and ferry service across the Saskatchewan River was initiated. While such progress was inevitable, it was not without its costs. Along with the new facilities and services came the news that a hydroelectric dam would be constructed upstream from the community.

THE SQUAW RAPIDS DAM

The Squaw Rapids Dam was perceived by the Government of Saskatchewan and the Saskatchewan Power Corporation as the first step in a thirty-year plan to harness electricity from the Saskatchewan River and other northern rivers to meet an increasing provincial energy demand, estimated in 1962 to have grown sixfold in the preceding decade.[8] The Squaw Rapids Dam would also be the province's very first hydroelectric dam feeding power into the provincial energy grid, dominated at the time by thermal generating facilities.

The first mention of hydro projects in general on the Saskatchewan River occurred in the SPC annual report of 1955.[9] In the report of 1956, potential hydro sites were named: Squaw Rapids, Nipawin, and Fort-à-la-Corne.[10] It is apparent that at this time the Fort-à-la-Corne site was favoured as the best site for the first project, and in 1957 the engineering firm of Crippen-Wright was hired "for the purpose of bringing up-to-date previous studies of the Fort-à-la-Corne site and investigating at least two other possible sites on that river."[11] By September 1959, however, the Squaw Rapids site had emerged as the favourite, and a public announcement was made that the project would begin immediately.[12] It was estimated that the project would cost some $46 million.

Construction on the dam and related facilities began early in 1960. Construction activity reached a peak in July 1961, when a maximum of 1,700 men was employed at the site.[13] Also in 1961, the Saskatchewan River was closed off and diverted in order to facilitate construction. By October 1962, the dam had been completed and final closure of the river was executed. The forebay area, known as Tobin Lake, subsequently began to fill.

At the time the Squaw Rapids Dam was officially opened by Premier W.S. Lloyd, in June 1963, virtually no consideration had been given to any potential negative effects the dam might have. The construction of the dam was seen as a heroic effort, a triumph of "man over nature," and a triumph that could only benefit the residents of Saskatchewan. Premier Lloyd made this clear in his address at the commissioning of the station: "We may look upon this great complex of machines and masonry as a symbol of many things. In one sense it is a symbol of man's control over his environment and of man's use of his opportunities. In another sense it is a symbol of the growth of our province. The use of power is one of the measurements of economic growth and of growth in our standard of living."[14] The heroic struggle was echoed in the press: "Man is bending the mighty Saskatchewan River to his will as the province's first hydro-electric project nears completion on this rugged, isolated site," declared the *Regina Leader Post*.[15] *The Commonwealth* echoed this view: "Saskatchewan, once the dry land, drought-ridden bread basket of Canada will be transformed into a diversified, increasingly vital province in which the people, by controlling a river, exercise a substantial control over their entire economic and social environment."[16]

Missing in all of these pronouncements of technological triumph was any consideration that the Squaw Rapids Dam might cause harm to the environment, or to people, particularly those of Cumberland House some ninety-seven kilometres downstream. Although Premier Lloyd stated in his address that "we should not today overlook the history of our river and of the people who first encountered and used it,"[17] he generally described the river's role as a "hindrance" to the development of the province. There would be a great many advantages to the construction of the dam, he affirmed, stating clearly that an improvement in the standard of living was inevitable.[18] The hinterland and its resources were to be made to serve the metropolis of the province, and even more directly would serve those individuals who had invested in SPC. Lloyd stated:

This mighty generating station is set down here in the fringe of our forest area to serve cities, towns, villages and farms separated from it and from each other by hundreds of miles. . . . Your investment in the Saskatchewan Power Corporation is a productive investment. Your investment is in comfort and convenience for thousands of homes; in employment for thousands of people, in sources of power for old and new industries. It is an investment which has value in terms of the hardest economics but, much more important, an investment which has value in terms of human welfare.[19]

Needless to say, the residents of Cumberland House were not likely holders of Saskatchewan Savings Bonds.

The communities in the Squaw Rapids area were absolutely delighted with the announcement of construction plans. Prosperity would surely be brought to the region, with construction jobs and spin-off benefits to the local economy. So keen on the project were these communities that two of them, Nipawin and Carrot River, squabbled over the naming of the new hydro facility.[20]

Other advantages were cited frequently by the SPC. The corporation grew fond of highlighting the immense recreational potential that would develop behind the dam, in newly created Tobin Lake, while seemingly ignoring the fact that the dam might seriously harm the recreational potential downstream. The provincial newsletter, *Saskatchewan News*, stated, "The new lake will provide excellent recreational facilities in the heavily-treed northeast as nature's bonus for storing water."[21] *The Commonwealth* went even further when it stated, "The new lake formed by the dam opens up new vistas of recreation, and downstream communities can now look forward to more reliable water supply."[22] Such assertions were, however, merely speculative, as no impact studies had been done.

The Squaw Rapids Dam, in addition to providing Saskatchewan with power, was designed to generate power for export, especially to Manitoba. In fact, construction of the dam was accelerated, and more generating units were installed than were necessary for provincial use, in order to sell power to Manitoba, while the latter began construction of its own Saskatchewan River hydro project at Grand Rapids.[23] The two projects were clearly tied together as part of a giant scheme to extract power from the Saskatchewan River, and it was believed by hydro officials that regulation of the river's flow by the Squaw Rapids Dam would "greatly enhance" power production from Grand Rapids further downstream.[24]

The first generator at Squaw Rapids began operating in April 1963, and four were in operation when the station was officially commissioned by the Premier the following June. Two more generating units were added in 1964, and two more again in 1965, for a total of eight. The total generating capacity of the Squaw Rapids Dam is 280 megawatts. The dam is now operated by remote control from the Queen Elizabeth Station in Saskatoon. However, since the Squaw Rapids Dam was designed as a "peaking station" to provide electricity during peak demand periods, this maximum generating capacity is only periodically achieved.

CONSIDERATION OF DOWNSTREAM EFFECTS

The possibility that a hydroelectric dam at Squaw Rapids could have a negative downstream effect was discussed as early as 1958, when the Squaw Rapids site began to emerge as the most viable. In a confidential memo, the Deputy Minister of Natural Resources instructed members of his department to begin considering the issue. In a reference to Cumberland House residents, he wrote: "It is suggested that there is some sturgeon fishing by a group of Indians at the confluence of the Torch and the Saskatchewan Rivers. Since the plan might involve the diversion of the Torch into the Saskatchewan above the dam, we should consider what affect this might have on the sturgeon fishery at that point."[25] The diversion mentioned in this memo was not undertaken. Most of the memo in general referred to possible effects of the dam in the forebay, or reservoir, area where farmland and timber would be submerged. Non-Native farmers and settlers would have to be compensated and perhaps relocated. The Department of Natural Resources was expected to "examine the whole proposition and indicate how the project will affect resource management in the [forebay] area."[26] The issue of downstream effects, while broached, was clearly of secondary importance. Cumberland House, a Native community, was the only Saskatchewan community in the downstream area.

There is ample evidence to suggest that, as the project was planned and as construction forged ahead, only cursory attention was provided to the potential downstream effects, or to the community of Cumberland House. For instance, the Saskatchewan Power Management Advisory Committee rarely discussed the issue during their meetings. Whenever the Squaw Rapid Project was discussed, the committee usually concentrated on problems developing at the construction site itself, for example, roads, housing and construction contracts. Cumberland House was rarely mentioned, and there was no discussion of downstream effects. The one exception to this was a damage claim submitted by an outfitter based in the Cumberland Delta, Les Voyageurs Outfitters Ltd. The Management Advisory Committee did consider the issue of compensation for damages or loss of land in the area of Tobin Lake. Acting promptly, the committee established a figure of 2.5 times the assessed value of expropriated land as well as compensation for both movable (one-half the depreciated value) and unmovable (full depreciated value) buildings.[27] The non-Native farmers were to be dealt with expeditiously.

In 1960, a special committee was formed to deal with a variety of hydro-related issues. Known as the Squaw Rapids Hydro Electric Liaison Committee, its function was outlined at the first meeting on 25 January 1960: "The Chairman reviewed the need for a liaison committee to act: a) as an information centre; and b) to provide a contact between SPC and the various Departments of Government so that specific problems encountered can be handled as promptly and efficiently as possible." Like the Management Advisory Committee, the Liaison Committee focused on the Squaw Rapids site and the forebay area, and paid little attention to the downstream effects or to the community of Cumberland House. There were, however, a few exceptions: at the second meeting of the Liaison Committee, a member of the Department of Natural Resources "introduced the problem of flooding Cumberland Lake and Sipanok Channel which may destroy considerable fishing area."[28] It was not clear how, given the design of the project, Cumberland Lake and Sipanok Channel could be flooded, and the issue was not pursued.

A letter from the engineering firm of Crippen-Wright Ltd. to the SPC, dated 17 May 1960, confirms that even at this early date the SPC believed "the Squaw Rapids Development itself will have relatively little effect on downstream flow and the levels in Cumberland Lake."[29] Not everyone was convinced, however. Ducks Unlimited, an international conservation group which operated a number of projects in the Cumberland Delta area, was concerned about the possible negative effect of the dam: "Ducks Unlimited has expressed concern over the possibility of the drying up of Cumberland Delta areas. Such a result would adversely affect wildlife as well as the livelihood of local trappers. It was noted that PFRA [Prairie Farm Rehabilitation Administration] may have information as to water levels in this area. Department of Natural Resources is requested to report on this problem."[30]

At the next meeting of the Liaison Committee, the concerns expressed by Ducks Unlimited were again considered. A general lack of information concerning the project led to much speculation, and the prospect of negative downstream effects was treated as a relatively minor issue: "No further information has been received on the effect of the project on the Cumberland Delta area. It was noted that biologists in the Department [of Natural Resources] expect more advantages than disadvantages from the Project. In any event, *problems will most likely appear only after completion of the project"* [emphasis added]. Failing to take the issue of downstream effects seriously, the following comment was then added: "Someone suggested that Dr. Gallup be requested to conduct a poll among the muskrat population as to their future in this grey area."[31] Despite the allusions to investigations of downstream effects, I have not been able to uncover any evidence that such studies were, in fact, undertaken.

While the Liaison Committee functioned as an information centre for the project, the information at hand was not always complete and accurate. An excellent example of this occurred during the twelfth meeting of the committee, on 23 November 1962, and represents one of the few instances in which the committee discussed potential downstream effects and the operation of the Squaw Rapids Dam. The minutes of the meeting record, "The Chairman noted the possibility of loss of beaver and muskrat population downstream from the Powerhouse due to sudden fluctuations in the flow rate. SPC will co-ordinate Generator testing in 1963 as fully as possible in order to minimize damage."[32] A minor flurry subsequently erupted, not around the issue of downstream effects, but about the operation of the Squaw Rapids facility. E.B. Campbell, Assistant Chief Engineer of the SPC, wrote to the Chairman of the Liaison Committee (who was also an employee of the SPC) saying:

I am somewhat disturbed by a statement in the minutes of the recent meeting which appears to be attributed to you. . . . I do not think that we can be expected to limit operations at the Squaw Rapids site to protect beaver and muskrats. In future years the Squaw Rapids project will be operating as a peaking plant, at least during heavy load season, and this will result in extremely large daily fluctuations in discharge. These will vary from whatever minimum flow is established up to about 24,000 cfs. Any restriction on this in the interests of wildlife will, no doubt, result in economic losses to the hydro project that will greatly exceed the value of any fur bearing animals.[33]

The offensive passage in the minutes of the twelfth meeting was subsequently amended, at which time the following new passage was added:

The meeting was fully informed by SPC that unknown fluctuations in water levels below the Powerhouse will be a permanent reality and will take on whatever pattern is made necessary from the day-to-day or even hour-to-hour requirements of the system, as soon as the powerplant is fully operational. It is expected that fluctuation in water levels immediately below the Powerhouse and for some ten to twenty miles downstream will be considerable.[34]

As part of their mandate to communicate information about the project, meetings were held by the Liaison Committee. Delegations were received from various communities in the Squaw Rapids area, such as Nipawin, Carrot River and Whitefox. The purpose of these meetings was to explain the project and its potential effects and to learn the concerns of the residents. The major issues of concern to the residents seemed to be compensation for lost lands and the enhancement of economic benefits to the communities from construction activity. There is no evidence from the minutes of the Liaison Committee meetings that representatives from Cumberland House attended or that the committee held any meetings in the community.

THE COMMUNITY VIEW OF THE DAM PROPOSAL

While it is apparent that some representatives of the government and/or the SPC came to Cumberland House to discuss the dam, there appears to be no documentary evidence concerning the date, the number, or the purpose and content of these meetings. In interviews, only a few Cumberland House residents could recall such meetings having taken place or the general pattern of discussion. Unfortunately, the recollections were often vague. For instance, one resident stated: "There was a bunch of guys came in here. We had a bunch of promises but we never seen anything. It was a big meeting. I can't remember any promises but we did get many promises. They fooled us."[35] Other residents recalled some of the promises that were orally made. These included:

1 The community would receive electricity by land-line to replace two diesel generating units. Power bills would be lower.

2 Residents would find employment on the dam construction and related activities.

3 The water levels would remain stable, and conditions downstream from the dam would probably improve.

As could be expected, the discussion on the part of the government or the SPC seemed to centre on the advantages Cumberland House residents would gain from the hydro project. Some comments made by residents highlight this: "They told us that they would have a better system about controlling the water"; . . . "I heard it [the dam] was going to be good because we would have electricity. Never mentioned it would be [i.e. cost] so much in the future. No more coal lamps"; . . . "They said electricity would be good for the community. Sure, that is good, but the damage of our lake is not good."

None of the residents interviewed could recall being told about any potential downstream effects. One resident commented, "No, they never said anything about harming the lake. They told us they were going to build a dam, and that was it. They also said the dam would not have any effect on our lakes and rivers." Only one resident recalled the issue of compensation being discussed, although it may have occurred after the dam was built. Since none of the residents recalled being told of potential negative downstream effects, it was unlikely that the issue of compensation would have been broached. Another said, "We didn't know what was going on. Because the people from Sask Power or the Government never said anything about what could happen in later years."[36]

It is unclear from the interviews and available evidence when these meetings took place. It would seem that the plans for the dam, and even the construction itself, were well under way before the issue was formally brought to Cumberland House. Consider these comments: "It wasn't until after they started building it that we heard about it"; . . . "Only found out that the dam would be built when the actual work began." Further, there is no indication that the community was given the opportunity to participate in the planning and construction phases. Some interviewees said: "They did not consult the community"; . . . "They said they were going to build and that was it"; . . . "Nobody said what the effect would be. We believed what Sask Power said, that water levels would remain stable"; . . . "Mistake has been that no studies were done. The people in the community were not asked for their knowledge."[37]

EMERGING PROBLEMS

Despite the private concerns of various members of the SPC and the Saskatchewan government, the SPC publicly maintained that there would be no negative downstream effects. In October 1962, as the Tobin

Lake reservoir was being filled, concern was voiced over the related low-water levels at The Pas, Manitoba, which is downstream from Cumberland House. The *Regina Leader-Post* published the following: "The Saskatchewan Power Corporation in Regina said in a statement Wednesday that its dam across the Saskatchewan River at Squaw Rapids in the northern part of the province is causing only temporary inconvenience to downstream users, including those at The Pas, Manitoba." Quoting the SPC statement, the article continued: "Following construction at Squaw Rapids, river control will provide supply stability for downstream users. The reservoir will refill from spring floods while the turbines, discharging water downstream during periods of otherwise low river flow, will tend to even out downstream flow."[38]

Despite these assurances, a claim against the SPC emerged very quickly. Les Voyageurs Outfitters Ltd., through its solicitor, made a claim in November 1962, just after the reservoir was filled. This company, based in the Cumberland Delta area, employed between six and fifteen Cumberland House residents as guides during the eight-week fall hunting season. According to Les Voyageurs, "The river became so low it was impossible to negotiate it even with light canoes, or to land float-equipped aircraft on it." As a result, three weeks of the season had to be cancelled, at an estimated loss of $10,000. According to the solicitor for Les Voyageurs, R.P. Rendek, "The SPC action contraven[ed] the Navigable Rivers Protection Act, which guarantees that the public right to navigation on navigable waterways will not be interfered with." Further, he "contended that SPC assured federal authorities that it would compensate anyone adversely affected by its actions."[39]

The SPC's initial reaction was to publicly deny legal liability since Les Voyageurs had been warned of the water level change and the construction schedule of the Squaw Rapids facility.[40] Privately, however, the SPC began immediately to investigate their legal options. Les Voyageurs' claim was discussed during the Management Advisory Committee meeting on 27 November 1962, at which time the option of allowing the claim to go to court was entertained.[41] However, by the meeting of this committee on 15 May 1963, the SPC had decided to reach a settlement with Les Voyageurs by providing compensation. A decision was reached to offer the outfitter $1,500 in return for a promise "not to proceed against the Corporation for any action of the Corporation arising out of operation of the reservoir at Squaw Rapids or regulation of stream flow."[42] Further, if Les Voyageurs were able to "show some convincing evidence of having suffered loss in excess of $1,500," the SPC would offer up to $5,000.[43] Clearly, the SPC had acknowledged responsibility for negative downstream effects and their obligation to provide compensation.[44] Yet, the residents of Cumberland House would not receive the same consideration when their claims were presented.

The claim by Les Voyageurs Outfitters Ltd. was followed very quickly by a rash of other complaints by Cumberland House residents. In 1963, when the community was asked to explain its failure to pay taxes, the Cumberland House Ratepayers Association executive responded by letter: "Another cause for the failure of payment of taxes can be attributed directly to the lack of money due to the fact that our sources of money have been cut down considerably. The fur and fishing industry is almost completely finished for the Squaw Rapids development just a few miles up from our settlement has greatly affected our water supply which caused the same industries possible. There is worse to come yet."[45]

The Hon. Bill Berezowsky, MLA for the Cumberland House region, also raised the issue with the government. With respect to the possibility of summer employment, the problem raised in caucus by Berezowsky "was that the way in which the Squaw Rapids Dam has affected the water level will in turn have a disadvantageous effect on fishing and other sources of income, consequently the possibilities of summer employment." The Saskatchewan government was also forced to deal with the need for a ferry crossing at Pemmican Portage. The changing water conditions in the Saskatchewan River had made crossing very hazardous, with the loss of some equipment and one life during the winter of 1963. The problem was clearly acknowledged by the government. In a memo from the Office of the Director of Northern Affairs to J.W. Churchman, Deputy Minister of Natural Resources, it was agreed that "the development of the Squaw Rapids hydro programme is thought to have created considerable hazard and an unreliable crossing at Pemmican Portage. The variance in water levels at this crossing caused by the hydro programme is responsible for the formation of poor ice on the river. Significant reductions in the flow of water at the dam invariably make the river crossing unsafe and hazardous." Subsequently, the Minister of Natural Resources himself acknowledged that the Squaw Rapids Dam was the cause of the problem: "The construction of the Squaw Rapids power plant has increased the hazard of crossing on the ice. The variance in flow in the river causes formation of weak ice."[46]

On 13 July 1964, the new Minister of Natural Resources, Hon. J. Cuelenaere, was informed by the President of the Cumberland House Fisherman's Cooperative of the problems caused by the dam. This letter, quoted here in full, is significant in that it details the nature of the problems being experienced in much the same terms that, twenty years later, Cumberland House residents would also use in formal interviews with the author. The problems, as seen by the president, have been consistent, yet solutions have not been forthcoming:

Honourable Sir,

We, the Fisherman's Co-operative of Cumberland House, have found it necessary to draw the attention of the authorities to the disastrous effect the inconsistent flow of water has meant to our livelihood. From the time the Squaw Rapids dam has been operational, we have noted the following:
Fish have been caught in deeper holes in rivers and lakes, when the water flow is suddenly reduced. Fishing operations carried on elsewhere have had to be abandoned. If the situation is reversed, the fish drown on sudden high levels. We suffer heavy losses both ways.
Sudden high water destroys nests of waterfowl during nesting seasons. Income usually derived from this source of guiding and hunting by natives is lowered.
At this time of writing, the species of wildlife suffering most from the consequences are big game. Their young are being caught in lowlands and drowned in the rise of water. The latter effects on fur bearing animals will also be greatly felt. The unsteady flow is definitely hampering with conservation.
We trust that our plea will reach sympathetic ears. We are a people depending on these sources for a living. We ask for more consideration from the management of the dam and your support before our plight is increased.[47]

In response to this letter, Cuelenaere indicated that officials in the Department of Natural Resources would investigate the matter with the SPC. He explained, "If further investigation reveals that damage is being done, I sincerely hope that we shall be able to take remedial measures."[48] However, some officials had already considered the issue and had concluded that the Squaw Rapids Dam was responsible, at least partially, for some damage. Acknowledging the problem, G.R. Bowerman, Fisheries Supervisor for the Department of Natural Resources in Prince Albert, informed the Chief of the Resource Program in the Department of Natural Resources: "There has been considerable reaction to the fluctuation of water levels from the Squaw Rapids Dam. There is little question that such reduced flow of water that has been experienced on occasions is detrimental to aquatic and marine life."[49] However, the Director of the Wildlife Branch of the Department of Natural Resources stated, "I do not have any definite reports of damage caused to wildlife through the release of waters from Squaw Rapids dam."[50] Other than the complaints offered by Cumberland House residents, no one had yet investigated in any systematic way the extent of the effect of the dam on wildlife and fish populations.[51]

In response to the concerns being raised by both Cumberland House residents and some members of the provincial government, research into problems in the delta region was finally undertaken. In April 1972, a government-appointed committee, the Committee on Saskatchewan River Delta Problems, completed a confidential report which substantiated many of the claims of the Cumberland House residents, but generally failed to discuss cause and effect in specific terms. Remedial measures were suggested for further investigation, including the stabilization of Cumberland Lake levels and major rivers in the delta through the regulation of water patterns or through the construction of various control structures.[52]

The subsequent four years saw the Saskatchewan government make little attempt to implement the committee's recommendations. Frustration at the community level intensified until, in the spring of 1976, the community issued an ultimatum: the government had sixty days to deliver concrete proposals to remedy the community's problems or the community would take legal action against the government and the SPC. Included in the litigation would be a claim for "damages for destruction of the northern wildlife habitat; alienation of native rights to hunting and fishing; and a claim for loss of tourist industry." The SPC, for its part, remained largely quiet on the issue, although Gordon McKay, SPC Power Production Superintendent, acknowledged, "There certainly appears to be a problem there, but just how big a problem I don't honestly know."[53]

By the time the sixty-day deadline had arrived, the community apparently had been satisfied that progress was being made. A new committee had been formed by the community, the Saskatchewan River Delta Committee, and discussions with the government had been productive. The government had agreed to conduct environmental and engineering studies on the construction of weirs across the Tearing River and at the outlet to Cumberland Lake, as well as an investigation into the feasibility of adjusting the operation of the Squaw Rapids plant to improve downstream water conditions.[54] At least three studies were produced as a result of this action.

An engineering study, conducted by the Prairie Farm Rehabilitation Administration (PFRA), acknowledged that "the fluctuating water levels have had a detrimental effect on trapping, hunting and fishing in the Cumberland Lake area, and have increased transportation problems on the lake and surrounding areas."[55] However, none of the engineering alternatives investigated were viewed in a totally favourable light, and no other recommendations were made.

In an environmental impact study, conducted by the Saskatchewan Research Council, the authors also acknowledged the problems caused by the Squaw Rapids Dam, but concluded that none of the mitigation proposals would have the acceptable balance of positive and negative effects.[56]

A third study was conducted on the implications of limiting the discharge from the Squaw Rapids Dam so as to lessen the effect upon the downstream area.[57] The report concluded that the maintenance of a constant discharge from Squaw Rapids would require a capital expenditure of some $30,000,000 to 1990. Presumably, this was a prohibitive amount. No recommendations were offered.

While generally supporting the assertions being made by the community concerning problems caused by the Squaw Rapids Dam, the three studies failed to offer any concrete proposals for mitigation. This ambivalence essentially allowed the government to delay further the negotiation process.

THE CHURCHILL RIVER STUDY

In the meantime, while studies and discussion were under way, plans for a proposed hydro dam at Wintego Rapids on the Churchill River in the northern part of the province had been announced. The Saskatchewan government's approach to this development was a cautious one, but not because of the problems associated with the Squaw Rapids Dam. Rather, the government was anxious to avoid the public outcry that had accompanied the recent announcements of hydro projects on Southern Indian Lake, in Manitoba, and in the James Bay region of Quebec.[58] In an effort to stem the potential backlash, the government created the Churchill River Board of Inquiry, to examine all aspects of the proposed development, social, economic and environmental, and to make recommendations about whether the project should proceed.[59] Premier Allan Blakeney went to great lengths to convince the province's citizens that the study was not "a public relations exercise designed to persuade the public to go along with a development decision that has already been made."[60]

Despite these actions, almost immediately after the announcement, concerns were expressed by both northern Natives and southern residents that the hydro project might seriously damage the environment of the north and the economy of the Native people who were dependent upon the lakes and rivers that would be harnessed for electricity. In response to these concerns, Fred Ursel, General Manager for the SPC, declared, "We do . . . accept the responsibility for compensation" for damages caused by the Wintego Dam. Further, he stated, "We do know that the corporation is adding to existing problems in the north and as good corporate citizens, which we believe ourselves to be, we should not be penalizing northern residents for making power available to the south."[61] However, despite these good corporate intentions, the SPC still could not come to grips with the damage they had caused in the Cumberland Delta by their Squaw Rapids facility, and were still reluctant to admit liability.

Cumberland House residents were granted the opportunity to vent their anger when the Churchill River Board of Inquiry arrived in town in January 1978. At this session, nine briefs were presented and 174 pages of text were produced. For the most part, the briefs emphasized the problems that the Squaw Rapids Dam had caused for Cumberland House residents and argued against the Churchill River Project. For example, local councillor Leon McAuley told the board: "You will realize that the community of Cumberland House here, you might get some bitter comments about power generating stations because this community is affected every day, I'm not kidding, every day, by the power station up the river. So you are not going to be looking at a book by somebody trying to predict what will happen. You will find out exactly what has happened by the residents, people in here will tell you exactly what has happened and that is not forecasting."[62]

Members of the community went on to explain in great detail the manner in which Squaw Rapids had affected the community. The lack of consultation with the community in the pre-project period was emphasized, and the post-project problems caused by low and fluctuating water levels were detailed. The overall sense of frustration was expressed by Leon McAuley:

We have met with SPC on a number of occasions. The local people and SPC got into a lot of violent exchanges of comments but they say their mandate was to provide power to the residents of Saskatchewan at the cheapest cost and they haven't got no moral investigation responsibilities. That is their way of thinking and that is exactly how they stick to their thoughts. One area, at one time we had one civil servant that was sent in here by SPC from Regina, accidently [sic] slipped out, that we don't give a damn what happens below the dam. He was pretty up tight when he realized that our tape recorder at the meeting was running and we have his taped voice saying that this is exactly what their attitude was. They don't give a damn what happens to the people here.[63]

As the Churchill River Board of Inquiry travelled throughout the North, similar concerns were raised by the Native people. Further, the commissioning of an impact assessment, under the auspices of the Churchill River Study Board, raised some fears of a whitewash. In response, the Federation of Saskatchewan Indians sponsored their own impact study. Their report, *Aski-Puko (The Land Alone)*, adopted a much different perspective on the hydro issue, by arguing that the Indian people of the north surrendered by treaty the "land alone," and not the resources, and that they therefore retained ownership over these resources, including the water.[64] The Churchill River Board of Inquiry eventually recommended against the construction of the Churchill River facility, for a variety of reasons, leaving the government with little option but to cancel their plans, at least for a time. Public pressure clearly played a prominent role in this decision.

MORE STUDY – NO ACTION

Meanwhile, evidence that the Squaw Rapids Dam was having a negative effect on the Cumberland House region continued to mount. In 1979, the Winnipeg firm of Damas and Smith was contracted by the Department of Northern Saskatchewan to develop a comprehensive development plan for Cumberland House. The consultants were forced to acknowledge in their plan that "low water levels in Cumberland Lake and fluctuating water regimes have adversely affected the fishing, trapping, outfitting and transportation in the delta area of the Saskatchewan River,"[65] and they recommended the raising of the level of Cumberland Lake.

By January 1980, Jerry Hammersmith, Minister of the Department of Northern Saskatchewan, was "prepared to recommend construction of a weir which would raise water levels in Cumberland Lake in order to assist in the preservation of traditional lifestyles." The proposed weir would cost an estimated $3.3 million and would be constructed across the Bigstone Cutoff, raising Cumberland Lake by almost one metre. According to the *Prince Albert Herald,* "Mr. Hammersmith said studies conclude that if the water levels are raised, the areas' economic potential will improve. . . . According to minutes of the meeting, Mr. Hammersmith said the government is working to 'resolve how much Saskatchewan Power should contribute' and added that 'we might have to lean on SPC, if need be.' " In the same article, Bill Kennedy of Damas and Smith Ltd., the consultant who had conducted the development study, stated, "SPC . . . admitted its liability in part, when it paid compensation claims submitted by trappers in the area, a number of years ago. Only a few claims were submitted."[66]

For their part, the people of the community were pleased that it appeared as though some action would finally be taken, but were apprehensive enough to once again emphasize the community's resolve to take the issue to court if need be.[67] Key members of the community had met on 20 January 1980 to form the Local Resource Allocation Committee. The goals of this committee were outlined in a letter to Jerry Hammersmith: "The number one priority of the Committee is to see that action is taken about raising the level of water in Cumberland Lake. Other priorities include improving the fishing, trapping, hunting, agricultural, forestry and tourism industries in Cumberland House."[68] Members of this committee included the President of the Saskatchewan Trappers Association, the Mayor, the President of Delta Outfitters Mutual Ltd., the President of the local Native women's organization, the President of the Association of Métis and Non-Status Indians of Saskatchewan (AMNSIS), the Area Director of AMNSIS, and the President of the Fishermen's Co-op, all of whom were Cumberland House residents. Surely such an influential committee would be taken seriously.

Faced with the prospect of more studies, the Local Resource Allocation Committee resolved on 4 July 1980: "If there is any additional studies required on lake levels then they should only go on during construction of [mitigation] dam. That the community forsees [sic] a raise of four feet [1.2 metres] water level increase."[69] In response, the Deputy Minister of the Department of Northern Saskatchewan, Don Murphy, informed the committee that no work could commence on any structure to alter Cumberland Lake levels until all of the impact studies had been completed and plans approved, a process he estimated could take two to three years. He did, however, offer some advice: "Any outstanding compensation claims for damages relating to trapping, fishing or resource development should be pursued with the appropriate authorities whom the injured party feels to have caused the problem."[70]

By late August 1980, no firm decision had been taken by the government, which was still insisting that an environmental impact assessment be required. Once again, the community raised the possibility of legal action, stating that over the previous ten years some $225,000 had been spent on studies in the Cumberland House area with no tangible results.[71] While this figure is likely somewhat of an exaggeration, it nevertheless underscores the pessimism with which Cumberland House residents had come to view the negotiation process. In an open letter to the Saskatchewan government, Premier Allan Blakeney, Jerry Hammersmith and Jack Messer (the Minister-in-Charge of the SPC), the community outlined its frustrations with the "more study-no action" approach of the government:

The first formal complaint to the Premier was made in 1964 by the President of the Cumberland Fur Co-op. Since then, there have been hundreds of complaints about a shortage of water in the lakes and fluctuating water levels in mid-winter. The Government responded to these appeals for assistance by doing studies of the problems in Cumberland House. First, a Government Committee was set up to prepare plans for the development of the resources and the land and for assisting education and employment in the area. Most of these plans were never implemented and did not address the problems of hydro-electric development on the Saskatchewan River. Then the Saskatchewan Water Resources Commission did a study. They recommended further studies. PFRA did another study of the water level problems and recommended another study. Even the Saskatchewan Research Council got into the act. . . . Over the last 18 years, there have been hundreds of thousands of dollars spent in producing reports and holding Government meetings about the problems in Cumberland House. Our people have been involved very little in the studies and reports and in the Government committees. This is not surprising because we were never involved in the planning of the Squaw Rapids Generating Station either. But we have tried hard to get action going to improve our situation. Our leaders have written letters and asked for assistance for years. Even our MLA's [sic] have supported us in our requests over the years, but nobody seems to be able to take on the challenge and effect positive change. Even the lawyers seem to be afraid of Saskatchewan Power. In the meantime, the lake level continues to drop and our fishermen and trappers are up in arms. . . . After all this time, we have tried to do things the proper way by going through the right channels and dealing with our political representatives in Senior Government, but to no avail. Now we are in a position where we feel we must go to Court to resolve the situation and correct the damages that have been done to our community over the past eighteen years.[72]

Despite these concerns, Hammersmith was once again able to convince the community to keep faith while new studies were conducted.[73]

LEGAL ACTION

By 1983, it appeared that the SPC was finally willing to acknowledge their responsibility for damages caused to the community by the Squaw Rapids Dam. At a meeting of the Cumberland House Local Community Authority in January 1983, attended by SPC officials, it was agreed: "SPC will study the issue of compensation re: loss of livelihood, find out what others are doing and will talk further with the LCA about the issue."[74] Subsequently, SPC officials began an investigation into compensation programs in other provinces, raising hopes that the matter would soon be resolved. A committee of local trappers and SPC officials was formed "to more closely study all trapper issues arising from impacts of the Squaw Rapids and Island Falls Hydro stations, . . . to identify all impacts and recommend possible solutions."[75]

In a letter dated 13 May 1983, O.W. Hanson, Senior Vice-President of SPC, informed the Mayor of Cumberland House: "SPC agrees that operation of the Squaw Rapids Hydroelectric Station possibly contributes, on occasion, to flooding at the ends of the ice road."[76] While the letter was extremely ambiguous, the SPC appeared finally to be admitting liability for the flooding of the winter road across the Saskatchewan River to the community. It would follow, therefore, that the same dam operations created the problems that the trappers, fishermen and outfitters had been complaining about for twenty years.

The renewed hope generated by the SPC's willingness to discuss the issue soon dissipated. The new Mayor of Cumberland House, Winston McKay, had discussed the community's problems with reporters for the television program, *The Fifth Estate*, in hopes that favourable publicity would help the community. However, according to McKay, the SPC wrote to the local members of the negotiating committee, stating, "If we are going to continue to discuss your problems you must agree not to include the press in any way or we will refuse to continue to meet with you."[77] The Mayor then explained subsequent events: "We upheld our end of the bargaining agreement and SPC agreed to discuss compensation for damages. However, as we explained, SPC changed negotiators following this agreement and then came to us on 13 May 1983, and we were told that 'no one in SPC is willing to discuss compensation and that the only issue that they would consider is the matter of our winter ice crossing flooding.' "[78]

As the dam's lifespan edged toward two decades, and with a myriad of studies resulting in little action on the requests and recommendations of community residents, the level of frustration in the community peaked. Finally, in the fall of 1983, after much local discussion and debate, the Cumberland House LCA, in conjunction with the local fishermen's and trappers' associations, instructed their lawyer to commence litigation against the SPC and the Government of Saskatchewan for compensation for damages caused by the Squaw Rapids Dam.

The Statement of Claim filed by Prince Albert lawyer Peter Abrametz on behalf of the community on 19 December 1983 charged that the Saskatchewan Power Corporation and the Government of Saskatchewan "negligently and recklessly proceeded with the construction of the Squaw Rapids Dam, which caused and continues to cause severe and continuing damage" to the Cumberland House residents.[79] Among other things, the Statement of Claim argued:

1 The Construction of the Squaw Rapids Dam was conceived, planned and implemented without input or representation from those within the downstream impact area.

2 The Defendents failed to provide adequate information to the Plaintiffs concerning the effects of the dam on the downstream impact area and the residents therein.

3 The Defendents failed to do sufficient and adequate studies to determine whether the project would cause damage to the Plaintiffs, in terms of both their lives, and livelihood, and how such damage could be minimized.

4 The Defendents failed to recognize or protect the interests of the Plaintiffs in the impact area downstream from the said dam, and/or to make the Plaintiffs a party to any information or negotiation or compensation, or adjustments which were necessary and/or efficient to indemnify the Plaintiffs for the damage caused by the Defendents to the Plaintiffs by the said project.

5 The Defendents erected the aforesaid Squaw Rapids Dam without any consideration whatsoever for the downstream impact of the aforesaid dam, and in particular without consideration for the damage that would result to the lifestyle and livelihood of the residents in the said downstream impact area.

6 The Defendents erected the said Dam after giving to the Plaintiff false assurances and promises as follows: (a) the assurances that the building of the Squaw Rapids Hydro-Electric Dam would have minimal downstream impact and consequences upon the Plaintiffs; and, (b) assuring and promising that should any detrimental consequences arise from the construction of the said Dam, that the Defendents would compensate the Plaintiffs for such consequences, all of which assurances and promises the Defendents have neglected and failed to keep, all of which has been detrimental to the Plaintiffs.

The Statement of Claim outlined the economic loss sustained by the community as a result of the dam, including the destruction of wildlife and fish habitat, the drowning and freezing of animals and fish, the increased travel difficulties, and the damage to or loss of equipment caused by low water levels. The claim also included costs of miti-gative structures to alleviate the problems in the delta area. The total claim against the SPC and the Government of Saskatchewan, includ-ing legal costs and punitive damages, amounted to $200 million.[80]

The Statement of Claim also made mention of the possible nega-tive consequences of the construction of the Nipawin Dam, some fifty kilometres downstream from Squaw Rapids. While still hoping for an out-of-court settlement in the Squaw Rapids case, the community's strategy shifted on advice from their lawyer: they would seek an injunc-tion to prevent further construction of the Nipawin facility until the Cumberland House claim had been resolved. While fears that the Nipa-win Dam would cause further damage certainly influenced the action, the community and its lawyer firmly believed that the legal action would force the SPC to officially discuss both the effect of the Squaw Rapids Dam and the potential effects of the Nipawin Dam.[81] The in-terim injunction application came to court in March 1984, but was denied on a "technicality," according to lawyer Peter Abrametz.

The lawsuit and injunction authorized by the Cumberland House LCA generated some ill feeling between them and the band council representing the Cumberland House Indian Band. While members of the band had supported the lawsuit through their participation in the trappers' and fishermen's associations (who were co-plaintiffs with the LCA), the band Chief, Joe Laliberté, and the council saw things differ-ently. In July 1984 they ordered the LCA's researcher (who was in-volved in a socioeconomic impact study to support the Statement of Claim) not to enter the reserve or to speak to band members even if they had signed the claim. Laliberté believed that the status Indians had a better chance of settling their claim if they worked through the Department of Indian Affairs, using their treaty rights under Treaty Five as a lever. However, throughout the entire dispute, the federal government had been conspicuous by its absence, despite the existence of the Indian band and reserve land in the downstream impact area.[82] The extent to which they would now enter the fray was questionable.

In September 1984, the Cumberland House Indian Band announc-ed its own intention to seek compensation for "the lost way of life and the lost livelihood" they had suffered as a result of the Squaw Rapids Dam and other water control facilities along the Saskatchewan River.[83] To this end, the band retained University of Saskatchewan law professor Richard Bartlett, a recognized authority on Indian treaty water rights. Like the LCA some twenty years earlier, the band expressed a desire to negotiate a settlement. But one year later, when no progress had been made, the band was forced also to threaten legal action.[84]

MEDIATION

In response to the LCA's legal action, the Saskatchewan government filed an intent to submit a Statement of Defence, and, though one was prepared, it was never filed. The government had hoped to resolve the dispute through negotiation,[85] ironically a process for which the people of Cumberland House had been lobbying for over twenty years. In December 1985, the Saskatchewan government announced that it was willing to appoint a mediator to settle the dispute, and in the spring of 1986 the nomination of mediator Val Longworth of Prince Albert was agreed to by the LCA, the band and the SPC. The initial meeting held between the LCA, the band, their lawyers, and representatives of the SPC and the newly created Saskatchewan Water Corporation took place on 19 and 20 August 1986. Designed primarily as an orientation session and to establish the procedure for the mediation process, the meeting was apparently significant enough to encourage the LCA to announce that their lawsuit was "on the back burner," though not withdrawn. Similarly, the Cumberland House Indian Band, which had made application for a hearing before the Saskatchewan Water Corporation, also announced that their action would be "put on hold." Although all parties agreed that a final settlement would take a great deal of time to negotiate, probably more than two years, Longworth did say, "Ultimately there will be fairly substantial amounts of monies involved."[86]

The Cumberland House saga continues to this day with no real end in sight. While many consider the move to mediation as significant in finally resolving the dispute, only time will tell if the government and the SPC are indeed prepared to deal squarely with the issue. The appointment of the mediator is now viewed by some Cumberland House residents as just another delaying mechanism. In fact, in the year and a half following the appointment of the mediator, only two sessions with residents were held. The frustration of the community members again peaked, and this time they threatened to construct a dam of their own across the Tearing River in an effort to raise the level of Cumberland Lake.[87] When the government failed to respond to this threat, the people began construction of their dam. In August 1987, under the watchful eye of the RCMP, who arrived to take photographs for possible prosecution, about one hundred Cumberland House residents began to place rocks across the Tearing River. Ironically, the Saskatchewan government's Department of the Environment expressed concern that not only was the dam illegal, but also that it could cause environmental damage. By the end of August 1987, a low-level dam structure was complete, and plans were under way to widen it and to build it higher.[88] The desperate actions of the Cumberland House residents seemed to wake the sleeping provincial government, and in October 1987 the Saskatchewan Power Corporation offered the community a compensation package worth approximately $10 million.[89] In return for their withdrawal of their lawsuit against the SPC, the community would receive a bridge across the Saskatchewan River, safe drinking water, compensation to trappers and fishermen for lost and damaged equipment, and assistance to complete the dam across the Tearing River. The latter offer was particularly surprising since the government has, for many years, refused to consider this option, citing high costs, likely environmental damage, and numerous reports which argued that a dam would have only minimal effect. But the compensation proposal fell short of what the community felt it required, and within a week of the offer it was rejected by the people. They did, however, make a counter offer, adding to the SPC's list an additional weir to stabilize water levels in Cumberland Lake, a recreation complex, and a road to Sturgeon Landing.

In response, the SPC requested that the community draft a document rationalizing their new demands, with emphasis on how they relate to the Squaw Rapids Dam, and provide cost estimates for the requested structures. The community agreed to do this. By February 1988 this document had yet to be completed, but the people of Cumberland House seemed optimistic that the long-running dispute would soon be resolved.

The inability or reluctance over the years of the Government of Saskatchewan and the SPC to deal with the Cumberland House people very much reflects the province's attitude toward Métis people in general. The expeditious manner in which the concerns of the non-Native farmers in the Tobin Lake area were addressed contrasts sharply with the twenty-four-year grievance process undertaken by the Métis. The effect of the dam upon them was rarely considered in the pre-project period, and their post-project concerns have been handily side-stepped. Just as in 1885 when it took the imminent threat of Métis insurrection to spark the scrip process, so in 1985 did it take the modern democratic form of insurrection, the lawsuit, to spark the Saskatchewan government into action. The Métis, of course, did not benefit from the scrip commissions, and they may not benefit from the mediation process. With respect to the Squaw Rapids Dam at least, the people of Cumberland House have, for over two decades, truly remained a "forgotten people."

Easterville and the Grand Rapids Dam

4

Over there we had everything. Here we have nothing. Nothing.[1]

The people of Cumberland House were unprepared for the construction of the Squaw Rapids Dam. But the people of Chemawawin, prior to their relocation to Easterville, were the focus of a great deal of attention during the planning and construction phases of the Grand Rapids Dam, since virtually the entire town would be submerged. But despite federal and provincial government intervention (and some would say because of government intervention), the relocation was remarkably unsuccessful. The post-project years have seen the people of Easterville in conflict with the Manitoba government and Manitoba Hydro over alleged and documented promises issued at the time of the relocation.

THE COMMUNITY OF EASTERVILLE

Easterville is a Swampy Cree and Métis community located along the south shores of Cedar Lake in mid-northern Manitoba. It is centrally situated within the Province of Manitoba on the Saskatchewan River system and is approximately fifty-one kilometres southeast of the original settlement of Chemawawin. It is accessed via Provincial Road Number 327 from Highway Number 6, one of the main north-south arteries in the province.

Like Cumberland House, Easterville is found just north of the established boundary demarcating the Subarctic ethnographic area. The region is characterized by extensive muskeg and limestone, and thus has little agricultural potential. However, found on the north shore of Cedar Lake is the Summerberry Marsh, a renowned wildlife habitat which provided the Native people of the region with excellent waterfowl and game hunting.

The community of Easterville consists of an Indian reserve, where the members of the Chemawawin Indian Band reside, and a smaller, adjacent Métis community. The Indian band currently comprises approximately 548 people, while the Métis community comprises approximately 300. Politically, the Indian band and the Métis community are separate entities and, although the boundary between the two is simply a road, the two sides have demonstrated increasing difficulty in mounting cooperative activities.[2] The political efforts of the people of Easterville have been largely carried out by the Indian band, due perhaps to their better organization and more established support network (especially through the Swampy Cree Tribal Council, an organization representing the five Swampy Cree bands in the region).

Commercial fishing is the basis of the local economy, although it has occasionally suffered because of the hydro project.[3] Trapping and hunting, significant activities prior to the construction of the dam, have been even more seriously affected, and today they contribute minimally to the local economy. Periodic wage-labour activities provide an additional source of cash to the residents, but these activities are generally non-productive "make-work" schemes implemented by the federal or provincial governments, designed to temporarily alleviate the stresses of poverty.

COMMUNITY HISTORY

Because of the location of Cedar Lake, with its excellent east-west and north-south water transportation network, the region became prominent in the competition between the earliest fur-trading enterprises to enter into the inland area. La Vérendrye, in 1741, was probably the first explorer in the region, and he established a fur-trade post, known as Fort Bourbon, on Cedar Lake (the exact location of which is a matter of debate).[4] While the various posts established around the lake were originally under the control of the North West Company, the Hudson's Bay Company eventually came to dominate the region.[5]

The original community of Easterville was called Chemawawin,[6] and is today affectionately known by the people as the "Old Post." Located at the point where the Saskatchewan River emptied into the western end of Cedar Lake, the community was directly adjacent to the Summerberry Marsh, not far from The Pas. While the Saskatchewan River provided an excellent transportation route to this developing centre, the community was nevertheless isolated, and forays to The Pas were rare.

It is not possible to establish an exact date for the formation of the community at Chemawawin, but we do know that a group of people was unexpectedly found living there in 1876 when Thomas Howard passed by on his way up the Saskatchewan River to conclude a treaty with the Indians at The Pas.[7] It became apparent to Howard that, although these Indians were directly related to those at Moose Lake, they had some time earlier removed themselves to Chemawawin and had come to think of themselves as a separate social entity. Howard wrote: "Noticing a large encampment of Indians there [Chemawawin], I landed and found they were part of the Moose Lake Band. They desired that I should treat with them where they were, and not bring them to The Pas, but upon my telling them that I could only treat with them at the appointed place of meeting, they readily assented to follow me up."[8] When Howard and the Indians reached The Pas, he once again attempted to have the Chemawawin Indians sign Treaty Five as part of the Moose Lake Band. Although he had stopped only briefly at Chemawawin, Howard used as his reasoning for this action "the unfitness of the locality for a reserve."[9] Although Howard was successful in forcing the Moose Lake and Chemawawin Indians together under a single chief for the purposes of signing the treaty, the Chemawawin Indians returned immediately to their homes along Cedar Lake. Recognizing the reality of the situation, Lieutenant-Governor Alexander Morris wrote to Howard saying, "The Moose Lake Indians . . . will probably desire the recognition of two separate Chiefs and the allotment of separate reserves to them."[10] The land at Chemawawin was first surveyed for a reserve in 1882, but was not actually granted reserve status until 1930.[11]

Chemawawin grew only very slowly after the treaty was signed, and the people remained dependent on the harvesting of the natural resources of the area. The harvesting of furs was particularly lucrative, overseen as usual by the resident Hudson's Bay Company trader. By the 1940s, however, the fur and dry-goods business in Chemawawin was no longer viewed as economically feasible by the Hudson's Bay Company, and in 1941 they halted their operation there. The void did not last for long, however. A free trader by the name of Armand Pouliot, who had been transporting fish from Chemawawin to The Pas for sale, saw a golden opportunity and made his move. According to Pouliot, "They [Hudson's Bay Company] were too much in the books. So I decided that I would try it. I went over there while they were trapping and made a few bucks. So why can't I come down here to stay? I asked the chief for permission. The Indian agent wanted a store there. I started with nothing, building up. All of a sudden, they give me a five-year lease. So I built a house. The whole thing took a long time."[12] The "whole thing" was, in fact, a rather amazing economic mini-empire, in which the trader controlled virtually every aspect of the Chemawawin economy. In addition to operating his general store, he managed the commercial fishery, the lumber and sawmill operations, and the trapping industry. As a result, he embedded himself as the broker between the Native residents and the outside world, and through this role became very powerful. However, he was viewed by most as benevolent, and the paternalism with which he governed the affairs of the community, though obvious, was never seriously challenged. Pouliot said:

> I was creating work for the Indians. I never had an Indian on relief. If he was capable to work, I gave him a job. A government man would come in, and an Indian would say, "I've got to have some relief." So he'd say, "Okay, I'll look into it," and he'd come and see me. He'd say, "This man wants some relief." And I'd say, "No, no, tell him to come see me, and I'll give him a job." After he was gone, the fellow would come and see me and I'd put him to work. I could always fit in one more.[13]

In addition to having complete control of the local economy, Pouliot acted as doctor and law enforcement agent, and was thus able to maintain a pattern of economic and social life in the community which enhanced the viability of his economic operations.[14]

Politically, the Indian and Métis people at Chemawawin were unsophisticated. Since the trader controlled almost the entire network of communications with the outside world, he exercised a great deal of political control. Although a band council existed to represent the Indians with the Department of Indian Affairs, government officials only rarely visited the community, and the council had little to do. Further, it is evident that, insofar as the federal government needed contacts with the Indian community, the contacts were frequently made through the trader, bypassing the band council. An even looser organization represented the Métis residents. When the provincial government and Manitoba Hydro first approached the community about their plans for the Grand Rapids Dam, they found a community with little experience at governing their affairs at the local level and with virtually no experience in dealing with the government. Their last major decision had been made some seventy-five years earlier, when they signed on to Treaty Five. When the trader was excluded from the hydro negotiations, the people were without their patriarch, their mentor, their broker. They were on their own.

THE GRAND RAPIDS DAM

Although serious planning of the project began as early as 1957, and discussions concerning it date back at least to 1953, the Grand Rapids Project was not officially announced in the Manitoba Legislature until January 1960. The project, located on the Saskatchewan River system at Grand Rapids, between Lake Winnipeg and Cedar Lake, represented the first phase of a massive hydroelectric development scheme which, the Manitoba government hoped, would harness the most powerful rivers in the north and turn Manitoba into the "electrical province." Premier Duff Roblin made this fact perfectly clear at the official opening of the station on 13 November 1965 when he stated, "We shall not stop here; . . . there are other challenges ahead."[15] This obvious reference to the Churchill and Nelson rivers largely went unnoticed by both the media and the public.

The immediate purpose of the dam was to supply power to the mine and mill complex of the International Nickel Company (INCO) in Thompson.[16] Toward this end, the four turbines installed at Grand Rapids, built at a cost of $117 million, were designed to produce 472 megawatts of electricity.[17] Although not particularly large by today's standards, in the 1960s it represented something of an engineering feat. In order to facilitate this development it was necessary to raise the level of Cedar Lake behind the dam some 3.5 metres; the area would be turned into a huge reservoir whose level would be regulated as water passed through the turbines. It became apparent that the community of Chemawawin would be submerged with the rising waters.

THE GRAND RAPIDS FOREBAY
ADMINISTRATION COMMITTEE

As early as 1953, when the Grand Rapids Dam was first being discussed, the potential disruption in the Cedar Lake–Saskatchewan River region was also discussed. A 1955 provincial report on the project stated: "The threat of this development faces the federal and provincial Administrations with serious problems with those whose economy is directly linked with the area. These problems should be studied immediately and steps taken to find new employment for these people."[18] One of the first reactions of the Manitoba government to the official announcement of the Grand Rapids Dam was to designate key individuals in both Winnipeg and The Pas to begin considering the implications of the development for the residents of the Cedar Lake area. Initially, two small committees were established, one in each centre, to commence the investigation. The committee in The Pas was charged with the responsibility of informing the Native residents of Chemawawin and Moose Lake of the project, and the possibility that partial or total relocation might prove necessary. Although officials in the Department of Indian Affairs expressed their opinion that residents should actually sit or be represented on the The Pas committee, the Manitoba government felt such representation to be unnecessary.[19] At this early date no one seemed to have a clear idea of the enormity of the task confronting them.

As the inevitability of relocating the 280 Native residents of Chemawawin became clear, in October 1960 the Manitoba government took steps to form a new committee to act on its behalf in all matters pertaining to the consequences of the project, including the negotiation of a proper compensation agreement.[20] As planned, the community was to be relocated by the spring of 1964, giving the Grand Rapids Forebay Administration Committee (hereafter the Forebay Committee) only four years to achieve these broad aims. In an attempt to ensure some continuity in the process, however, the committee was granted a ten-year lifespan from the date at which the maximum forebay elevations were achieved. As this occurred in 1965, the committee was formally disbanded in 1975.[21]

Officially, the Forebay Committee's terms of reference were: "(a) To co-ordinate all government agencies involved; (b) To negotiate with the people affected by the project; (c) To keep the people informed of the developments concerning the relocation and the power projects; (d) To inform the residents of Chemawawin and Moose Lake of decisions made in Winnipeg; (e) To provide administrative services for the relocation."[22] Clearly, the function of the Forebay Committee was to be much different from that of its counterpart in Saskatchewan, the Squaw Rapids Liaison Committee. However, despite the fact that the Forebay Committee's *raison d'être* was the relocation and subsequent well-being of the Native people in the Cedar Lake region, the committee proved unable to successfully fulfill its mandate, or incapable of it.

Initially, the Forebay Committee consisted of only two members. It was expanded shortly after its creation, due to the unexpected workload involved, and eventually grew to a size of nine or ten. The committee lacked a sense of continuity, since membership fluctuated considerably over the years. Furthermore, the Forebay Committee consisted primarily of senior-ranking civil servants seconded to the committee. Expected to maintain their separate departments while serving part time on the committee, these individuals quickly became swamped by the task at hand. Further, there were no representatives from the community of Chemawawin (in fact, there were no Native people at all on the committee). As the terms of reference indicated, decisions were primarily made in Winnipeg, largely in isolation from those who would be affected by them.

The lines of communication between the Forebay Committee and the people of Chemawawin were fragmented throughout the entire lifespan of the committee. Between these two was a chain of people and departments all involved in some way with the negotiation process. Indeed, one vital function of the committee was to coordinate the activities of these various parties, a task which may have consumed much of their time. At any given moment, a directive from the Manitoba government had to be relayed through the Forebay Committee to the community where it was received by the Indian Superintendent, the Community Development Officer, or the local trader. The communication was then offered to the band council and the local flood committee, who in turn informed the people. There was little actual contact between members of the Forebay Committee and the people of Chemawawin or their representatives.

Although the Manitoba government clearly hoped that a new organization with allegiances to no particular government department would facilitate the planning of the relocation, they in fact created a body which drifted helplessly, never certain of its responsibilities or powers, and pulled in different directions by the various interest groups that quickly arose. The members of the Forebay Committee were also clearly in a conflict-of-interest situation. While charged with the task of successfully relocating the community, and by inference representing its interests, the members were also federal and provincial civil servants with long records of loyalty to their respective departments. To support too strongly the Native position in their roles as Forebay Committee members would be to invite criticism from their colleagues and superiors (and possible dismissal). To support too stringently the governments' position would also lead to criticism, from the community and Native organizations. In the final analysis, their allegiance to the government apparently won out, and the committee became, in the words of one critic, "a bargaining agent of government with responsibility for limiting the demands of those affected by the flooding."[23] A modern-day version of a treaty commission had been unleashed.

LAND SURRENDER AND SITE SELECTION

Although the planning of the Grand Rapids Dam had commenced in 1957, the residents of Chemawawin were first approached in late spring of 1960, and were not officially notified of the relocation plans until later that fall. On the first visit of the Forebay Committee to Chemawawin, in October 1960, the people were told that by the spring of 1964 they had to be living in a new place. The Forebay Committee agreed that the people had rights which they would "try and recognize" throughout the process of negotiations.[24] The fact that their community would be submerged and the realization that they would actually have to move were ideas that the people came to understand only very slowly.

Significant discussion had ensued behind the scenes before the residents of Chemawawin were informed of their fate. In fact, extensive dialogue is evident between the Indian Affairs Branch (known after 1966 as the Department of Indian Affairs) and the Province of Manitoba on a variety of issues, including some very fundamental ones, such as the need to negotiate with the Indians, and the manner in which the negotiations would be conducted. The two major issues to be discussed – surrender of reserve land to allow flooding and compensation for the relocation – were seen at this time by the province as two somewhat separate issues. Since approval by the Indian Affairs Branch was necessary before any agreement could be reached, the branch was able to insist on a "package deal," involving both the allocation of new lands and compensation.[25] However, despite the insistence on a package deal, to which the provincial government appeared to acquiesce, the actual negotiation process followed two separate agendas: first, the land surrender; and second (once the land was secured), the development of a compensation package.

The most urgent matters faced by the Forebay Committee were the securing of the reserve land at Chemawawin to allow for the flooding behind the dam, and selection of the new community site. Of course, federal government approval was required under the Indian Act before reserve land could be taken. The 1951 Indian Act provided two methods whereby the land could be obtained. In the first method, land could be surrendered to the federal government and then transferred to the province.[26] This method required formal consent of the band to surrender. In the second method, the federal government could, in effect, expropriate the land without the Indians' permission and transfer it directly to the province.[27] Both methods required the consent of the Governor in Council (in effect, the Minister of Indian Affairs), who could attach whatever terms he wished. The federal government thus held the "trump card" in the transaction, and was in a position to ensure that the rights of the people were protected. It is apparent, however, that in most respects the Indian Affairs Branch abandoned its responsibility and allowed the Manitoba government to control the negotiation and surrender process.

It was essential that the members of the Forebay Committee familiarize themselves with the land-surrender process, and requests for information were made to Indian Affairs.[28] While the federal government considered the need to expropriate the Indians' land if they refused to surrender it, expropriation ran counter to their policy at the time.[29] This option may have represented the substance of at least one internal debate consuming Indian Affairs officials. Another likely debate concerned the issue of the exchange of land. According to A.G. Leslie, the Indian Affairs' Regional Supervisor in Winnipeg, a land exchange was the only option, "because the reserves are part of the Treaty obligations."[30] However, the head of the Chief Reserves and Trusts for Indian Affairs, directly responsible for the welfare of Indians, had serious misgivings about a land exchange. His concerns in many ways foreshadowed the post-relocation story of the Chemawawin people. He wrote: "Compensation by way of exchange of land is probably not the best method of protecting the Indians in this instance. Usually land available in areas of this kind is not of the best and it might be better to consider compensation in cash. Land could then be purchased, selected by the Indians themselves."[31] The decision was eventually made to promote a direct exchange of land.

The actual selection of land for the new community site is perhaps the most controversial of the Chemawawin events. Controversy about it still rages, and is fueled by the fact that the site chosen has proven to be horribly inhospitable; it is in fact the opposite of the original Chemawawin site in virtually every respect.

While the government has insisted that the people were allowed to choose freely the new location, other evidence suggests that this was not the case.[32] The selection of the new community site (eventually named Easterville after the Chief of the Chemawawin Indian Band, Donald Easter) was not a free choice by the residents. It is quite clear from the evidence that, even at the outset, the Manitoba government and the Forebay Committee had taken on the responsibility of determining at least the best sites in the area, according to their own criteria. The site selection process adopted by the Forebay Committee was described in an internal Indian Affairs memo:

Mr. Schortinghuis [Chairman of the Forebay Committee] stated that Mr. Wells [of Manitoba Department of Mines and Natural Resources] has been supplied with aerial photograph maps and will examine possible sites for relocation. Information on this will be provided to higher authorities by Mr. Wells and it is expected that a number of these can be rejected for good reason. The result will be to narrow the choice down to four which could be regarded as feasible. The resulting four sites – two for each band [Chemawawin and Moose Lake] – would then be turned over to a firm of town planning consultants who would examine them in the light of their specialized knowledge, and would endeavour *to sell the Indians on one or the other of these sites*, and have the Indians choose the one which they regarded as preferable [emphasis added].[33]

Just as Thomas Howard the previous century had passed judgement on the Natives' ability to select a site for the community, so too did the Manitoba government feel compelled to "sell" the people on a site.[34] Although the Department of Indian Affairs was concerned that such a process did not "go far enough in involving the Indians themselves in consultation and planning"[35] (in fact, the proposal really only called for the Indians to rubber stamp a pre-selected site), their weak protests were largely ignored.

The number of potential sites offered to the people by the Forebay Committee is difficult to determine, and estimates have ranged from one (i.e., the present site) to eleven. Some sites were proposed by the people themselves; others were submitted by members of the Forebay Committee. The evidence shows that three sites were seriously considered. Of these three, one site was rejected by the people because road access was questionable; the second was rejected because of excessive muskeg and steep banks; the third site was perceived as the best because of the possibility that both a road and electricity could be provided. These two features were the most important considerations, and it appears that the Forebay Committee promoted the Easterville site as a sort of Indian Utopia. As Walter Mink, a member of the community, explained,

What I understand, the promises were too good, because at that time we never used a light. We used to use gas lamps. Wood stoves. That's all we used to use over there [at Chemawawin]. And now, those promises. They said, "You gonna have a highway there, and everybody will have a car. And whenever you want to go somewhere, your car sitting there, you go where you want to go. And a stove like that [points]. You're going to have an electric stove. A coffee-pot, and things like that. You're not going to have to use any wood. No wood stoves." So that's what I said. The promises were too good, I guess. We never seen anything like this before [motions around kitchen]. "You're going to live in a town, a nice town. You're going to have your own store." These are what the promises were. "Everything you need you're going to have. You're going to live in a town."[36]

It is evident that the Easterville site was discussed among the Forebay Committee members and Manitoba government officials as if it were an *a priori* fact that the community would select it. It has even been suggested that the plans for the relocation of the people to the Easterville site were under way before the people officially accepted it.[37] Similarly, a brief presented by the community of Easterville to Manitoba Hydro in 1975 declared, "We did not make the original choice on our own, and Easterville was the location promoted by the provincial government as the best choice."[38] The same thought is also evident in a 1975 passage from a presentation given by a former chief at Easterville to the Panel of Public Inquiry investigating Manitoba Hydro's proposals for flooding Southern Indian Lake: "When we moved over we really didn't want to move to the place that was chosen for us, but at that time we did not really know or understand and the people who advised us told us that we really didn't have much choice in deciding as to where we should live. The decisions as to where we should go were not made by us."[39] While visits to the various sites were facilitated, it appears that for only one, the eventual Easterville site, did the Forebay Field Representative, H.E. Wells, and the Indian Affairs Regional Superintendent, J.R. Bell, accompany the visitors. Furthermore, when favourable comments were offered concerning this site, "the committee men took advantage of the surge in favour . . . and held a meeting to promote the climax, which became the meeting of decision" in which the Easterville site was approved.[40]

The Easterville site was discussed at a community meeting in May 1961. According to the transcripts of this meeting, the Chief, Donald

Easter, began by noting that "the government promised us everything; . . . I think the government is very good to everybody."[41] The notes on this meeting give no indication that any site other than the eventual Easterville site was under consideration. Furthermore, there was virtually no discussion of the pros and cons of the site. The tone is one of a people reluctantly coming to the realization that they had to move, almost as if the particular site was not an issue.

The Easterville site was officially selected by community vote in June 1961. A piece of paper was circulated at a community meeting, and the people simply signed their names under the preferred site.[42] The Chief and council were the first to vote, and indicated their support of this site. In fact, many residents voted for Easterville primarily because the Chief supported it: "We should never have come here where the water's high. We supposed to run away from the high water, but the leaders, they wanted to come this way. We followed our leaders."[43] This theme is recurrent in the minutes of the May and June meetings. Clearly, the paramount influence was that of Chief Easter, a fact which became abundantly clear when the new townsite was named after him. Both Chief Easter and other members of the local committee supported the Easterville site. Although the reasons for this support are not abundantly clear, inference can be drawn from these meetings where the Chief and committee members made constant reference to the "promises" of the government, which were clearly linked to the Easterville site. Quite likely they believed they were making the best of a bad situation, and they pressured the electorate to go along. In fact, notes taken at the "meeting of decision" and passed on to Wells were clear on this point: "The local Committee men, in verbally reporting to the writer [Wells] on the meeting of decision, pointed out that although the result was overwhelmingly in favour of Site 2 [Easterville], that many appeared reluctant to vote, as if in doing so they might seal their doom. And the fact that they all did vote was the result of hard work and pressure put on by the committee. This, they said, was justified because otherwise these people would have *never* made up their minds and selected any site [emphasis in the original]."[44]

Although the Chief and council, and those community residents who so desired, had been taken to the potential site prior to the vote, its obvious drawbacks were not readily apparent. The site chosen is, without question, one of the most uninhabitable and depressing places one could imagine, and fully deserves its nickname "the rock pile." There is a popular belief among the residents of Easterville that the site was visited by the community leaders in the winter, and therefore the obvious drawbacks were not visible. For example, one resident had this to say: "They went about three or four places . . . and they come here in the winter time. So this is where they chose. In the winter time. There was deep snow, and it looks good. High land, that's what they wanted."[45] By late spring, it became painfully obvious that the site was not as good as it seemed. As the snow melted, the limestone ridge upon which the community would be built seemed to dominate the area.[46] Yet, the initial disappointment appears to have been tempered again by the vision of a new community rising phoenix-like from the rock: "Oh, everybody said it was good land. But it was still rocky. I could see rocks all over. And yet they chose that. . . . They said there's going to be a highway, a town, a bus will be running here. Everybody glad. So after we settled, well, everybody didn't like it. 'Too rocky,' they said."[47]

Gordon George, eventually elected Chief in the new community, offered an interesting perspective on the selection of the Easterville site: "I don't see why we took this place at that time. Well, I think it was, well, we were kind of fooled by the government people. They said this was the best place. I don't know if the Band Council agreed to this place, but they were forced to. There's a lot of better places around the lake but I can see now that the government people, they didn't want to spend too much money moving us, you see. See, it's much cheaper here."[48] It is apparent that the potential problems with the site were well known among Forebay Committee members and Indian Affairs. In a memorandum to A.G. Leslie, Bell noted: "The area has one distinct drawback in that there is very little soil coverage, the ground, from two to six inches below the surface, being composed mainly of fractured limestone, . . . I am not too impressed with the fur and game potential as the area is almost entirely Muskeg with swamp spruce cover."[49] Although the Easterville site may have seemed the most cost feasible at the time, this report foreshadowed the severe social and economic problems it was likely to cause, and the enormous expenditures that would be required for rehabilitation.

NEGOTIATING AWAY A HOME

The first official negotiating meeting between the members of the Forebay Committee and the people of Chemawawin did not take place until 22 March 1962. By this time, the people had formed a local flood committee to negotiate on their behalf, the site for the new community had already been selected, and plans for its construction were under way. The purpose of these negotiations was to obtain an agreement between the Forebay Committee and the people of Chemawawin with respect to the surrender of the reserve land and the development of the new community. To this end, a letter was mailed early in 1962 to the local committee outlining a number of commitments that the province was willing to make to the community in return for their relocation. The local committee expressed dissatisfaction with some of the items listed, and requested clarification for others.

At the initial meeting on 22 March 1962, the Chairman of the Forebay Committee read a revised list of promises to the representatives of the community. Although this meeting marked the first face-to-face negotiations between the two parties, it became immediately clear that the Manitoba government was in no mood to tolerate an extended period of bargaining. The Chairman of the Forebay Committee stated bluntly at the outset: "We must all remember that we have not much time. A lot of these things take time and we should finish our negotiations soon. When I say soon, I would hope certainly not more than two months." Another member of the committee, in addressing the leaders, made the point even clearer:

We did not conceive the dam. The government decided it. I would like to say this is in the public interest and affects many people, and whether or not you reach agreement, it will go on. We have spent upwards of 20 million dollars, and other projects of greater magnitude are planned for the near future and this must be dealt with before we go on to these. You will have to go along with us and reach agreement by negotiating or some other means. The job is going to be built. One final word, we all earnestly hope that we can settle this by June first and be underway and you will have to trust us.[50]

It was, in fact, made clear that the committee wanted to have an agreement finalized at the next meeting. The people of Chemawawin were being asked to negotiate their future in the span of two meetings over less than three months, all the while faced with the constant threat that "the job is going to be built" regardless.

There is no question that the people were, in the formative stages, rushed into making decisions that they have since regretted. These were decisions totally unlike any they personally had ever confronted, although the legacy of the treaty-making process was still in their minds. They were not provided with legal counsel, and even the trader was barred from the negotiation meetings.[51]

In early 1962, a community development officer was stationed in Chemawawin at the request of the Forebay Committee. This act was primarily the result of the lobbying activities of one man, Jean Lagassé. Lagassé's 1959 report, *The People of Indian Ancestry in Manitoba,*[52] had been well received, and he had convinced the Manitoba government to officially adopt the community development approach as its strategy for dealing with the socioeconomic problems of the Native people in the province. Basically, this approach emphasized the involvement of the local community in effecting positive change. Unfortunately, certain officials of the government in general, and the Forebay Committee in particular, were not especially receptive to the community development philosophy. This fact was of great concern to Lagassé, who saw as part of the problem the Community Development Services' inability to effectively communicate its ideas to the Forebay Committee. In a memorandum to the Minister of Welfare, he said: "If we are not able to communicate successfully to the Forebay Committee when we talk the same language and can freely exchange visits and phone calls, is it surprising that the Forebay Committee could not communicate with the local people?"[53] Lagassé became increasingly upset at the ineffectiveness of his program, and especially about the refusal of the Forebay Committee to accept his recommendations. At one point, in a meeting with the committee, he reprimanded its members for violating "good community development practices" and for the lack of coordination between government departments in dealing with the requests of the Chemawawin people.[54] Lagassé subsequently resigned from the Community Development Services program.

The local Community Development Officer at Chemawawin, Joe Keeper, also had his problems. He had, in effect, been dropped into the community well after the time that his services were really needed, and was forced to "mop up." His official function was to inform the people and prepare them for their imminent relocation. However, he quickly became a community advocate. Most of the crucial negotiations had already been completed by the time Keeper was assigned, including those in which the band consented to the Letter of Intent, and by inference lost their reserve land. Although Keeper attempted to have the band rescind the respective band council resolution, the Manitoba government officially accepted the agreement only three weeks later, and the agreement was history.[55]

When Keeper arrived in Chemawawin, he found that the people were both confused and bitter about what was happening to them. As

Lagassé wrote, "There is no doubt that the Indians and Métis of these two areas [Chemawawin and Moose Lake] will come out of their relocation experience with increased bitterness towards the white man and his agencies of government. . . . This might have been prevented if a Community Development Officer had been assigned to that area two years ago to explain to the people what was happening. It is too late now that they are being physically displaced."[56]

Soon after his arrival in Chemawawin, Keeper made it clear to the Forebay Committee that they were expecting too much from the people. The Forebay Committee was, in fact, assuming that the people would fully comprehend what was happening, coordinate the activities at the local level, and plan for their future. However, according to Keeper, "The whole idea of planning is strange to most of the people as they are used to asking or being told. The idea of planning itself must be the first one to get across. They can do this, but they can find this difficult to do in relation to the white man."[57]

The communication gap between the Forebay Committee and the people certainly hindered any progress at the local level. Much information was withheld, and other information was transmitted fragmentally. This fact was periodically pointed out to the Forebay Committee and the government. Lagassé wrote to the Minister of Welfare: "I believe the Committee has underestimated the difficulty there is for Indians and Métis to understand what they are talking about. They hope to achieve by intermittent visits what it would have been difficult for a resident Community Development Officer to achieve."[58] Joe Keeper wrote to the supervisor of field services: "Each time they have asked for clarification of points or have made a request from the Forebay Committee they have either been evaded or refused. This is making them very discontented."[59] Again, he wrote: "The people are beginning to wonder, after making requests and being verbally promised many things, what to believe and what not to believe. They do not believe what Mr. Schortinghuis [Forebay Committee Chairman] tells them any more."[60] Damaging rumours also circulated around the community and undermined the whole process.[61]

There is clear evidence that the local people were not provided with the available information concerning the likely effects of the dam on their lake and their economy. Although a study had been commissioned by the Manitoba government to consider the environmental effects of the project (the study was executed by biologists from the United States Wildlife Service), S.W. Schortinghuis, eventual Chairman of the Forebay Committee, requested that the report be treated "as very confidential as any rumours about the findings of the U.S. Wildlife people would only cause problems."[62] Needless to say, the findings were not very favourable toward the future of the region. Furthermore, despite the fact that many federal and provincial government officials concurred with J.R. Bell that "many of the resources from which the people derived a livelihood . . . will be lost or seriously depleted for a number of years and in some cases, possibly forever,"[63] the people were apparently being told the opposite. The Regional Director for Indian Affairs, A.G. Leslie, wrote to his superiors, saying, "There is no convincing factual information being fed to the people."[64] Even Premier Duff Roblin became a party to the deception, quite likely unwittingly, saying to the people that a newly formed economic development committee would ensure that the "people are not hurt by the Forebay Development but will in fact be able to earn as good a living as before, and we hope, a better living."[65] The people were denied accurate information about the effects, and were simply asked to trust the Manitoba government. And this they did: "We were told we had nothing to worry about as we were dealing with the Government of Manitoba."[66]

For the most part, the Forebay Committee meetings occurred at two separate levels: the local level, between members of the Chemawawin Flood Committee, the Indian Superintendent, and the Community Development Officer; and in Winnipeg, between members of the main committee. Joint meetings were occasionally conducted, but usually these were scheduled for a location other than Chemawawin, especially after the agreement had been signed.

At the local level, as the date of relocation neared, the frequency of meetings increased, again largely in the absence of members of the committee. Manitoba Hydro paid the community members to attend meetings, though whether they actually understood what was happening is questionable. Armand Pouliot described the meetings: "These hydro meetings, they met pretty near every day for awhile. They got paid five dollars every time they went to a meeting. The Hydro was [paying them]. Just to go. That's a lot of money. Thirty of them would go in, just to get that five dollars. And I bet you none of them understood what the hell they were talking about."[67] Certainly there was a language problem which hindered the progress of these meetings. The Chief himself spoke little English, and the other flood committee members spoke even less. While translators were occasionally used, evidence indicates that the translations were very crude. The language barrier also inhibited the participation of the local leaders in the relocation planning process. Further, the Forebay Committee apparently did not really allow these leaders to participate. The Community Development Officer wrote: "It seems that the people themselves have not had anything to say, really, in any of these decisions. They are involved in meetings, but not in decision-making. These meetings are not council meetings, they are meetings where the people are talked into approving decisions that have already been made by Mr. Schortinghuis and Mr. Wells. A great deal of the mix-up in the Forebay can be attributed to this."[68] And: "Since coming to the Forebay I have commented many times upon the mechanical way things seem to be proceeding here. At meetings of the local committee, the local members never take any active part in the discussion of methods (planning). They are usually asking things to be done or are being told certain things will be done."[69]

For many members of the local committee, the meetings held outside of Chemawawin, especially those in Winnipeg, were a new experience for them, one which was vividly recalled by Walter Mink, a member of the committee:

We had meetings, to talk about this moving. And after that we go to Winnipeg. That's my first time I go to Winnipeg. When we had these meetings . . . and when we got to Winnipeg . . . I was kind of scared. The town it was big, and all those people there when we went to the meeting. I believe there was 1,700 people there. That's the first time I see a lot of people before my eyes. And I was standing on the top of the stage there, talking to the people. And I couldn't talk English at that time. I had an interpreter. And then at that time I said we don't want to move unless we have everything that they promised. We'll move when we see those things.[70]

Whethor or not these joint meetings were productive can be questioned. Certainly the culture shock to which Mink alludes was an inhibiting factor, as was the language problem. Joe Keeper, who attended one of the joint meetings, wrote: "My main impression of the meeting in Winnipeg is one of confusion and I am more than certain that this was the impression of the Cedar Lake and Moose Lake delegates."[71]

The meetings of the Forebay Committee continued for many years after the relocation, and it quickly became evident that the people were not satisfied with the provisions of the agreement, their new community, or the activities of the Forebay Committee.

THE ROLE OF THE FEDERAL GOVERNMENT

The role which the Department of Indian Affairs assumed through-out the negotiations was primarily that of "interested observer." Very early in the negotiation process they did attempt to exert some influence by dictating to the province the procedure whereby the Indians would be allowed to surrender reserve land, according to the Indian Act. Although the possibility of expropriation of reserve lands was discussed, the province was warned that agreement by the Indians was essential and that a full compensation package supported by the Indians would likely be required before any land transfer could take place.[72] But even these warnings were hollow threats, and there is no indication that the Department of Indian Affairs was prepared to play anything more than a passive role in the process. In fact, a contradiction does emerge in the role which Indian Affairs adopted. For instance, the Special Assistant to the Director wrote in a memorandum: "While in favour of the Province playing the major role, the [Indian Affairs] meeting was of the opinion that in our position as trustee for the Indians we would have to take an *active* part in seeing that the future well-being of the Indians was not subrogated to the interests of non-Indians who may have to be relocated as a result of the power development"[73] [emphasis added]. But a short time later another senior Indian Affairs official detailed a different approach: "The matter of compensation and relocation is the responsibility of the Manitoba Hydro-Electric Board and the main functions of this Department are to act in an *advisory* capacity to the Indians and agents of the Board, and to see that the provisions with respect to Indian lands in the Indian Act are followed"[74] [emphasis added]. Hence, while acknowledging on one hand the existence of the trust relationship between the Department of Indian Affairs and the Indians and the road for the Department to actively defend the interests of the Indians, on the other hand the department seemed prepared to allow the province to negotiate directly with the Indians, providing only advice as necessary. As it turned out, Indian Affairs adopted the latter approach. Only later, after the agreements had been signed, did Indian Affairs consider "whether or not we should change our role with respect to assuming responsibility for negotiations with the Forebay, rather than having the Indians involved."[75] In instances where they did actively intervene on behalf of the people, they were often rebuked by the provincial government. In one such case, after Indian Affairs representatives advised the Chemawawin people not to move to the new site until deficiencies

in the newly constructed houses were amended, they were accused by
the Manitoba Deputy Minister of Mines and Natural Resources of being "irresponsible, occasionally even antagonistic, to what we were
trying to do, and in any event, completely negative and detrimental
to any progress that we might make in our dealings with the
Bands."[76]

The task of safeguarding the interests of the Native residents of
Chemawawin essentially fell to one man, J.R. Bell. As the local Indian
agent operating out of The Pas, he had some familiarity with the community. Recognizing that his new role would consume much of his
time, he was relieved of his other duties and officially seconded "to act
as advisor to the Indians in all questions relating to Operation Grand
Rapids."[77]

It is apparent that Bell spent a great deal of time in Chemawawin,
and attended many of the local committee meetings. In fact, it is quite
likely that he became closely attached to the community because he
began to advise, and some would say bully, the Native residents to
resist many of the province's overtures. At one point, he even suggested
to the local committee that the people remain in Chemawawin until
they were fully satisfied with the compensation agreement.[78] However, his alteration of an official role as advisor into one of advocate
was not well received by his superiors. According to Armand Pouliot,
the trader at Chemawawin, "his [Bell's] hands were tied. Indian
Affairs, . . . they worked pretty much with the Hydro. And they didn't
get along too well with him. Well, he got transferred out of here. I guess
he talked too much. But his hands were tied. He used to tell me, 'They
don't like what I'm doing,' he'd say."[79] Other reactions to Bell's role
are diverse. The Community Development Officer at Chemawawin
described him in paternalistic terms, noting that he had "decided that
he must make the decisions for the Indians of the Forebay as to where
they should move, and all decisions affecting their livelihood."[80] The
Forebay Committee saw him in a similar light, although to them his
paternalism was interference more than anything else. Subsequent
research into Bell's role also suggests that, at times, he was extremely
authoritarian in his dealings with the local people, effectively denying them the opportunity to actively participate in the negotiations.
For instance, it has been alleged that "Mr. Bell threatened the Indians,
informing them that they would be flooded anyway if they did not sign
the agreement."[81]

Members of the community firmly believe that Indian Affairs officials should have been more active in protecting community interests.

Furthermore, they feel that the federal government abandoned its responsibility to the people during the period of negotiations and subsequent events. As one resident explained, "We made all kinds of mistakes. Because nobody helped us out. We should have had Indian Affairs people working with us, who could help us, who could give us ideas. I don't see why they weren't working for us."[82]

The refusal of the Department of Indian Affairs to become actively involved on behalf of the community is viewed by residents as tacit support for the methods and policies of the Forebay Committee.

THE FOREBAY AGREEMENT: A LETTER OF INTENT

Perhaps the most controversial aspect of the Easterville case was the agreement that was signed between the band and the Forebay Committee. Referred to as both the Letter of Intent and the Forebay Agreement, this document has all the ingredients, and elicits all of the emotions, of the treaties signed generations earlier.

Since reserve land was to be flooded, it was necessary for the Manitoba government to first properly obtain the land under the provisions of the Indian Act. It was the Indian Affairs Branch that first suggested that a "package" of commitments be prepared and presented to the Indians for their consideration. While retaining the right to ultimately consent to this package, and in effect the terms of the surrender, Indian Affairs essentially abdicated its responsibility to negotiate on behalf of the band, and instructed the Manitoba government, through the Forebay Committee, to negotiate directly with the people of Chemawawin.[83]

Negotiations with the local committee at Chemawawin had begun in the spring of 1962. These first negotiations were conducted orally; the Forebay Committee obviously saw them as a necessary precursor to a written agreement, but the Native people saw them differently. The oral discussions, interpreted as promises by the Native people, became entrenched in their minds as significant components of the agreement. Even after a written version was received, the original perspective remained unchanged in the Natives' minds. Further, the oral discussions preceding the agreement, and in fact all of the oral discussions with the Forebay Committee and government representatives, became attached to the community's body of knowledge about the agreement.[84]

The Letter of Intent was mailed to the Chief of the Chemawawin Band on 18 April 1962. In general, this letter detailed some of the promises made verbally at the first meeting with the Forebay Committee. A few issues arose, however, and the Chief proposed a number of changes. These revisions were made, and another letter of intent was sent to the Chief, this one dated 7 June 1962. The band council accepted the offer and passed a band council resolution to that effect on 14 June 1962.[85] The federal government gave its approval to the letter by Privy Council Order Number 1962-1617, passed on 15 November 1962.

It seems that, as soon as the band resolution accepting the agreement was passed, the Indians began to express their increasing reluctance, concern and suspicion. In a letter to the Forebay Committee, the local people demanded clarification on a number of points, including the question of the provision of electricity to the new community. In concluding the letter, they wrote: "We feel that this letter [i.e. Letter of Intent] is similar to a Treaty. We cannot accept what we do not think is right, as it is not we who will suffer for our mistake, but our children and our children's children."[86] For its part, the Forebay Committee was perturbed. Believing that the negotiations had been satisfactorily concluded, they wrote back, "This is no time for you or for us to reconsider our Agreement as this would delay the great deal of work to be done."[87] This assertion had little effect on the community, nor did a letter from Premier Duff Roblin reaffirming the province's intent to fulfill all of the commitments in the agreement. The people declared their intent to remain at Chemawawin until their concerns were adequately dealt with.

In early 1964, as the date of relocation neared, the band council passed a resolution requesting that Indian Affairs intervene on their behalf in negotiations with the province.[88] The federal government apparently rejected the request. About the same time, the people put their concerns in a letter to the Chairman of the Forebay Committee:

We, the Council of the Chemawawin Band, and our people have had many meetings with you, the representatives of your Committee and other Provincial Government officers in regard to our move from Cedar Lake to Easterville. In all these meetings we have asked for one thing and another which, we feel, are very necessary to our future well-being and economic stability. In almost all cases verbal or written confirmation to our requests has only partially been given, refused outright or an alternative proposed. . . . It is only fair to advise you now of what we must have before we will move from our present location on the Chemawawin Reserve.[89]

Then, in June of the same year, less than one month before they were to be relocated, they detailed a new list of concerns and grievances to be dealt with before relocation. Among these, they demanded that: "(1) the new reserve boundaries be established; (2) the land exchange be completed; (3) electrical power by hydro line, not generator, be provided; (4) houses be available for all families at Easterville at the time of the relocation."[90] At a meeting with the Forebay Committee in Easterville shortly thereafter, the people were apparently satisfied that these issues would be resolved eventually. However, it was too late for any action prior to the relocation. Given the fact that many of these issues did remain unresolved for many years, and some issues are still not resolved, the decision to move over to the Easterville site instead of holding out for firmer commitments proved to be a mistake.

From the moment the Letter of Intent was received, confusion surrounding its meaning developed. The letter was written in non-legal language so that it could be easily understood, but proved to be so vague in meaning as to stymie even the Community Development Officer.[91] The Letter of Intent was fraught with ambiguous, open-ended clauses that even later members of the Forebay Committee found difficult to comprehend and interpret. Wrote committee-member R.M. Connelly in 1970: "Admittedly, a letter of intent was developed and became the basis of a mutual agreement as to what was to be done. However, it is a document written in layman's language which can easily be interpreted in different ways."[92]

The Letter of Intent is reproduced in its entirety in Appendix 2. A few of the more substantive elements are:

1 The provision of new or reconditioned homes with pit toilets and electricity;

2 The construction of a new school;

3 The establishment of a forest management unit for the exclusive use of the community;

4 The establishment of a "planned" community, part reserve for the Treaty Indians, and part non-reserve for the non-status Indians and Métis;

5 The construction of a road to the community;

6 The use of local labor "as much as possible" in the construction of the townsite;

7 The exchange of land in the ratio of two acres of new land for each acre of reserve land taken;

8 The payment of $20,000 into the Band's account;

9 The undertaking of "scientific and engineering studies and investigations in order to assure maximum economic development of the interior and fringe areas of the forebay for wildlife propagation";

10 The undertaking of "every step possible to maintain the income of the people of Chemawawin at the new site."[93]

Although the Letter of Intent was primarily designated for the status Indians, the Métis residents of Chemawawin were also included in a number of provisions, particularly those pertaining to housing. While the Métis were, in effect, told that they had few specific rights (they were, technically, squatters on provincial crown land, and this fact was emphasized), they were allowed all of the "benefits" of the agreement.[94] Both Indian and Métis were concerned that the community remain intact as a social entity, and the Forebay Committee endeavoured to fulfill this request. Furthermore, the Chemawawin Band Council, and the elected representatives of the Métis people, worked well together, and most committees at the local level consisted of both Indian and Métis members.[95]

Many issues arose over the Letter of Intent in subsequent years. Paramount among these was the fact that at no point in the negotiations was a lawyer made available to the community to advise them of their legal rights and aid them in understanding the legal technicalities involved. Harvey Pollock, a lawyer hired by the Chemawawin Band in 1968 to investigate the Forebay Agreement, was openly astonished that no lawyer had been provided. Pollock testified:

In my meetings with these people and my discussions with them, I said, "Well why didn't you get legal counsel?" The answer was, "Well, Hydro and the Government made us promises and they said they were going to do this and they were going to do that, and we took them for their word, and we didn't feel that we required legal counsel." I would have thought that at that particular time the Government and the Hydro would have taken some steps to adequately protect these people's rights. . . . You see the whole point here is that there [was] no representation by these people and this is just awful. This is the most inequitable situation I have ever come across.[96]

It is not at all clear why the people of Chemawawin were allowed to negotiate without legal advisors. Evidence suggests that representatives of the federal government discussed this issue amongst themselves, and decided against providing legal representation. Even after the agreement had been accepted, and the people were threatening to remain in Chemawawin, the Regional Supervisor of Indian Affairs was forced to ask, "If the Indians are to negotiate, should they not have legal counsel at all meetings with Forebay officials?"[97]

Although not evident at the time, it would appear that the reserve land at Chemawawin was expropriated by the federal government and transferred to the Province of Manitoba. A close examination of relevant documents supports this view. In the Letter of Intent itself, S.W. Schortinghuis, Deputy Minister of the provincial Department of Mines and Natural Resources, himself "authorized by the Province of Manitoba and Manitoba Hydro," wrote: "*We* will — (a) exchange all of the Chemawawin Indian Reserve . . . for vacant provincial land . . . (e) survey the boundaries of the new reserve . . . at provincial cost" [emphasis added].[98] The band council resolution passed by the Chemawawin Indian Band on 14 June 1962 stated that, in a previous resolution, the province had "agreed to transfer certain Reserve Lands to the Province of Manitoba under the terms and conditions outlined in Mr. Schortinghuis's letter."[99] Finally, the Government of Canada consented to "the taking of the land . . . subject to the terms and conditions set out in the said exchange of letters, the administration and control thereof to be transferred to Her Majesty in right of the Province of Manitoba."[100] Unorthodox, yet apparently legal, the direct transfer of Indian land to the province through expropriation underscores both Manitoba's pressing need for resolution of the issue and the federal government's willingness to expedite the matter on behalf of the province.

One area of frustration for the people was the fact that, aside from the negotiating and signing of the agreement, the Forebay Committee actually had little if any authority to fulfill the terms of the agreement or to act upon their requests. This is especially true with regard to problems which arose in the new community, and there were many. While the committee proved to be very efficient in securing the agreement, its efficiency declined markedly when it came to fulfilling the promises outlined in the agreement. For example, at two separate meetings of the Forebay Committee where "requests for action" were submitted by the local committee, the Forebay Committee denied their responsibility or indicated another government department as the responsible party in more than half the requests. At one point the Chairman of the committee "informed the meeting that the function of the Forebay Committee is to approach other government agencies, not to carry out actual work itself."[101] However, in most cases the local committee was directed to approach these agencies on their own.

LEGAL ACTION

In the years following the relocation, the community became frustrated at the lack of action on the part of the Forebay Committee in fulfilling its obligations under the Forebay Agreement. Particularly frustrating was the fact that, not only had the band not received all of the land owing to it under the agreement, but also the land upon which the community sat at Easterville had yet to be officially granted reserve status.[102] It seems that, in considering additional lands to fulfill the land exchange provision of the Forebay Agreement, the province and the band could not come to any agreement; the band came to feel that the province was willing only to release marginal, unproductive lands. In 1968, the Chemawawin Indian Band, using funds provided by the Manitoba Indian Brotherhood, hired Winnipeg lawyer Harvey Pollock to investigate the conditions surrounding the signing of the Letter of Intent and the relocation of the community. Specifically, his task was "to carry on negotiations on their behalf in respect to obtaining for them proper compensation for the taking of the Chemawawin Reserve, . . . to determine whether or not the discussions preceding the letter of commitment were unilateral on the part of the government, or whether or not the Indians entered into an agreement with the government, and in this regard, if, on the surface, there appears to have been an agreement, whether or not the Indians truly understood the nature of the agreement."[103]

Fundamental to the investigation was the lawyer's belief that the Letter of Intent, or Forebay Agreement, was a legal agreement which was not being fulfilled.[104] Further, according to Pollock, "the Indians had no outside counsel to advise them and the letter of intent went largely unread and uncomprehended."[105] The analogy between this agreement and an Indian treaty was not lost on Pollock, who noted, "It reminds me of my studies of the treaties of 1870 and '71, '72 and '73 and the situation that prevailed in our country at that time when the Indian gave up his birthrights; . . . this was the attitude that was taken [in negotiating the Letter of Intent]."[106] Foreshadowing the type of support that Indian Affairs was likely to provide, one department official responded to Pollock's assertions with the incredulous statement: "I am very surprised the Indians did not insist on legal counsel at the outset."[107] Clearly, it was not the Indians' responsibility to insist on legal counsel; it was the responsibility of the federal government to provide such representation as a part of its trust relationship with the Indians.

In his attempts to uncover the facts of the case, Pollock immediately ran into obstacles in his investigation. As he had not been a party to the original agreement, he requested from the Forebay Committee all files pertaining to the hydro project. However, as a result of the legal action, these had been turned over to the committee's own solicitor, J.D. Raichura, who refused to allow Pollock access to them. Pollock's request was denied, first because it was "impractical, time-consuming, and expensive" to comply with, and later because such documentation was "privileged." However, Raichura did agree to supply specific documents, but only if Pollock could identify them. Confidentially, Raichura was of the belief that Pollock did "not know what he is talking about."[108]

Although this action on the part of the Forebay Committee proved a great hindrance, Pollock did manage to obtain enough information to file a Statement of Claim on 15 August 1970. Listing the Government of Manitoba, the Manitoba Hydro-Electric Board, and the Grand Rapids Forebay Committee as defendants, the claim asserted that, among other things: (1) . . . the commitments of the Province of Manitoba and Hydro set forth in the said letter [Letter of Intent] are not the same as originally orally agreed on, and moreover offers and commitments have not been honoured; . . . (2) . . . the Province of Manitoba and Hydro, through pressure exerted on the Band, forced the Band into the selection of Easterville as the relocation site, and as a result of this forced move, the Community as a whole sustained severe damage to its social, economic and financial structure."[109] In addition to the costs of the legal action, the band claimed damages for breach of contract and a "rectification" of the Letter of Intent allowing for both performance of some provisions and revision of others.

While the Forebay Committee decided to "continue to function as heretofore" even though the claim had been submitted, they were soon advised to terminate all discussions with the community concerning forebay matters.[110]

On 30 October 1970, the Government of Manitoba filed its response to the claim of the Easterville people, expectedly denying all of the claims made by the community.[111] According to the Statement of

Defence, the Forebay Committee could not be taken to court because it was not a legal entity. In other words, it had no legal responsibility to the people of the community and was, therefore, technically speaking, not responsible for its actions or its inactions. For the Indians, the negotiations had been conducted, and an agreement signed, with a body that was not legally responsible to fulfill the conditions of the agreement.[112] The Government of Manitoba and Manitoba Hydro, however, were legal entities and therefore subject to possible lawsuit. The Statement of Defence also argued that the band could not bring an action against the Manitoba government because the band was not a legal entity. The federal government would have to initiate the action on behalf of the band.

In addition to refuting the claims made, the Statement of Defence stated that the Government of Manitoba should not be liable because "the relocation of the plaintiffs at Easterville was negotiated and carried out with the advice, knowledge and consent of the Government of Canada."[113] In other words, the fact that the federal government concurred with the agreement, whether it was right or wrong, ostensibly absolved the provincial government of all responsibility.

The federal government seemed puzzled by the legal action. Although it had released twelve thousand dollars from the band's capital funds to pay for the lawsuit, some officials of the Department of Indian Affairs doubted the band's claims. One such official was R.M. Connelly, the individual closest to the case; he was the Manitoba Regional Director for Indian Affairs, and simultaneously a member of the Forebay Committee. In a letter to Ottawa, Connelly stated his position clearly, and it was contrary to his responsibility to represent the interests of the Indians: "Having been a continuous member of the committee since 1964, it is my personal opinion that the Province of Manitoba has steadily but surely been bending every effort to meet its commitments to the Chemahawin Indian Band. True, there are a number of matters still pending, namely, those pertaining to economic development and to land transactions. As a member of the committee, but even more important, as an official of the Department of Indian Affairs which has special interest with respect to the Chemahawin Indians, I can say that I agree with the Statement of Defence prepared by Mr. Raichura." Mr. Connelly did not think much of Harvey Pollock's representation either, commenting: "The action of the two bands [Chemawawin and Moose Lake], in my opinion, stems as much from Mr. Pollock's wanting to spend the $12,000 retainer each band has set aside for legal fees, as from the Indian's understandable impatience about the Province's delays, some inexplicable, in finalizing its obligations." Still unable to see the substance of the Indians' cause, he concluded his letter by asking "why the bands and our department allowed negotiations to proceed without securing adequate legal counsel for the Indians."[114]

Pollock worked for about four years on the case, but for a variety of interrelated reasons the action failed to make it to court. According to Pollock, certain officials of the Manitoba government used very effective stalling tactics, especially in refusing to disclose relevant documents in the preparation of the Indians' case.[115] As the case dragged on, the people of Easterville became disenchanted with Pollock's efforts. Their disenchantment stemmed as much from their lack of understanding of the legal process and the lawyer's task as it did from their exasperation at a never-ending process of negotiation and confrontation. Community input was essential in Pollock's preparation of the case, but, according to Pollock, the people failed to adequately direct him; they apparently assumed that once he had been hired, he would resolve the issue on his own. The severe social disintegration which was occurring at the time was no doubt instrumental in hampering the community participation which was urgently required by Pollock.[116] Ironically, this disintegration was caused by the declining economic potential of the region, the subsequent unemployment, and a general community-wide depression, all of which were the result of the hydro project and relocation.

The people of Easterville, for their part, do not feel that they received adequate representation from Pollock, and some have openly questioned what he did for his money.[117] However, though disenchanted with the legal process, the people were not ready to give up. Faced with the ongoing frustration of dealing with the Manitoba government and the Forebay Committee, the band council refused to let their claim die, and it was resurrected in early 1978.

THE SPECIAL FOREBAY COMMITTEE: A NATIVE REACTION

As the lifespan of the Grand Rapids Dam passed one decade, the bitterness of the people of Easterville failed to subside. Their grievances were many; they were essentially the same as those communicated in their earlier Statement of Claim, and little progress had been made in resolving them. Further, much to the consternation of the Easterville people, the Forebay Committee was dissolved in February of 1975, according to its mandate. In the Manitoba government's view, the terms of reference of the committee had been carried out "to the extent that ongoing government programs can now service the needs of Moose Lake and Easterville.[118] From the perspective of the community, however, very little in fact had been accomplished, and the dissolution of the Forebay Committee while there were still many outstanding issues was seen as a further attempt by the Manitoba government to circumvent its responsibilities.

Although the people of Easterville had many grievances, perhaps the most significant to them was the lack of progress in the allotment of new lands to replace those surrendered at Chemawawin. According to the Letter of Intent, reserve land was to be replaced at a ratio of two acres of new land for each acre surrendered. This meant that approximately 11,626 acres were to be provided to the band.[119] At the time of the dissolution of the Forebay Committee, only 655 acres had been selected by the band and agreed to by both the federal and provincial governments. However, this land, the Chemawawin Band's new reserve at Easterville, still had not been officially granted reserve status. Although attainment of such status was imminent, the people were at a loss to explain the continual delay. In their minds, how could the Forebay Committee be dissolved when even the most fundamental aspect of the Letter of Intent, the granting of their new reserve lands, had yet to be enacted? Walter Mink, a Chief in Easterville, eloquently put the whole issue into perspective: "The letter of intent from the province of Manitoba covered only a 10 year period. Now I have often thought of this and I wonder whether if after ten years if the letter of intent doesn't provide for more than 10 years. What the Manitoba government and Manitoba Hydro is planning to do? Are they going to open the dam and let the water go because if it's only for 10 years well then there should be no more flooding and we should be back the way we were."[120]

The problems associated with the granting of new lands in fulfillment of the provisions of the Letter of Intent were unforeseen at the time the agreement was made. Although a zone for the land exchange had been indicated at the time, that there were additional constraints was not so indicated. The Chemawawin Indian Band was obviously concerned that it obtain land with economic potential, and the Letter of Intent certainly supported such an idea, at least in spirit if not in letter. But when land selections were made by the band, they were frequently denied. It seems that the province was not prepared to lose prime land or locations to the band. In one case, the band wished the road leading down to the fish plant, and the plant itself, to be established as reserve land. This would have had the effect of eliminating income tax for the status Indian fishermen, since the fish plant would be considered their place of employment, and income tax is not payable on income earned on the reserve. The Manitoba government rejected this request. In another case, the band selected land at the junction of Highway 6 and Highway 327, an important intersection leading, alternatively, to Grand Rapids and Thompson, The Pas, and Winnipeg. The band hoped to establish a gas station/restaurant complex at this key location. The province, however, also recognizing the significance of the location, rejected the request, although they offered to lease the land to the band. This offer was rejected.[121]

The residents of Easterville were not alone in their discontent. Similar letters of intent had also been accepted by the Indians and Métis of Moose Lake and The Pas, and they too had outstanding grievances. Furthermore, the Native residents of Grand Rapids, immediately below the dam, had never been offered any compensation, nor had they signed an agreement, and they felt that they had been unfairly ignored. Certainly the Easterville people had borne the brunt of the negative effects of the dam, but that did not make the discontent of the other bands any less significant. Through the establishment of an umbrella political organization called the Swampy Cree Tribal Council, the four bands – Chemawawin, Moose Lake, Grand Rapids and The Pas – were brought together.

At the time of the initial negotiations in the early 1960s, few residents of these communities experienced any sustained contact with the residents of the others. Despite the fact that there was some intermarriage among them (and of course the Chemawawin and Moose Lake bands were closely related geneologically as they had only separated around the time of the signing of Treaty Five), contact was infrequent and almost exclusively social in nature. There existed no pantribal political organizations to bind the bands together in common interest. Each band experienced the negotiation process largely as an isolate, unaware of the very similar problems the others were having.

In December 1977, Swampy Cree Tribal Council Chief Henry Wilson called for a meeting with representatives from each of the four communities to consider the formation of a flood committee to pursue negotiations and, if necessary, legal action, to settle the outstanding claims of the Forebay Agreement.[122] This committee, called the Special Forebay Committee, was officially formed at a meeting in Easterville early the next year, and after hiring Winnipeg lawyer Ken Young, himself a northern Manitoba Indian, it launched a new legal campaign.

Fortunately, the new Special Forebay Committee had some unexpected ammunition in its struggle. A report prepared for the Department of Indian Affairs and released confidentially in May 1978 legitimized many of the grievances that the bands had.[123] Although not accepted by Indian Affairs as anything more than a "discussion paper," the effect of the report was such that the federal government had little option but to provide funding to the fledgling Special Forebay Committee to finance negotiations.[124]

The tactics of the committee, under Ken Young's guidance, were to initially seek redress through negotiations, and pursue legal action only if necessary. To that end, they formally requested that negotiations with the Manitoba government and Manitoba Hydro be reopened. In addition, they made it clear to the federal government that the latter was not in the clear on this issue. The Deputy Minister of Indian Affairs was informed that "the letter of intent was hinged on the bands agreeing to transfer Indian reserve lands to the Government of Manitoba which consideration was clearly a violation of a federal statute, Section 28 of the Indian Act."[125] The Deputy Minister was then left with the question of "how the federal government of that time allowed this whole sordid episode to proceed in the manner it did."[126] According to Ken Young, the federal government became more and more an accomplice in the Grand Rapids fiasco: "I must reiterate that what the federal government allowed to take place during the stages of negotiations had all the ingredients of breaches of trust in its responsibility to the Treaty Indian people of the four communities which were impacted by the Grand Rapids Hydro Project."[127] With the statute of limitations on submitting a claim apparently running out, Young filed claims in the Court of Queen's Bench on behalf of the Moose Lake, The Pas and Grand Rapids Indian bands. The 1970 claim filed by Harvey Pollock on behalf of the Chemawawin Indian Band was retained.[128] The Manitoba government, Manitoba Hydro, and the federal government were all named as defendants.[129]

In filing the claims, Young clearly was unsure of the direction the action might take. While challenging the legality of the various letters of intent, he was faced with the responsibility that, should he be proven correct, there might not be any agreement on which to sue for breaches.[130] Furthermore, while an impact study had been undertaken by a Winnipeg consulting firm, it was a preliminary study that still left many questions unanswered. Young hoped that if the action went to court there would be sufficient time available to garner all of the needed evidence to substantiate the case.[131]

The threat of legal action seemed to have the desired effect, especially after the province's attempts to have the claims struck were unsuccessful. Both the federal and Manitoba governments indicated their desire to sit down and renegotiate the agreement. It was decided that all sides should consider the issue of loss of hunting caused by the dam before any other. However, the province's participation was conditional, as long as "major costs" were not involved.[132] Furthermore, the request by the Special Forebay Committee for provincial funding was denied. The federal government then reappeared on the scene, committing $581,000 to the bands to research their claim and finance negotiations. At a time that the Guerin case was before the Supreme Court (and it seemed likely that the federal government would be found guilty of the breach of fiduciary or trust relationship to a British Columbia Indian band), the federal government adopted a new role in support of the Indians' cause.[133] In a letter from the Minister of Indian Affairs to the Manitoba Minister of Natural Resources, the federal government's position was outlined. It was willing to concede, among other things, that injustices had been done by the Manitoba government and Manitoba Hydro in failing to satisfactorily implement the various letters of intent. For its part, the federal government noted that it was not responsible for compensation to the bands because it "was not a party to the agreements."[134] This position was, of course, antithetical to Manitoba's position that the federal government had consented to the agreements when it passed the order-in-council transferring the land to the province; the federal government's role in supporting the agreements, though passive, was clear. The federal government was prepared to acknowledge that "should, during the negotiations, definite evidence arise proving a failure by Canada to fulfill its legal obligations, the Government is prepared to examine and negotiate a reasonable and just redress with the Forebay Bands."[135] The onus of proof, of course, would lie with the bands.

The optimism surrounding the upcoming negotiations did not last for long. New chiefs were elected in Easterville, Grand Rapids and The Pas, and the legal action took a new direction. Young and his firm were released from their retainer, and a new firm was engaged. Files switched hands, and the residents of the forebay once again found themselves "back at square one."[136] A new direction was conceived, one that called for a re-evaluation of the position of the bands and the development of a coherent blueprint of grievances, compensation, and negotiation tactics.

The grievances of the people of Easterville have, in recent years, been partially resolved. Despite some fundamental disagreements with the Manitoba government concerning eligible land for selection as replacement for the surrendered reserve land, progress in this area has been made. In 1981, the band and the province agreed to the transfer of 1,000 acres of provincial crown land near the community.[137] In 1985, the band selected their final lands due them under the Letter of Intent, a parcel of some 11,000 acres near Denbigh Point. At present, this land is in the process of being transferred to the federal government to be made into reserve land. But the band is not happy with the quality of the lands that were made available to them. There are indications that the band may now request additional lands as well. Unfortunately, many other grievances stemming from the Letter of Intent remain outstanding. The economy is still suffering. Social life has deteriorated significantly. And Cedar Lake is still over three metres higher than their Creator originally intended. The people of Easterville, while both bitter and angry, have come to understand why they have suffered so much: "We are not pointing the finger at any particular government or political party. When we look at the development of the North, we can say that all governments of whatever political stripe have been callous and indifferent to the needs of Indian people when the choice has to be made between the welfare of Indian people and the short-term benefits of a society and a system which appears to measure benefits using money as its chief standard. If it had to be a choice between money and Indians, it seems the Indian always loses."[138]

South Indian Lake and the
Churchill River Diversion Project

5

The Hydro has no thought of the people of South Indian Lake, only of the power he can get out of it.[1]

As the 1960s came to a close, it was apparent that a new movement was afoot in Canada. Individuals from all walks of life had begun to express their concerns about the damage being caused to the environment by developers. Pollution too was becoming an issue, and the extent to which the pristine northlands was being affected had become an open question. More than anything else, the image of the northern Native emerged in this period as the symbol of the environmental movement. Here were individuals who, it was believed, continued to live in harmony with nature, and did not abuse it. Yet, industrial projects in the North threatened to disrupt the balance that the Native people had struck with the land. When plans for another, even larger, hydroelectric project for northern Manitoba were announced, the Native people of the North became the centre of a controversy which raged on national and even international fronts.[2] Unlike that of the Cumberland House and Easterville cases, the intense media attention which surrounded the flooding of Southern Indian Lake ensured that this case would be different. The controversy over the flooding would be fought in the public eye, and the Natives were to be at the forefront of a political struggle to stop the project.

THE COMMUNITY OF SOUTH INDIAN LAKE

South Indian Lake is a small Native community in northern Manitoba, some 1,200 air kilometres north of Winnipeg. It remains semi-isolated on the southeastern shore of Southern Indian Lake. The community is accessible by road from Leaf Rapids, forty-eight kilometres to the southwest, and then by boat or ferry across South Bay. The mining centre of Thompson is found 129 air kilometres to the southeast.

The tenth largest lake in Canada, Southern Indian Lake is in effect part of the Churchill River, and is the last major water body found on that river before it reaches Hudson Bay. The community of South Indian Lake is located along its shores in the boreal forest region of the Precambrian Shield. The surface cover consists primarily of dense, yet relatively short, black and white spruce, jack pine, and white birch. The extensive tree cover, combined with thin soils and discontinuous permafrost, render the region largely unsuitable for extensive agriculture.

There are over 900 Native residents in the community, of which approximately three-quarters are treaty status Indians. The remaining residents are primarily non-status Indians who have, in large part, adopted the term *Métis* to identify themselves. The treaty Indians are descendants of those who signed the adhesion to Treaty Five in 1908, and are currently members of the Nelson House Indian Band. The community of South Indian Lake itself is not a reserve, despite the preponderance of treaty Indians living there, a fact which is of great significance in understanding their political struggle.

The people of South Indian Lake are, in ethnographic terms, properly described as Rocky Cree, a division of the Western Woods Cree peoples who dominate much of the subarctic regions of the western provinces.[3] Their contemporary economy, like that of Cumberland House and Easterville, is pluralistic, involving a combination of traditional and modern pursuits. While wage-labour activities and government transfers have become increasingly important to the community since the dam was constructed, hunting, fishing and trapping have remained important as both commercial and domestic activities. However, the overall negative effect of the project has seriously undermined the viability of these industries.[4]

COMMUNITY HISTORY

South Indian Lake is a relatively new community, although habitation of the Southern Indian Lake region dates back some 6,000 years.[5] The region itself marks the historic boundary between the Cree and the Chipewyan, and it is quite likely that the name Southern Indian Lake refers specifically to the Southern or Cree Indians (in contrast

to Northern Indian Lake, and the Northern or Chipewyan Indians).
After the establishment of the fur trade, this boundary shifted extensively as one group, then the other, gained superiority in the new economic activity and expanded its territory.[6] With the subsequent collapse of the fur trade and the advent of the treaty-making process, the
boundary became stabilized and the conflict was terminated.

It is not possible to determine the exact date in which a community was formed in the Southern Indian Lake area in post-contact
times. There were some people in the region in the early 1800s who
were involved intensively in the fur trade, and this fact prompted the
Hudson's Bay Company to establish a post there in 1803. The rich
potential of the region at this time is clearly indicated by the quick reaction of the North West Company, which opened a competing post in
1805.[7] Although the Hudson's Bay Company post closed in 1824, followed by that of the North West Company, the region remained important to the companies. The Indian people from the Footprint Lake area
(later the Nelson House Reserve) continued to travel into the region
on trapping and hunting expeditions.

By the early twentieth century it was likely that a small but relatively stable population of Indians was living in the region. With the
signing of the adhesion to Treaty Five in 1908, these people were encouraged to resettle at Nelson House, where a new reserve was to be
created. Many chose to do so, but quickly found the social and economic
conditions of the reserve intolerable. At the same time, a number of
non-Native trappers, primarily Americans, moved into the Southern
Indian Lake region in search of the lucrative white fox. Many of these
individuals established permanent residences and married Indian
women.[8] Subsequently, many of those who had resettled at Nelson
House began to drift back north and take up more or less permanent
residence. With the establishment of a small but growing and apparently permanent population, the Hudson's Bay Company in 1919 reopened an outpost in the area. Staffed by a trader who travelled up periodically from Nelson House, the new business was relatively
successful. Consequently, in the late 1930s, the Hudson's Bay Company made the decision to re-establish a permanent post on Southern
Indian Lake.[9] The community of South Indian Lake became a permanent fixture from this point onward.

For many years the economy of the community revolved around
the trapping industry and the production of fish and animal products
for food and other domestic uses. However, in 1942 a commercial fish-

ery for Southern Indian Lake was established by northern entrepreneur Tom Lamb, heralding a new era of economic prosperity for the residents.[10] And when a fishing cooperative to replace Lamb's enterprise was established in the late 1960s, the aggressively self-reliant people of South Indian Lake found themselves on the verge of yet another progressive step.

When the news of the Churchill–Nelson River Project first reached the residents, they were not especially concerned. Similar to the situation at Easterville, the scope and magnitude of the government's plans for the Churchill and Nelson rivers were incomprehensible to the people, and they ignored the whole idea. But, unlike the people of Easterville, the people of South Indian Lake did not live on an Indian reserve, and were "squatters" on provincial land in the eyes of the Manitoba government. They were thus on the verge of a political struggle that was even more incomprehensible than was the project that was to disrupt their lives.

THE CHURCHILL RIVER DIVERSION PROJECT

It was not long after the Grand Rapids Hydro Project began operating in 1964 that Manitoba Hydro turned its attention to the enormous potential of the Churchill and Nelson rivers. In fact, even before 1964 the Manitoba government had begun preliminary investigations. In 1963, the Manitoba and federal governments signed an agreement to cost-share studies to investigate the power potential of the northern rivers.[11] Yet, many people were surprised when the Manitoba government announced phase one of the massive hydroelectric scheme in 1966. The Easterville debacle was still fresh in mind, and the Manitoba government initially vowed not to repeat the horrendous mistakes that had accompanied the Grand Rapids Project. They had "learned from the past."[12] Walter Weir's Progressive Conservative government insisted that the people of South Indian Lake receive independent representation in any compensation negotiations; the government could not and would not act as both developer and advisor, as it had done at Easterville.[13] Very quickly, however, these resolutions gave way to the development of strategies to deflate opposition to the project.

At the time of the opening of the Grand Rapids Dam in November 1965, then Premier Duff Roblin was already making plans for the Nelson River development.[14] Studies had indicated that the river was capable of producing an enormous amount of electricity because of its steep slope toward Hudson Bay. The Churchill River, on the other hand, with a much more gentle slope, was not considered a viable location for generating facilities. But the waters of the Churchill River would not be wasted altogether. Roblin's dream, and no doubt that of many innovative engineers, was to divert the water from the Churchill into the Nelson. The additional water flow in the Nelson would increase the capacities of the generating stations and render the total project more cost effective. A channel would be blasted in the rock of the Precambrian Shield, beginning at South Bay on Southern Indian Lake and continuing down to the Rat River, where the water would be carried on into the Burntwood River and then the Nelson.[15] It would be necessary to dam off the Churchill River in the north, at Missi Falls on Southern Indian Lake, to force the water to reverse its natural northward flow and proceed southward out the diversion channel. Southern Indian Lake would become a huge reservoir, and the water level would be raised some ten metres. The entire South Indian Lake community would be submerged.

The governments of both Manitoba and Canada saw the valuable contribution that extensive development of the Churchill–Nelson River system would have. The sale of export power was paramount in the minds of many, not only to offset the costs of the project but also to improve Canada's position in the balance of trade with the United States.[16] Furthermore, it was widely believed that the product of the development would be cheap electricity for all Manitobans, and most specifically southern Manitobans. Industry and consumers alike would benefit.

After much controversy, the final construction plan somewhat altered the configuration of the project. When the diversion was implemented, the level of Southern Indian Lake was raised only three metres, necessitating the relocation of only half the community of South Indian Lake. Nonetheless, over 1,500 square kilometres of boreal forest was flooded in an area of recognized ecological fragility.[17] To offset the reduced water flow available from the Churchill River, a plan was developed to regulate Lake Winnipeg, thereby further expanding the volume of water pouring into the Nelson River.

At present there are four generating stations in operation on the Nelson River. The first of these to be constructed, Kelsey, was completed in 1960 specifically to supply additional power to the INCO mining and smelting complex in Thompson. Since then, three more stations have been added: Kettle, completed in 1970; Jenpeg, completed in 1977; and Long Spruce, completed in 1977. The Limestone Generating Station, presently under construction, is scheduled to go into service in 1990. With this new facility, the total generating capacity from the Nelson River will have exceeded 3,000 megawatts.

ANACHRONISM IN A TECHNOLOGICAL AGE

In 1966, Premier Duff Roblin officially announced that the Churchill–Nelson River Project was ready for government approval. The announcement was met in most quarters with enthusiasm. The *Winnipeg Tribune* referred to the project as "a billion dollar dream," and stressed the number of jobs it would create.[18] But little actual planning had been done, and in many ways the project was still very much at the dream stage.

The euphoria which surrounded the announcement was not felt by everyone. The Manitoba Wildlife Federation voiced the need for environmental impact studies, but its suggestions went largely unheard. However, when a group of University of Manitoba professors spoke against the project, the media picked up on the story and the controversy commenced.

In March 1966, Stuart Anderson, the Deputy Minister of Mines and Natural Resources, and D.M. Stephens, Chairman of Manitoba Hydro, approached the University of Manitoba concerning the possibility of an impact study of the hydro program. Subsequently, an agreement was made between Manitoba Hydro and the University, and a small group of professors was commissioned to "appraise the problem and suggest the various aspects of it that should be examined later and in greater detail."[19] Headed by H.E. Duckworth, Academic Vice-President of the University, this group's investigations eventually caused some members of the study team to become bitter opponents of the plan.

Duckworth and his associates completed their study and submitted their report early in January 1967. The Reconnaissance Study (or the Duckworth Report) was extremely critical of Manitoba Hydro's plans. Their primary recommendation was that the level of Southern Indian Lake not be raised at all, but if absolutely necessary it should be raised much less than planned. The report also noted that there were alternatives to the flooding of Southern Indian Lake, and that these alternatives should be thoroughly investigated. The authors were not optimistic about the future for the people of South Indian Lake under the proposed scheme. They calculated that the community would experience a minimum economic loss of over $11 million, and predicted that their lifestyle would be seriously disrupted. They concluded: "Without attempting to be melodramatic about it, we feel that relocation of this Indian Village would be unjust to the present inhabitants and unworthy of the Province, although it might be in keeping with much past treatment of the Indians."[20] The Manitoba government was unimpressed with the Duckworth Report, and refused to make it public. Their belief that the report was both superficial and unscientific seemed justification enough. But the group of professors would not stay quiet. The confidential report soon surfaced in public, and opposition to the project began to mobilize. The publication of an open letter to Harry Enns, Minister of Mines and Natural Resources, by some of the professors, now joined by others, condemning the government's plans, was the spark that ignited the controversy.[21] In their words, under the proposed plan, Southern Indian Lake would become the "biggest man-made swamp in the world."[22]

In rejecting the Duckworth report, the Manitoba government appeared to view more favourably a consultant's report prepared for the Manitoba Development Authority, a body under the jurisdiction of the Department of Mines and Natural Resources.[23] Prepared by two leading consulting firms, Van Ginkel and Hedlin Menzies, the report argued that northern Native people were in "transition" from some kind of primitive past to a technological present. The lack of skills, proper training and locally available resources had resulted in widespread poverty in the North. The report described the people of South Indian Lake as "anachronisms in the present age of technology," and argued that the effect of the hydro project would do "nothing more than move forward in time the break-up of this community and way of life." The overall perspective of the report, and one which Manitoba Hydro apparently adopted, was stated succinctly in the covering letter to the Deputy Minister of the Manitoba Development Authority: "The consultants wish to make very specific their unqualified conclusion that the communities of native people that exist throughout Manitoba – and this is equally true of all parts of Canada – have no future and the interests of the native people of the total community will be gravely prejudiced if those resources of money and creative thought are not dedicated to solving the problem of the remote Indian settlement and the Indian reservation."[24] The sentiment expressed in this passage was echoed throughout most of Manitoba Hydro's negotiations with the affected communities.

NEGOTIATIONS AND PUBLIC HEARINGS

Inevitably, rumours of the hydro scheme reached South Indian Lake, where the people formed an *ad hoc* flood committee to begin discussion amongst themselves. But virtually nothing was known about the project, and the committee was largely inactive until the spring of 1968. At a press conference in January 1968, Harry Enns had announced that the project was "an imaginative major development in the interest of the people of Manitoba," adding, "Let there be no mistake about the importance of this project to all Manitobans."[25] He also announced his intention to grant Hydro an interim licence to proceed with the project, even though its engineers were still putting the finishing touches on their licence application and had not yet submitted it. In April 1968, it was decided that a meeting with the South Indian Lake people was in order: "It was felt that since the people were going to be directly affected they had the right to know at least as early as the rest of Manitoba and it was felt too that Manitoba Hydro had an obligation to make a direct announcement to the people rather than have them learn of it at second or third hand."[26]

The initial meeting was convened at South Indian Lake on 22 April 1968. Present were Kris Kristjanson, Manitoba Hydro's Assistant General Manager, and a number of other individuals from Hydro and the Manitoba government. Although the purpose of the meeting was to inform the people of the hydro plans and their progress in obtaining the necessary licence from the Water Control Branch, Kristjanson, in his opening remarks, spoke for only a few minutes. While acknowledging that "the people of South Indian Lake would be making a sacrifice for the rest of the people of Manitoba," he was not in a position to detail in any specific terms the magnitude of that sacrifice.[27] Further, while he was prepared to answer whatever questions existed in the minds of those in attendance, it soon became clear that neither he nor the other government officials had the necessary background information with which to respond.

Angus Bonner, a retired lay minister in the community, best summarized the concerns of the local residents as expressed at this meeting. He stated: "Ever since people have started for a livelihood on this lake our grandfathers have used this lake for their livelihood and our fore great grandfathers as well. This is South Indian Lake. This is where an Indian found to make a living. Now this is the lake that is going to be destroyed. It is going to affect us a lot. Not only us grown up people but our children and our grand-children.[28]

All those present acknowledged that the Native residents had rights, although no one was able to say what these were. However, the government was prepared to provide funds to ensure that these rights were protected, once defined. To this end, it was suggested that the community hire legal representation, and that the government was prepared to facilitate such action. In stressing the need for representation, Kristjanson's words, prophetic and succinct, failed to elicit any response: "In my opinion the white man is not as honest as the Indian but he would like to be."[29]

Clearly, at this time the idea that the people might fight the project was not taken seriously by the government. Indeed, the residents were warned: "You people here have the arguments against giving them [Manitoba Hydro] the licence but there are a whole lot of arguments – the whole of the rest of Manitoba wants the electricity – so there are lots of reasons for giving them the licence."[30] Such a view was echoed by the people themselves. Basil Colomb, a prominent member of the local flood committee (and eventually Mayor), was resigned to the fact: "Yes, we won't fight but we don't want no flood here, understand, but what's the use? We are just a handful of people here when there's millions of other people that are going to have the benefit of the light so I think we have one poor chance to try to fight on that [Manitoba Hydro's licence application].[31]

The Water Control Branch received Manitoba Hydro's licence application on 26 April 1968. Two days later, a representative of the branch met with the people of South Indian Lake to explain the licence application process. At this meeting, the representative for the government stated that the major question to be asked was whether or not "this is the best thing for the province of Manitoba because you and I are the ones that form the province.[32] In his mind, the Native residents of South Indian Lake were not being asked to do any more than non-Native residents in other parts of the province had been or might be asked. The unique culture and lifestyle of the northern Natives was equated with that of southern farmers, all of whom were, in the end, just Manitobans.

Subsequently, the local people began to get organized. A new flood committee was formally convened, and its members were flown to Winnipeg to interview four lawyers who had expressed an interest in the case. One in particular, Harold Buchwald, caught their attention and, on 5 July 1968, he was officially retained. Exactly what he was to do was not yet clear. The government's position in funding the representation focused on the application before the Water Control Branch. Once this issue had been settled, presumably the lawyer's services would be terminated. Certainly they did not anticipate that the legal relationship between Buchwald and the community would span close to seven years.

Once he was hired, it was necessary that Buchwald acquire as much information about the project as possible, and take direction from his clients. At the June meeting, George Bowman, the Province's Director for the Nelson region, poignantly explained the lawyer's role to the people: "He has a great deal of work to do; . . . he has to build up the case for you. . . . *He* is then *You*, he is your one voice and you have to feed him with the information he needs so that he can do this job effectively" [emphasis original].[33] But as a relatively isolated community, South Indian Lake had had little direct contact with the larger Canadian society, except for those who visited the community from time to time. Particularly, the people had had no experience whatsoever with lawyers and the legal system, and it proved difficult for Buchwald and his associate Yude Henteleff to explain their role in the hydro controversy. Eventually, a Cree word meaning "the one who speaks for others" was utilized to describe them, but even still the people were not entirely certain of the lawyers' role in the dispute. Furthermore, as Buchwald states, "They were blissfully unaware that they could say no [to the project], that they didn't have to accept automatically what the Great White Father gave them."[34]

In spite of the fact that the people of South Indian Lake lacked any concrete details concerning the hydro project, they were able to provide a wealth of information to Buchwald and Henteleff as the lawyers began to prepare their case. Henteleff himself spent over a month in the community, interviewed every family, and obtained the community view of the likely effect of the project.[35] Requests for specific information were still made, but the government representatives who met with them, ostensibly to provide such information, were themselves largely in the dark, leading to such ludicrous statements as the following one offered by George Bowman of the Manitoba Development Agency: "Certainly nobody at the moment can be quite sure of what is going to happen. I think all of us that are reasonable will know that there must be some fish in the lake, and it's going to be a bigger lake so it should be able to carry more fish."[36] This kind of information was of little assistance to the local flood committee, and points out the absolute dearth of reliable information which existed at this time. As Basil Colomb remarked at one of these early meetings, "We are still holding our meetings blind-folded."[37] It remained that way for some time.

The lawyers' early work with the community was greatly facilitated by the federal Indian Affairs Development Officer, Oscar Blackburn. Based in Lynn Lake, Blackburn had previously been a trapper, trader and school teacher in the South Indian Lake area, and his sympathies were clerrly with the local people. Indeed, in his active support for the community, he frequently risked reprimand from his superiors. He provided a great deal of advice to the local flood committee, as well as to Buchwald and Henteleff, and made the required arrangements for visits to the community by these lawyers.[38] The gratitude of the people was expressed when they named their new school after him.

On 19 June 1968, Manitoba Hydro's licence application was officially published, and "protests or objections" were invited.[39] Shortly thereafter, Harold Buchwald and his associates, particularly Yude Henteleff, filed a "conditional protest and objection" to the application on behalf of the South Indian Lake community.[40] The primary concern of the community at this time was that a compensation package be determined before the licence was granted, and most certainly before construction commenced. Manitoba Hydro seemed sympathetic. According to Yude Henteleff, Hydro's Kris Kristjanson had noted at a meeting held early in December 1968, "Manitoba Hydro is terribly concerned about having articulated to them the real position of the Indians."[41] In Henteleff's words, "He [Kristjanson] indicates that they thought they had done this more than adequately in respect to the Easterville situation but it now appears that such was not the case."[42]

As the year 1968 was drawing to a close, the protest against Hydro's licence application was slowly heating up. Once again, it was a group of University of Manitoba professors who took the lead. Forming an *ad hoc* "concerned citizens group," they wrote to Harry Enns, Minister of Mines and Natural Resources, saying that the hydro plans would surely prove "disastrous for the community."[43] In proposing alternatives to the flooding of Southern Indian Lake, they warned the Manitoba government: "Similar disregard for the future in the single purpose exploitation of our natural resources has already caused irreparable damage to the quality of our environment; . . . the real costs and potential losses associated with the present flooding proposal may far exceed the apparent saving in the cost of power production."[44]

The issue moved into the public forum in January 1969 when, according to provincial statute (the Water Power Act), Manitoba Hydro announced its application to proceed with the project and the holding of public hearings on the application. The first hearing began at South Indian Lake on 2 January 1969.

Most of this initial hearing was taken up by Harold Buchwald's questioning of Ed Overgaard, Manitoba Hydro's Chief Engineer. The questioning, at some points grilling, brought out a number of disturbing facts for the people of South Indian Lake to consider. First, Hydro had seemingly discounted a number of possible alternatives to the flooding of Southern Indian Lake without extensive investigation. Second, both Overgaard and Kris Kristjanson were unable to discuss in specific terms either the costs of the hydro plan under consideration or the costs of these alternatives. Third, Overgaard was forced to admit that no studies had been done on the likely effect of the diversion project on the fisheries and wildlife resources on the lake. Henteleff later commented: "The fact is they [Hydro] were totally ill-prepared. They approached the situation with considerable arrogance, and felt that anybody who questioned them was, in effect, questioning God. . . . Somehow, they were touched with infallibility in terms of decisions. Who had the temerity to question them?"[45]

The initial hearing produced another surprise: Manitoba Hydro officially tabled their compensation package for the community. Looking suspiciously like the Letter of Intent (or Forebay Agreement) signed with the Chemawawin Band at Easterville only a few years before, the package focused on a variety of structural commitments. Among other things, the Manitoba government, through Manitoba Hydro, agreed to provide: new docking facilities; replacement of fish camps; reimbursement for the cost of relocation; electricity "on the standards which now apply in other comparable communities"; work training programs; and $60,000 for a floating fish plant and an electronically-equipped boat to search for fish (see Appendix 3 for the complete text).[46] The people of South Indian Lake rejected this proposal outright. At the close of the hearing Buchwald made the community's position clear: answers to their many questions would be expected at the next round of hearings.[47]

The second round of hearings was scheduled for Winnipeg on 27 January 1969. However, shortly after the conclusion of the South Indian Lake hearing, Harry Enns announced that an "interim licence" would be granted to Manitoba Hydro to proceed with the diversion. According to Enns, the Winnipeg hearings were designed primarily to address the concerns and needs of the residents of South Indian Lake; they were not to decide the fate of the project, nor to question the engineering or economic aspects of it.[48] Buchwald and Henteleff were shocked at the news. In the wake of the public outrage that followed, stories began to circulate that Manitoba Hydro had in their possession a "secret" report which refuted all engineering and economic rationale for the planned project. The rumoured secret report was actually a series of reports (including the aforementioned Duckworth and Van Ginkel reports), and it was believed that the cumulative effect would be sufficient to stop the project. Harold Buchwald responded to the rumours by arguing that the reports "should come under scrutiny of the people who are going to be affected by this scheme before a fair enlightened decision can be made."[49]

Enns reversed his decision to issue the interim licence under a barrage of criticism from the media and the public. Furthermore, he provided a glimmer of hope for the people of South Indian Lake when he effectively agreed with the position of their counsel that the onus was on Manitoba Hydro at the Winnipeg hearings to convince the people of the province, and his government, that the Churchill River Diversion was the right project.[50]

An enormous crowd turned out at the Winnipeg hearings; there were so many people that a change of venue was required. With only one exception, everyone who chose to speak did so against the project. It was a scene not often witnessed: there were scientists and housewives; Natives and non-Natives; amateurs and professionals; all offering the same perspective, that the diversion should not be built. The people of South Indian Lake should not be made to suffer.

From the opening salvos, Manitoba Hydro was on the defensive. Leonard Bateman, Manitoba Hydro's Chairman, began by summarizing Hydro's position: the power was urgently needed, and the high-level diversion was the most economical way of attaining it. In fact, since 1965, the diversion had "been counted on" by Hydro in its plans to extract power from the Nelson River. Kristjanson echoed these views, and commented: "As in other cases where the public and private interests appear to be in conflict, the people of South Indian Lake are being asked to leave their homes and establish themselves in new surroundings for the benefit of all the people of Manitoba."[51]

Then, in a curious twist, Manitoba Hydro presented itself as the protector of Native rights. Bateman stated, "It is our earnest desire that we do provide every facility that is possible for these people so that there would be no one in Manitoba that would be ashamed of the treatment that these people received." He then addressed the issue of compensation by subtly chastizing Buchwald and Henteleff, who had taken the position at the previous hearing that Hydro should develop a compensation proposal for presentation to and discussion by the community. Stated Bateman, "Now, it's a shame, ladies and gentlemen, that you should think in terms of citizens of this province [South Indian Lake residents] as not knowing or as not being as knowledgeable in what they want as you are or as to what you think they want. Now certainly they are entitled to the same laws and rights as you and I are and I don't think they are entitled to anything less." For his part, Kristjanson once again produced the list of compensation promises, unchanged from the South Indian Lake hearing, and reaffirmed Hydro's "responsibility to compensate the residents of Southern Indian Lake who are displaced or otherwise suffer damage through the raising of the level of South Indian Lake [sic]." He too spoke in conciliatory terms about the need to work out "constructive programs which can enhance human values," and in effect presented the diversion project as opportunity rather than calamity. Hydro's benevolence was not limitless, however. According to Kristjanson, "Manitoba Hydro's position . . . is that to the greatest extent possible all factors should be considered and when I say to the greatest extent possible, in any decision of this kind *there are always pressures of time to move on* with a particular development" [emphasis added].[52]

Even though Manitoba Hydro clearly acknowledged their need to get the project under way, it once again became painfully obvious that they either had not yet fully planned out the project, or were unwilling to provide anything more than its barest details. When the lawyers for the community asked for specific information on the hydro project, they again met with reticence on the part of Hydro. Manitoba Hydro spokesmen, especially Bateman, insisted that since many contracts had already been tendered for the construction of the project, it would not be appropriate for Hydro to publicly disclose detailed information, especially concerning cost estimates. This, of course, prevented accurate comparison with the alternate projects considered by Hydro or those presented by the University of Manitoba group.

Also appearing at the Winnipeg hearings were a number of scientists, including engineers, biologists and anthropologists (many from the University of Manitoba group) who argued vehemently against the high-level diversion scheme. Cass Booy, of the Faculty of Engineering at the University of Manitoba, argued, "It is not a matter of money and houses, it is their independence, their self-sufficiency, their self-respect that is at stake." Anthropologist C.T. Shay described the Easterville fiasco in detail to the hearing, concluding that while "change may be inevitable, . . . the changes that took place at Easterville and the changes that may be taking place at South Indian Lake are in the direction we are trying to avoid."[53]

Buchwald and Henteleff were provided the opportunity at the hearings to once again detail the South Indian Lake position on Hydro's licence application. They argued that Hydro had to make their case beyond any doubt that the engineering and economic merits of the proposal were sound, and that a compensation program was in place prior to the granting of the licence. Buchwald and Henteleff stated: "We are irrevocably committed to the proposition that the fundamental requirements and protection of the human resources represented by the people of South Indian Lake and Pickerel Narrows – as individuals, families, and as communities – must at all times remain paramount and never sacrificed to the expediency of electric power requirements."[54]

As the hearings closed, it was clear to all in attendance that Manitoba Hydro's licence application was on shaky ground. The community had once again rejected outright the compensation proposals, and public opinion was stacked against the project. Sidney Green, who at the time was an opposition New Democratic Party Member of the Legislative Assembly, seemed almost prophetic in his pronouncement at the hearing: "I submit that the denial of justice to the peoples involved at South Indian Lake will result in an inevitable erosion of the rights of every citizen in Manitoba. . . . I also know that historically societies have lived to rue the day that they have acted in a roughshod manner, with respect to the rights of groups of people who apparently have had little way to protect themselves. *These things have a habit of coming back to haunt you*" [emphasis added].[55]

The hearings subsequently ended in controversy. Henteleff presented a motion for adjournment until all available information, including the "secret" reports, had been made available. The Chairman of the hearings, Tom Weber, refused the motion. Furthermore, Weber indicated that his only obligation as Chairman was to issue a report on the proceedings for the Minister. He was not prepared to make recommendations. The hearings collapsed in a spasm of disagreement.[56]

Very soon after the Winnipeg hearings, the South Indian Lake lawyers started proceedings in the Court of Queen's Bench to secure an injunction against the granting of the interim licence to Manitoba Hydro. Furthermore, they sought through this action to have the public hearings declared null and void, on the grounds that at no time was the Chairman of the hearings officially appointed, an oversight that was in contravention of the Water Power Act.[57] The Government of Manitoba's reaction was swift: it immediately introduced Bill 15 into the Legislature, which would have the effect of superseding any previous legislation or hearings, including the Water Power Act, and which would allow the government to issue the licence to Manitoba Hydro without hearings. The legal action by Buchwald and Henteleff was subsequently held in abeyance by the judge, pending approval of Bill 15, since its successful passage would terminate the community's injunction request.

An enormous debate concerning Bill 15 erupted both inside the Legislature and out. While Finance Minister Gurney Evans confidently informed the Legislature of the "compelling economic factors" in support of the diversion plans, including "improved employment opportunities, better educational opportunities, better communications and a general improvement in . . . standard of living" for the northern residents,[58] the people of South Indian Lake were not so convinced. In an open letter to Premier Walter Weir, they expressed their dismay at the proceedings:

May 12, 1969

Open Letter to Premier Weir:

Through our advisors we have followed carefully the debate in the house on Bill 15.

It is now obvious that the facts being revealed are not the same as the information given to us originally.

We were led to believe that there were no alternatives to flooding Southern Indian Lake and that if we did not agree to move, the rest of the Province would risk a shortage of power. We were led to believe that we would be standing in the way of progress.

Under these circumstances, we decided not to oppose progress and reluctantly agreed to move.

Now we discover that we were not told the truth.

First, there are alternatives to the diversion of the Churchill River, which do not involve the flooding of Southern Indian Lake and raising its level by 35 feet. We had been told there were no alternatives.

Second, the Minister of Finance has admitted in the House that there is no danger of "black-out," "brown-out," or even "dim-out" because power can be produced by other means.

Third, the government does not seem to have conducted the basic minimum studies on the likely losses and costs involved in flooding Southern Indian Lake.

Under these circumstances, we want to repeat that we are not going to move until the government proves conclusively and publicly that all aspects have been properly studied, all benefits and losses considered and that flooding Southern Indian Lake is in fact necessary and is the best plan for all of the people of Manitoba.

Until the government proves this, WE WILL NOT MOVE [emphasis original].[59]

Despite the tremendous opposition to the project, and the threat of injunction, Manitoba Hydro began to call for tenders for construction. Furthermore, Hydro Chairman Bill Fallis made it clear that, having already spent more than $4 million on design, Hydro was beyond the point of no return.[60] The Churchill River Diversion Project would not be stopped.

On 20 May 1969, a special sub-committee of the Legislature commenced their review of Bill 15. In the course of this review, several individuals were called for questionning. Among them was Harvey Pollock, who had only recently been working on behalf of the Chemawawin Indian Band at Easterville in their struggle against Manitoba Hydro and the Manitoba government. Pollock outlined in some detail the social and economic situation at Easterville, and discussed the Letter of Intent with members of the sub-committee. The lessons of Easterville were not entirely accepted by certain members of the sub-committee, some of whom were clearly antagonistic to Pollock.[61]

Buchwald and Henteleff also had the opportunity to once again place the community's perspective before the government. It seems that with every new submission the people were becoming increasingly desperate, and in this submission they issued the most dramatic words to date. "Throughout the agonizing route that has finally brought us to this hearing and this moment," they wrote, "the communities have been the victims of deceit, deception and manifold breaches of faith as their democratic and fundamental rights have been usurped or overridden in the anxiety to grant Hydro this license."[62] If there was as yet any doubt that these lawyers had come to identify with the communities and their plight, it was dispelled when Buchwald resignedly admitted to the committee, "It has not been easy for me to hold up to the cold light of day the atrocities against the democratic processes perpetrated on these two communities by a government of which I personally am a supporter and by a great public utility I used to respect."[63]

At the same time, as the opposition to Manitoba Hydro's unilateral actions grew stronger, the Churchill River Diversion Project began to dominate the business of the Legislature. The debate became so intense that, right in the middle of the questionning before the sub-committee of Hydro's Bill Fallis, the government dissolved the Legislature and called for a general election.[64] Seeking in part a mandate to renew the high-level diversion scheme, the Conservative government learned the hard way of the unpopular nature of their plans.

NEW GOVERNMENT – SAME OLD STORY

In the election of 25 June 1969, the Conservatives were defeated by the New Democratic Party (NDP) in a move which rang the death knell for the high-level diversion scheme. At his first press conference, the new Premier, Edward Schreyer, stated firmly: "Manitoba Hydro surely cannot proceed without reference at all to the human factors and if the human, the sociological, the natural resource conservation factors weigh more heavily in the minds of my cabinet colleagues than the mill rate Hydro will have to charge, well then we'll have to reverse the present course Hydro is embarked on."[65] The new NDP cabinet quickly formed a special committee to examine all aspects of the Southern Indian Lake question, and the new ministers began the task of learning the facts. During the campaign, the NDP had spoken against the high-level diversion, and now that they were in power changes were surely in order. The spirits of the people of South Indian Lake rose.

After reviewing the facts, the Schreyer government cancelled the high-level diversion project. In the Premier's own words, "Can we . . . face up to the prospect of disrupting two communities of 700 people, completely upsetting the lake on which they depend for their livelihood making it quite impossible for at least some of them to continue to live independently?"[66]

The official announcement was made by Schreyer in the Legislature on 15 September 1969. In his speech, he reiterated the new government's development philosophy: "To look simply at the engineering cost aspect of the matter, Mr. Speaker, may have been enough fifty years ago, but in our time it is not. . . . In Canada and North America in recent decades, resources have been spoiled, usually for selfish financial gain, often in the name of progress – wrongly understood, I might add. . . . We owe it to the generations who will follow us to use our best knowledge and experience in order to avoid the kind of mistakes which our less well-informed predecessors made in years long past."[67] An obviously elated Harold Buchwald proclaimed that "the government decision would prove to the people he represented democracy works in practice as well as in theory."[68] According to the *Winnipeg Free Press*, "Minutes after being told the news, the lawyer was on the phone to the residents of South Indian Lake, telling them their homes would be spared."[69]

The early optimism was soon shattered. The government announced that, rather than reject the whole concept of diverting the Churchill River, they would go ahead with a new "low-level diversion" of

Southern Indian Lake that would flood the lake only three to five metres instead of ten. About half the homes at South Indian Lake would still have to be moved, and while the ecological damage anticipated under the new scheme would be lessened, the exact nature and extent of the damage was still not understood.

In assessing the implications of this new program, Michael Shouldice has written: "The provincial government treated the South Indian Lake issue as 'to move or not to move' the residents. The main point which they were overlooking was that the flooding would disrupt the environment and economy. It wasn't the amount of water at your doorstep which counted. Critics warned that even at the 850-foot level [i.e., an increase of three metres] soil erosion would occur on the shoreline and eventually mean the building of a new townsite."[70]

The people of South Indian Lake remained concerned about the government's plans, even though an official decision to proceed with the diversion component had yet to be made. It was not until May 1972 that such a decision was reached. In the interim, there had been little for the community and their lawyers to do, since in the absence of the official decision and public hearings or similar forums, their input was not accommodated.

Early in May 1972, the diversion issue once again began to heat up. Anticipating the announcement of a favourable official decision, the Premier informed South Indian Lake's lawyers, "The decision concerning the diversion is not subject to prior approval by any private interest group no more in this case than in the case of the many water control works carried out in the decade of the 1960's" [sic].[71] On 17 May, Manitoba Hydro's board came to its final conclusion that the Churchill River Diversion was the most feasible of various alternatives, and this was communicated to the Legislature on 25 May.[72] A few days later the Premier announced in the Legislature that South Indian Lake would not be provided with funds to contest the decision on the diversion. Funds would be available, however, for legal activity related to compensation matters.[73] The previous Conservative government had been content to allow the lawyers to use government money in the injunction action of 1969, an action which no doubt contributed to their downfall. The NDP did not wish to be so damaged.

The community was outraged by Schreyer's comments. Through their lawyers they prepared a position paper on the diversion project, in which they rejected the whole idea on the grounds that much information was still lacking, that impact studies were required, and that they would not be funded to challenge the project on these grounds.

The community dug in its heels. Buchwald informed the Premier that he had been instructed by the community "to resist to the fullest extent possible" the hydro proposal. Further, the lawyer wrote: "The people of the South Indian Lake community wish to remain together as a community. They do not want their community to be broken up as a consequence of the demolition of their economic base. Relocation of some to elsewhere is both divisive and potentially destructive. They have neither the financial nor the social mobility to survive. Money compensation means little without the ability to translate it into sustaining one's self with dignity and self-respect." With respect to the funding of the community's lawyers, Buchwald said that "underprivileged groups must have such assistance. Without it, they are not able to participate meaningfully in the decision-making process of our democratic system."[74]

In transmitting this position to Schreyer, the community had clearly lost faith in the ability of the provincial government to guarantee their rights. New avenues were needed, and to this end the Premier was informed that the position paper would be released to the media, and that a formal request for intervention would be sent to the federal Department of the Environment.[75] Until such time as the funding arrangements could be worked out, the lawyers offered to donate their time.

On 14 June 1972, Premier Schreyer responded by letter to the community's lawyers. He stated that his government had acted responsibly by rejecting the high-level diversion in favour of the low-level diversion and a new plan for the regulation of Lake Winnipeg. Further, he warned the lawyers that they should not expect any assistance from the federal Minister of the Environment, Jack Davis:

In that connection, I note that there is a hydro-electric project that has been approved by the government of Quebec relative to James Bay which involves the flooding of a territory many times larger in area and involving the dislocation of community and of hunting, trapping and fishing for several thousand people indigenous to the area, a problem which in terms of scope and number is dramatically much greater than what is involved here. Inasmuch as Mr. Davis has not seen fit to intervene in that project, it is difficult to understand how he would regard it as possible or fair to do so in the case of the Nelson River – a project which, when entered upon, was carried forward under the aegis of a Canada-Manitoba agreement which postulated, among other things, regulation of Lake Winnipeg and the diversion of waters of the Churchill River.[76]

On 15 June 1972, Schreyer visited South Indian Lake, and told the community that personally he wished the whole project could be disbanded, but that too much money had been spent to stop it now. And, he emphasized repeatedly, funding would not be made available for the community to fight the project. There was no way that the community's lawyers could stop it. Only $2,000 would be made available "to hire a lawyer or anything else" the community desired in their pursuit of compensation, but they were warned by Schreyer "that lawyers can expect large fees."[77]

In the meantime, in an effort to stem the tide of criticism against the project, the Manitoba government announced the signing of an agreement with the federal government to establish a study board to examine the likely effect of the diversion of the Churchill River and the regulation of Lake Winnipeg. The Lake Winnipeg, Churchill and Nelson Rivers Study Board was to complete their task within two years and submit their report. Critics, including the people of South Indian Lake, pointed out that by this time much of the project would already have been completed. If this was an attempt to appease the opposition, it was unsuccessful.

By the fall of 1972, the community was once again considering legal action to stop the project. This new threat forced the Manitoba government to move quickly. In November 1972, by order-in-council, the government eliminated the need to advertise the application for a licence to commence construction on the project. Subsequently, the government changed the Water Power Act so that the Minister of Mines, Resources and Environmental Management could issue the licence to Manitoba Hydro without hearings or passage by the Legislature. The government argued that the changes to the Water Power Act merely brought that legislation into line with the realities of Manitoba Hydro as a Crown corporation. Furthermore, in allowing the project to go ahead without advertising the licence application, the government was avoiding the public confusion which they believed would accompany the announcement of a project which had already been announced in 1970. The government vowed not to become involved in "window-dressing hearings concerning a program which has already been decided upon and whose implementation is in progress. . . . Such conduct on the part of the previous administration," they reminded, "was rightfully severely criticized. We do not intend to repeat such a process."[78]

In the eyes of Buchwald and Henteleff, the NDP government had adopted political tactics similar to, and in some ways even more drastic than, those of the previous Conservative government in order to force the issue, tactics which the NDP had actively criticized while in opposition. In a submission to the South Indian Lake town council, Buchwald and Henteleff stated:

> In this regard, the action which the government appears to be taking is far different than what the Conservatives attempted to do. You will no doubt remember that when we took them to Court last time, because they were afraid that we might succeed in Court they then were going to pass a Bill in the Legislature so that it wasn't necessary for them to have any further public hearings and they could grant the licence to Hydro without such public hearings. This time the NDP government intends to pass a regulation which would make it unnecessary for them to even have to go to the Legislature before giving the licence to Hydro to proceed. By doing it this way there will not even be the opportunity or the right to have the matter discussed in the Legislature.[79]

Later that December, the lawyers on behalf of the community filed a Statement of Claim in the Court of Queen's Bench.

LEGAL ACTION

In applying for an injunction to halt construction on the diversion under the interim licence, the people of South Indian Lake were attempting something that Native groups have rarely achieved. Despite the fact that their chances were slim, and that success would probably be unprecedented, the feeling nevertheless was that success was within their grasp. According to Henteleff, "They began to believe that their case was so just, that the truth was so clear, that how could they be denied. . . . In other words, they started from a position where there was no way they could win to a position where they felt there was no way they could lose."[80] The Statement of Claim outlined in detail the legal argument to be presented. It explained that the implementation of the diversion would cause a "private nuisance" in that, among other things, it would interfere with "the use and enjoyment of land."[81] Furthermore, the diversion would cause a public nuisance in that it would interfere with navigation and recreational and economic use of the lake and its resources. The diversion, it was argued, would "cause a trespass to the lands occupied" by the people and would breach a variety of statutes, particularly sections of the Fisheries Act, the Navigable Waters Protection Act, and the Water Power Act. Hence, they declared, the Manitoba government and Hydro were proceeding illegally with the project

The Statement of Claim also made reference to the Study Board Agreement, and argued that under the agreement a decision on the project could not be made until the impact studies had been completed. Finally, the lawyers pointed out that the government had refused to provide funding for legal action, even though some $100,000 for such representation had been set aside by the previous Conservative administration, and much of this had yet to be spent.

The question of treaty rights held by the majority of the South Indian Lake residents was not raised in the Statement of Claim, and was not considered by Buchwald and Henteleff.[82] They, along with many others in the province, accurately saw South Indian Lake as a non-reserve community, but probably inaccurately assumed that treaty rights were only reserve-based. While at this time the whole concept of treaty rights was relatively ill-defined, the people themselves readily invoked them in their own explanation of the reason for the legal action. In a letter to Henteleff, resident Charlie Dysart said: "The Hydro flooding Indian reserves, homes and lands is breaking a promise made by Queen Victoyer [sic], and the British Government to the treaty Indians, and if this matter were given publicity, and a strong protest made by the Queen and the present Government, I think the Hydro would reconsider doing so."[83]

The Manitoba government was not too concerned, at least at this point, about the injunction application. Hydro lawyer Steward Martin outlined his opinion in a communication to Premier Schreyer: "The other side to be considered is simply the longer this project proceeds and becomes patently irreversible, the more hesitant the Court would be to grant an injunction. Even at this point in time, with substantial contracts having been let, reversal would be at a horrendous cost."[84] Stalling seemed to be all that would be required.

APPEAL TO THE FEDERAL GOVERNMENT

Given the fact that many of the residents of South Indian Lake were treaty Indians with status under the Indian Act, and therefore the responsibility of the federal government, it was inevitable that the Department of Indian Affairs and other federal departments would become involved in the controversy in some manner. The federal government was simultaneously involved in the hydro development of James Bay, and were becoming sensitized (albeit slowly) to the issue of aboriginal rights. While the federal Minister of the Environment had been contacted regarding the environmental implications of the Churchill River Diversion Project, the Department of Indian Affairs would be brought into the dispute through the requests of the people of South Indian Lake for funding to continue their legal battle.

The Minister of Indian Affairs, Jean Chrétien, was first contacted by the South Indian Lake legal team in late February 1973. After briefly explaining the diversion project, the lawyers argued that Manitoba was violating the 1971 study agreement by proceeding with the project before the impact studies had been completed. They argued that "the federal officer most directly responsible for the well-being of Canada's Indian people should forthwith intervene on their behalf to protect their interests."[85] The Minister was asked to take legal steps, if necessary, to stop the construction. A similar letter was simultaneously sent to Jean Marchand, Minister of Transport and the individual ultimately responsible for certain legislation relevant to the legal case, particularly the Navigable Waters Protection Act. Later in March, the issue was brought to the attention of Winnipeg Member of Parliament James Richardson, who was asked to pursue it with Chrétien and Marchand.[86] The federal government was now fully informed, if not yet involved.

To Buchwald and Henteleff, the federal government was unduly slow to respond to the appeals of the South Indian Lake people. Henteleff subsequently lectured Chrétien on the lessons to be learned from the shootout at Wounded Knee, South Dakota, and asked, "What does it take, Mr. Minister, to have you intercede?"[87] Somewhat exasperated by the federal non-response, Henteleff in turn wrote to Keith Taylor, Member of Parliament for the Churchill constituency, one which included most of the project impact area:

It is absolutely beyond my comprehension as to why the people in Ottawa are taking such a namby-pamby attitude towards this matter. There is no doubt in my mind whatsoever that the issuance of the Licence by the Province of Manitoba to Hydro was in absolute contravention of the letter and spirit of the Canada-Manitoba Study Agreement entered into on the 24th of August, 1971.... Not only is there an unwarranted, unbelievable rape of our resources, but a horrible rape of the principles of democracy. I hope that you will do everything you possibly can to have the federal government immediately exercise its responsibilities on this matter.[88]

In his response to Henteleff, Taylor pointed to the apparently analogous situation in James Bay, Quebec, adding, "The situation there is even more confusing to all concerned."[89] Was the federal government only stalling for time while the hydro development problems in Manitoba and Quebec could be sorted out? This appeared to be the case.

It was in early April 1973 that the first evidence of intervention by the federal government emerged. Federal Minister of the Environment Jack Davis reminded Manitoba's Minister of Mines, Resources and Environmental Management Sidney Green that the Environment Department had completed a brief overview of the project and the controversy, and had concluded, "The Indians of South Indian Lake will likely suffer the greatest effect." However, Davis was not prepared to scold the Manitoba government about the issue, and his comments were deliberately designed to avoid confrontation. "Perhaps in view of these effects, consideration should be given to altering the construction time-table to enable our important joint studies under the Manitoba-Canada Agreement to be completed before the diversion of the Churchill River is made. . . . It seems to me that neither you nor I can, or should, hide the rather significant environmental effects that are likey to occur."[90]

About this time, Jean Chrétien also stepped cautiously into the fray. Initiating discussion with Premier Schreyer, Chrétien expressed an interest in learning "the steps the Province is taking to protect the interests of the Indian people."[91] However, it became clear that, for Indian Affairs, intervention on behalf of any northern Manitoba Indians was contingent upon the project threatening reserves; Indian "rights," it seemed, were only in effect on reserves. And, of course, South Indian Lake was not a reserve.

This fact became painfully obvious as further requests for intervention by the federal government went unheeded. The community was now desperate for financial aid to support their legal case, and since Schreyer closed the provincial avenue to them, they had no choice but to canvas Indian Affairs. But Indian Affairs was still wavering and they turned down the community's request for funding. An internal Indian Affairs document explained the reasoning:

The [legal] action appears to be predicated upon a concept of loss of livelihood for an entire community. The fact that the majority of the members of that community are of Indian status is not mentioned in the claim; nor is there any reference to loss of or impairment of any special Indian rights or of damage, by flooding or otherwise, to Indian lands. Indian people suffer more from the sort of disruption caused by a drastic change in the resource base upon which the community depends. It is recognized that such a drastic change as that feared with respect to the South Indian Lake fishery could lead to the almost total disintegration of community, family and personal relationships and life. Nonetheless the situation in Manitoba is substantially different from that which pertains in the James Bay area. In Manitoba, by reason of treaty agreements, the special rights of Indians within the area are defined. No known impairment of these rights has occurred as a result of the Churchill River Diversion nor can any future impairment be clearly identified.[92]

In a curious, even ironic way, the Indian people were not being provided financial support because their rights as Indians, as outlined in Treaty Five, were not, in the federal government's opinion, being violated. Yet, even a cursory reading of that treaty would have demonstrated that there was a threat to a number of important provisions. At the very least, a thorough investigation was warranted. In effect, the Indian people of South Indian Lake, and indeed across northern Manitoba, were being denied their rights because they had entered into formal agreements, the treaties, precisely to define those rights. And despite a federal government prediction that the "total disintegration" of the community was possible, the government refused to come to grips with the anomalous legal position of the community.

The community's lawyers continued to press for an injunction to halt the project, and also continued their canvassing of the federal government for support. They were not hopeful that funding would be made available for, as Henteleff wrote, "they say that since South Indian Lake is off reserve, even if the majority of the population is made up by Treaty Indians, they don't think Legal Aid Northern Affairs is obliged to give any assistance." The irony of the situation was not lost on Henteleff, who "pointed out that the community had been treated by Northern Affairs as a community of Treaty Indians for many years and it would be an absolute shame if they adopted a narrow view of the situation at this point in time."[93] The people were directed to the province for funding assistance, even though the Manitoba government had already refused.

South Indian Lake's application for an interim injunction against the diversion project was rejected in early July 1973, and a trial date was set for September. In rendering the decision, the judge declared, in Henteleff's words, "that whatever damages we were able to prove (which consisted of damage to traplines and a number of cabins by virtue of the construction already commenced) were damages which were compensable by [monetary] damages." According to Henteleff, "He [the judge] paid no attention whatsoever to the undisputed evidence presented by way of affadavit as to the irreversibility of the damage which might occur and the fact that by the time the matter proceeded to trial, contracts in such amounts and work to such a degree would have been entered into and proceeded with so that any subsequent order of the Court would be a farce." Furthermore, Manitoba Hydro, in their Statement of Defence, essentially argued that, again in Henteleff's words, "you [the people of South Indian Lake] have no legal rights whatsoever to the lands and therefore you have no right to object."[94] The federal government seemed to concur with this position. According to Chrétien:

It is difficult at this time for me to identify any precise grounds upon which I, as Minister of Indian Affairs, can urge intervention in the legal action by reason of the Federal Government's responsibilities to the Indian people. The community of South Indian Lake is not an Indian reserve; it is situated on Provincial Crown Land. The fact that the majority of the members of the community are of Indian status is not mentioned in any of the pleadings which have been made available to me. It seems to me that the action is based on a concept of loss of livelihood for the entire community, not just for the Indian segment of it. . . . I think that my intervention in the present court action would be premature, since there is, as yet, no evidence of any impairment of those rights.[95]

So, even while acknowledging that the majority of the residents were status Indians, Chrétien refused to become involved. The people were being penalized for their collective actions as a community in general, as opposed to an expressly status- or treaty-Indian community. Henteleff's response was well worn by now. He pointed out that the majority of the residents were treaty Indians, the federal government had always dealt with the community as if the residents were treaty Indians, and therefore they were entitled to Indian Affairs "assistance, guidance and support" as treaty Indians. Yet Chrétien continued to stress what by now must have seemed like a serious omission to the lawyers: federal assistance could only be provided "to Indian people on the basis that they are affected *as Indians*" [emphasis added]. Even the pleadings of the Mayor of South Indian Lake seemed not to move the Minister. As Tommy Thomas wrote, "We do not understand the legal technicalities of the case, we only know our livelihood is in severe danger and a beautiful pure lake is scheduled to be irreparably damaged."[96]

In a subsequent letter to Chrétien, Henteleff once again pointed out that, compatible with Indian Affairs policy, South Indian Lake was in fact a community of treaty Indians under federal jurisdiction, and therefore should qualify for financial assistance. No doubt exasperated, the lawyer let his true feelings be known to the Minister: "What really sets one back on one's heels is the enormous farce that is being played out here. It is time it was stopped and it is the view of the Indian community, Mr. Minister, that this can only be done, and it must be done, with your help."[97]

The loss of the injunction was a great blow for the people of South Indian Lake, an event which marks the beginning of the end of the relationship among Buchwald, Henteleff and the community. The people had become convinced, unjustifiably, that the lawyers would be able to stop the project. Reflecting back on an event that occurred over ten years before, Henteleff observed, "I guess we became just another part of White society that made the promise that's never been fulfilled."[98]

If there were any doubts that Premier Schreyer's attitude toward the project, and development in general, were markedly different from what he initially communicated during the provincial election campaign, those doubts were now dispelled. Seemingly abandoning his "humanity first" slogan of the 1969 election campaign, his new perspective reflected a more formalist economic view than before: "You have to weigh off the relative merits of hydro development versus ecology. Suppose, for example, a hydro project will cause $200,000 worth of ecological damage a year, while simultaneously creating a resource value of $80 million. In this case, I think the benefits of development far outweigh the drawbacks."[99] But without the completed Study Board impact assessments, there was absolutely no basis for Schreyer's loss estimate.

"JUST PEOPLE OF MANITOBA"

Opposition to the project continued to grow. In 1972, an organization known as The Friends of Churchill had been formed. And, in 1973, a group of clergymen representing the United, Anglican and Roman Catholic Churches began to mobilize behind the South Indian Lake issue. The United Church Minister resident in South Indian Lake spearheaded this new movement, and introduced a spiritual element into the controversy, as demonstrated in his letter to a fellow clergyman: "The people of Manitoba and especially the people of the Church must be made aware of the sin they are committing in destroying creation and people's lives. How many lives is the Nelson River Hydro scheme worth? . . . Once the water is allowed to rise, no power on earth can restore what God has given to the people of South Indian Lake and the people of Manitoba."[100] However, despite the increasingly vocal opposition to the project, and despite some flagrant violations by the government of democratic principles, the New Democratic Party was re-elected in 1973. With a new mandate, the government plunged ahead with the construction of the diversion scheme.

The furious exchange of letters and the pleadings for financial assistance continued throughout the fall of 1973 and on into 1974. Pleadings to Jean Marchand, Minister of Transport, to intercede even as the Churchill River was being dammed off at Missi Falls, met with the same fate as did the pleadings to Chrétien. Even though over $500,000 had been made available by Chrétien to the Cree and Inuit of James Bay in their legal action, the people of South Indian Lake remained totally without funding.[101] Chrétien continued to fall back on the position that Indian rights would not be abrogated, and that to provide financial assistance to South Indian Lake would be in violation of the spirit of the Canada-Manitoba study agreement of 1971.[102] This latter point may have been more significant than people realized at the time. When the Member of Parliament for the Churchill constituency, Keith Taylor, wrote to Chrétien stating, "I can only assume that it is the urgings of the Provincial government which have resulted in you failing to grant support to the Indians of South Indian Lake,"[103] he may have been very close to the truth.

Chrétien, apparently, was prepared to leave the fate of the Native residents of South Indian Lake in the hands of the provincial government, despite all indications that the latter was concerned with the community only insofar as they were potentially capable of blocking the project. His position remained unequivocal:

What is in question is the way in which the Province of Manitoba is prepared to deal with some people who live in a community situated on Crown Provincial land, and who in all respects come under Provincial jurisdiction; some of them happen also to be Indians who are members of a band of Indians who have Treaty rights, but these rights are not involved in this situation. . . . I can act only within my legal responsibilities. I cannot intervene between the Province and its residents in a matter which is solely within Provincial jurisdiction. As I have explained, there is no question here of Indian rights or Indian land or anything to do with people being *Indian*. It is just people of Manitoba [emphasis original].[104]

For its part, the Manitoba government continued to refuse to fund any legal action on the part of the community, indicating their willingness to provide only for the costs of determining proper compensation.[105] Further, and no doubt unhappy with the manner in which Buchwald and Henteleff had become personally involved in the case and continued to prosecute despite the lack of financial assistance, the province decided to withhold funds for independent compensation

advice and have the people work with Hydro-appointed lawyers to settle their claims.[106] These actions prompted Henteleff to write: "As
much as the Indian people of South Indian Lake are persona non grata
with Chrétien, Harold [Buchwald] and I are similarly persona non
grata with the Government."[107]

DIVIDE AND CONQUER: THE AGE-OLD STRATEGY

As everything seemed to be going the Manitoba government's way,
it began to operate at the community level with confidence. The Minister of Indian Affairs had clearly agreed that Manitoba had the right,
and indeed the obligation, to work out a compensation deal with the
people of South Indian Lake. However, rather than assuming that the
people had a collective right to compensation, the provincial government was of the view that each individual should be dealt with as a
separate entity. The residents did not agree.

Schreyer was alerted to this fact in January 1974. In a letter to the
Premier, South Indian Lake Mayor Basil Colomb noted, "Manitoba
Hydro is coming into our community and making settlements for property." It was emphasized that all matters of compensation were to be
handled by Buchwald and Henteleff. This feeling was reiterated at a
community meeting at which Henteleff implored the people: "We have
to fight together or we will lose. Hydro would like some people to give
up, as they hope the rest of the people may give up." Yet, some people
were already giving up. The battle had been raging for five years, with
no end in sight. The project was well under construction, and the hope
that it could be stopped had dissipated. As former South Indian Lake
Mayor Noah Soulier recalled: "Hydro came in once to talk to the trappers, but no agreement was made. They came in a second time with
cheques and started to pay off the individual trappers. A lot of men were
against it, but too many others took the money, and then the rest were
left to do so." Isabel Moose, one of the members of the local flood committee, described the scene this way: "The people were against Hydro
when the dam was planned, but Hydro got each separate family to
agree by offering them money. A thousand dollars was a lot of money
back then. They were going to build it anyway." In re-assessing the
situation, one of the elders of the community lamented, "We would
have been better off if we'd stuck together."[108]

The process of capitulation began in a small way, with one trapper
accepting a cheque for damage done to his boat by a Hydro tractor, but
began to snowball as Hydro's "easy money" began purchasing cabins

and other equipment. In a letter from the Mayor and council to Premier Schreyer, the anger of the community's representatives was apparent:

We are writing to inform you of a man who has been sent in here by Manitoba Hydro. . . . He says he has the right to pay compensation to individual citizens. We feel that this is [sic] unfair tactics on the part of Hydro, an attempt to break-up the unity of the community. We would urge you as the chief executive of our province to see that this man is told to stay away from our people and all other such people. We have a law firm who has our confidence and all matters of compensation should be carried out through them. Please use your influence to see that Hydro sticks to their own business, which is not the internal affairs of our community.[109]

Somewhat exasperated, and feeling that the community's resolve was slipping away, the community council passed a resolution, which they forwarded to Schreyer, and in which they emphasized that Buchwald and Henteleff were to represent them in compensation matters. They wrote, "Every free person has the right to choose his own lawyer." They also adopted a tougher stand with the provincial government, noting "that if Mr. Schreyer won't meet with us and if he won't give us this help so we can help ourselves then we will not have further meetings with anyone from government and Hydro and will go and tell all the people of Manitoba how we feel." In closing, they once again emphasized that "the people of South Indian Lake speak together with one voice."[110]

This show of bravado appeared to have some effect. Schreyer agreed to allow Buchwald and Henteleff to represent residents in compensation claims, and also agreed to meet with the community's representatives. However, the government remained unwilling to fund collective compensation negotiations or litigation.[111] And, not surprisingly, the government failed to invite Buchwald and Henteleff to the meeting upon which the people of South Indian Lake had insisted.[112]

The meeting with the Premier occurred on 2 March 1974, at which time a list of concerns and requests was presented by the community. South Indian Lake's United Church Minister, John McFarlane, wrote of this meeting, "Everything has been referred, turned down, or denied."[113] Among the requests was the provision of free electric service to the community. Schreyer responded to this request by stating that providing free electricity was not a policy of the government, and that "there are many communities that could make the same argument."[114] But McFarlane noted: "With regards to free electric service, we aren't asking to be treated like anywhere else where water has been raised in the province, and certainly don't intend to be treated like Easterville, although . . . this government is heading down the same path . . . disregard for the people's wishes and plans, and rigid adherence to Government ideas.[115]

The South Indian Lake situation deteriorated rapidly in the spring of 1974. The spirit of the people had been broken, and many were settling with Hydro on an individual basis. Attempts to include Buchwald and Henteleff in negotiating these settlements were being thwarted by threats that Hydro would be forced by such action to bring in its own lawyers, slowing down the process and likely leading to lower payments.[116] A pre-trial examination of Hydro Chairman Leonard Bateman had been thwarted by Bateman's refusal to answer in anything but general terms the questions put to him. The lawyers now had to decide whether or not to continue the legal action, designed primarily to force the Manitoba government to negotiate seriously with the community, and they were unsure that the community still supported their efforts. Henteleff articulated these views in a letter to Mayor Basil Colomb:

Harold and I are beginning to be of the view that the desire to continue with the court action represents only the feelings of a few people and no longer represents the views of the community as a whole. It may very well be that there are many members in the community that feel that they no longer feel it is important to have a decision by court as to whether the Indian people were right in continuing to oppose the project. It also may very well be that there are those who consider that it is to their personal disadvantage to continue to fight the government. There are also those no doubt who felt that the court action should be maintained only for so long as it was important to obtain from the government and from Hydro what is best for themselves and not necessarily for the benefit of the community as a whole.[117]

Without Jean Chrétien's help, the legal case seemed to be spinning its wheels. The lawyers needed some direction from the community, but the community was unable to provide it.

The stress on the Mayor, councillors and members of the local flood committee had been burdensome for some time. The decisions they were being asked to make were new to them, and they obviously were unable to grasp most aspects of the legal argument being presented by their lawyers. There was also a sense of betrayal, directed not only at their own provincial government but also toward Jean Chrétien and Indian Affairs. There was enormous public support for their cause, but rather than providing inspiration it is likely that the people felt overwhelmed. Visitors, on behalf of themselves or other southern *ad hoc* support groups, arrived daily to conduct their own investigations. Mayor Basil Colomb, the person who spearheaded the opposition at the community level, took to the bush, spending long periods in relative isolation at his trapline. In Colomb's absence, the other councillors, relatively unfamiliar with the exigencies of the political decision-making process, failed to hold the cause together. It seemed just a matter of time before all opposition would cease.

As a fall trial date approached, Buchwald and Henteleff had yet to receive any word from the community. Successive letters to Basil Colomb went unanswered, leaving the lawyers to assume that the community no longer desired their services.[118] Late in August, the lawyers officially requested that the community appoint other lawyers, and submitted a bill for $36,000 to cover their fees and expenses from 1972 to 1974.[119] But the community did not obtain new lawyers, and in October 1974, in the absence of legal representation, the legal action was dismissed by the court.

THE NORTHERN FLOOD COMMITTEE

By 1973, it was apparent that the focus of the South Indian Lake issue had actually shifted away from the community level and into the political arena on a provincial and national level. In some ways, the principle involved came to shroud the potential destruction of the way of life of the small community on the shores of Southern Indian Lake. Furthermore, other Native communities in the North had come to realize that they, too, were likely to be affected by the diversion project. The communities at Nelson House, Norway House, Cross Lake, Split Lake and York Factory, all of which were combined reserve and non-reserve Native communities, were particularly alarmed. Problems similar to those at South Indian Lake were developing in these communities as well, as Hydro attempted to make individual settlements and avoid community or legal representatives. Meetings were convened by the representatives of these communities to discuss mutual concerns and the possibilities of united action. The result of these meetings was the formation of the Northern Flood Committee (NFC) by the affected communities in April 1974.

The experiences of other Native communities confronted by hydro development were foremost in the minds of the founders of the NFC. In early 1973, they had drafted a resolution to commence organizing opposition in which they made reference to the Grand Rapids Dam and the "sad and negative results" its construction had had for the people of Easterville.[120] Representatives were invited from South Indian Lake to help organize the opposition, and the lessons from that experience were communicated by Yude Henteleff as they were unfolding.[121] It is ironic that, as early as 1969, South Indian Lake delegates had attempted to consolidate action of the northern bands to oppose the project, but had met with great reluctance. The other communities, it seems, were dissuaded by the Manitoba government from participating, with veiled threats that any provincial aid likely to be offered would be terminated if such action took place.[122] It is also likely that, with no previous experience at collective action, at this early stage the bands were unable to overcome the obstacles of poor communication and political antagonism. Certainly the South Indian Lake situation would have been greatly enhanced had the NFC been formed in 1969. By 1973, it was almost too late for South Indian Lake, and as the NFC did finally emerge, the South Indian Lake role remained peripheral.

The need for collective organization to deal with Hydro's compensation programs was discussed at the outset when the NFC was formed. Henry Spence, Chief of the Nelson House Indian Band and Chairman of the local *ad hoc* flood committee, told the community representatives, "Since it will affect all of us whether we're Indian, Métis, or white, it's a good idea to work together; . . . I hope we hear your ideas on this before we start to be divided on this important issue."[123]

The need for collective action became more focused in April 1974 at a meeting between the representatives of these northern communities and various Hydro and Manitoba government officials. Hostility quickly erupted over the issue of providing accurate information on Hydro's plans to the communities, prompting one delegate from Cross Lake to label the meeting "a ridiculous exercise." According to him, "If they were so concerned with the people of these communities getting affected by the flooding and the so-called democracy, then they would give these members of the communities a means to get their own experts and gather information on their own."[124] As South Indian Lake delegate John McFarlane described, "It was generally agreed that the present situation was comparable to the signing of the treaties some 100 years ago."[125]

Soon after, there emerged from Thompson a statement issued by the newly formed NFC:

Our major aim . . . is to fight for justice in the areas of Treaty land and Treaty rights and to fight for northerners in areas which do not fall into this category but who will face disruptive and negative effects due to the Project. Our aim is to try and keep these people united in their stand against Government and Hydro encroachments because it is only through strong, uncompromising unity that gains can be made by us. We believe that our people in the North have a very real right to participate in decision-making that affects them. The purpose of the Flood Committee is to inform these people in the North as to what is happening so that they can be better prepared to take part in some of the decision-making.[126]

The necessary information for such decision making was not forthcoming from either the government or Manitoba Hydro, however, and a strategy of confrontation was developed. At the meeting of the NFC on 23 April 1974, a decision was reached not to have any further dealings with Hydro, especially on the topic of compensation, until Hydro disclosed all information pertaining to the project and until the NFC could digest this material and decide on a course of action. Subsequently, when Hydro applied to the Nelson House Indian Band for permission to enter the reserve for purposes of exploration and surveying, the band council passed a resolution barring all Hydro employees from reserve land.[127] It was widely believed that many of the reports of the Study Board had been completed, but were being withheld by the government.[128] The government rejected this notion, and responded to the Nelson House resolution by failing to appear at a planned meeting with the northern communities concerning the hydro project.

Somewhat surprisingly, the federal government, and in particular the Department of Indian Affairs, moved quickly to support the fledgling NFC. Some resentment must have been felt by the South Indian Lake representatives when $65,000 was quickly made available to the NFC, along with the promise of technical expertise where possible.[129] Perhaps even more surprising was the intervention of Jean Chrétien. Hard-pressed to offer even moral support to the people of South Indian Lake for fear of alienating the Manitoba government, Chrétien adopted a pro-Indian stance with respect to the NFC. Quite likely, the Supreme Court of Canada decision in the Calder case in 1973, concerning the Nishga land claim in British Columbia, had a strong influence on the Minister. Although losing the appeal in a split decision, the Nishga's claim to aboriginal land title was not refuted. This led to a fundamental change in the attitude of the federal government regarding aboriginal issues and federal responsibility. The NFC was to benefit to some extent from this change.[130]

Writing to Premier Schreyer, Chrétien expressed both surprise and concern about the apparent lack of information being provided to the northern communities. According to Chrétien, "It is obvious that whatever steps have been taken by either the Province or Manitoba Hydro to keep the communities aware of the proposals has not been effective. . . . I am concerned, too, that perhaps Manitoba Hydro has not yet been able to identify the full impact of their project on Indian reserves. . . ." Then, in an obvious reference to the legal powers of the Minister, Chrétien emphasized "that there will be no commitment of lands on the Nelson House Reserve or any other reserve, without the agreement of the Band concerned."[131] Indian Affairs even went so far as to appoint a flood information coordinator to act as a resource person for the NFC. The battle lines were clearly drawn.

It is curious to note the extent to which Chrétien was willing to support the NFC. It is true that the organization represented a number of Indian bands from *bona fide* reserves, but it is also the case that non-status Indians and Métis, primarily from communities adjacent to the reserves, were also members. Indeed, the NFC emphasized to its membership that all people were to be represented; its appeals to the federal government, which stressed the likely flooding of Indian reserve lands, were aimed solely at obtaining funding.[132] To its credit, the NFC was successful. But one is hard-pressed to distinguish the NFC case from that of South Indian Lake. Furthermore, during its formative stages, South Indian Lake representatives were delegated to the NFC. While it is true that many South Indian Lake residents were members of the Nelson House Band, many others were not, and neither were some of the community's NFC delegates.

Manitoba, for its part, was largely unsympathetic to Chrétien's concerns or those of the NFC. While Schreyer felt comfortable describing to Chrétien the steps that his government had taken to insure accurate dissemination of information regarding the project,[133] the Study Board's impact reports remained confidential.[134]

The NFC communities, and particularly the treaty Indian residents, were acutely aware that they retained rights under treaty that were threatened by the project. As a possible legal strategy began to emerge, the question of treaty rights became more important. Aware that portions of the Nelson House reserve were likely to be flooded, Hydro's northern field representative was asked "what right you have, and on who's [sic] authority you have based your decision to flood Indian lands." Indeed, the NFC solicited financial and moral support from all the bands in Manitoba on the grounds that, should Manitoba succeed in violating Indian treaty rights, "it will pave the way for them to take away or damage Reserve lands or to take away our hunting rights in any part of the province or country." An important legal battle was brewing, and Winnipeg lawyer Charles Huband was retained to act on behalf of the NFC. As NFC Chairman Henry Spence noted in a letter to committee members, "I am not a bit scared to go against Manitoba Hydro or the Manitoba Government. . . . So far I have in no way backed down from our position and I don't intend to and I'm prepared to fight this issue all the way with your support."[135] At a meeting of the NFC in early July, the decision was made to seek a declaratory judgement that Manitoba did not have the legal right to flood Indian reserve lands, a judgement which would force the government to negotiate with the NFC and perhaps even stop the project.

THE NORTHERN FLOOD COMMITTEE'S LEGAL ACTION

To the members of the NFC, the significance of what they were attempting to do was not lost. Leonard Courchene, an assistant to Henry Spence, wrote to Huband: "The outcome of the case will affect all treaty Indians, our lands and treaty rights, all across this country."[136] The case was to be different from that launched by South Indian Lake, since Indian reserve land was clearly involved. And the NFC representatives were enthusiastic about their chances. They had acquired a good understanding of the South Indian Lake and James Bay situations. In some respects, the legal action would in fact be another "kick at the can" for South Indian Lake, since the community was still a part of the NFC, even if in name only.

The groundwork for the relationship between Huband and the Manitoba government was established very quickly. Huband informed Schreyer that, in light of the injunction application, Manitoba Hydro should desist from further construction activity. Should the corporation not heed this advice, in the event of a successful court case Hydro would be retroactively held liable for all "nuisance" caused by their actions. Schreyer was also informed that, by request of the NFC communities, all communications regarding the project, compensation etcetera were to be directed to him (with the exception of South Indian Lake, where Buchwald and Henteleff were still active). Individuals, and separate communities, were not to be approached.[137] Manitoba's response was to threaten to bring the federal government into the action as a co-defendant.[138]

Matters began to heat up by the early summer of 1974. The NFC continued to insist that any flooding of Indian lands was a violation of Treaty Five, while the Manitoba government continued to fall back on the Federal-Provincial Agreement of 1966 which, they believed, gave them that right. The NFC also continued to demand the disclosure of all information concerning the project. They clearly recognized the reason for the government's delay in releasing the study board reports: "What Hydro is doing is playing this game where they want the people to talk in terms of compensation before the people themselves know what the damages will be."[139] Earlier, on 19 June 1974, Premier Schreyer had indicated that these reports would soon be made available. The NFC was finding it difficult to build a legal case without these studies, and the time was too short for them to conduct research on their own (the proposed operational date of the diversion project was only a year away). Yet, when the reports finally were issued, they were only of marginal utility. Ken Young, now also working for the NFC, stated at the time: "Our engineer consultants were unable to complete an affidavit based on the reports. There seems to be important data missing."[140]

By mid-summer of 1974, the provincial government had yet to officially recognize the NFC as the negotiating body for the affected communities and they were furious at the federal government for legitimizing the NFC by providing funds to be used against Manitoba Hydro in a legal action. Although the federal government had stated that it expected the issue to be cleared up through negotiation, it became increasingly clear that negotiations were failing. In a confidential letter from Premier Schreyer to Prime Minister Pierre Trudeau, the Prime Minister was chastized for allowing his government to become involved in affairs that were none of its business. The Manitoba government, according to Schreyer, was proceeding legally with respect to the hydro project in accordance with the 1966 agreement. In the letter, Schreyer wrote: "The Manitoba Government takes the position that the federal government, in signing the agreement, obligated itself to do all those things that were necessary within its jurisdiction to facilitate the program being proceeded with. As a corollary, the federal government also undertook not to take any action which would hinder the development." While stating that discussion between the Manitoba government and the affected communities was still open, Schreyer added: "The only qualification is that the Manitoba Government will not negotiate as to whether or not it has the right to proceed with the Churchill River Diversion. We consider that right to have been established eight years ago" [i.e., 1966]. Finally, in administering the *coup de grâce*, Schreyer threateningly informed the Prime

Minister of the possible consequences of federal government interference: "It will therefore be our legal position to hold the Federal Government responsible for any damages suffered by the people of Manitoba as a result of federal actions inconsistent with their contractual obligations."[141]

Simultaneously, the Manitoba government's position was communicated to Huband by Steward Martin, the lawyer retained to handle the case for the government. According to Martin, the government believed it had the legal right to proceed with the diversion, and that proper compensation for the northern residents would be negotiated. According to Martin, it would be "futile" for the NFC to argue against the justification for the project; the project was simply not negotiable.[142]

By August 1974 the NFC was still making little progress in their negotiations and began to feel their case slipping away. It was apparent that Schreyer's letter to the Prime Minister had had some effect at the federal level, and the federal government began to scrutinize more carefully both the activities and the finances of the NFC. In a letter to Henry Spence, Huband described a meeting with the Assistant Deputy Minister of the Department of Indian Affairs: "The Assistant Deputy Minister emphasized, however, that he prefers to proceed along lines of negotiation rather than confrontation, and without saying so directly, he made it clear to me that if he feels that we are going too far down the route towards confrontation, our funds will quickly dry up."[143] In addition, it was now generally felt within Indian Affairs that the NFC was over-funded, and that some reduction in their budget was needed. Future funding would also likely be in the form of a loan, repayable when a settlement had been reached, rather than as a grant.

Pressure was also brought to bear on the NFC by Judd Buchanan, newly appointed Minister of Indian Affairs, who wrote to the NFC's lawyer indicating, "I am not prepared to support through federal funding any type of court action until there has been a sincere attempt during the next sixty to ninety days at a direct negotiation between the two parties."[144] While Buchanan agreed to continue funding the NFC, it was clearly not without strings attached. He informed Henry Spence that "funding of the Committee would be on a basis of monthly payments subject to a continuing review of progress in the discussions."[145] The NFC was directed to initiate negotiations with the province on matters of project effects and compensation.

By this time, the legal strategy employed by the NFC had changed. Rather than seek an interim injunction against the project, the committee and its lawyer decided to seek a declaratory judgement from the Manitoba Court of Queen's Bench that the flooding of reserve lands would constitute an illegal act. According to Huband, such a procedure would "avoid the trauma of an injunction and also avoid the problem of attempting to calculate or estimate damages long in advance of the time when the damages can properly be calculated and estimated."[146] In the meantime, while some minor issues could be negotiated, it would not be possible for the NFC to negotiate a comprehensive compensation program, since the extent of encroachment on Indian lands, and the likely effect of the project on socioeconomic conditions, had yet to be ascertained.

Once again, Judd Buchanan stepped in. At a meeting with Huband and members of the NFC, the Minister of Indian Affairs requested that the NFC refrain from bringing the legal action to the courts, at least for a time. The NFC agreed, hoping that a settlement could be reached through negotiation. To this end, they devised a draft agreement which included as a key element the appointment of an arbitrator with sole power to decide the issue.[147]

A CLASH OF DEMOCRACIES

Meanwhile, Manitoba Hydro remained confident that the project would remain on course, and continued to make overtures to the individual communities, hoping each would sign independent compensation deals and therefore undermine the support base of the NFC. Manitoba Hydro had yet to officially recognize the NFC as the bargaining agent for the northern communities, even though resolutions to that effect had been passed by responsible band and community councils. The strategy employed by Hydro and the government in the face of possible (though in their minds not probable) legal action was outlined by Steward Martin: "The whole project can be completed without Manitoba Hydro coming to terms with the Indian people at Nelson House. . . . I would recommend that Manitoba Hydro takes the bargaining position that time is on their side and that we do not bargain in panic in order to acquire the Nelson House land immediately. . . . Thus, instead of putting all our eggs in one basket and being dependent upon the Department of Indian Affairs, and/or the Northern Flood Committee, as the operative vehicle to attain results, we hopefully can move behind them and get direct community support."[148] Hence, by again employing a stalling tactic, combined with a "divide-and-conquer" strategy which was directly opposed by the NFC members, Hydro hoped to circumvent any legal or other opposition.

The NFC was of course aware that Manitoba Hydro representatives were contacting individuals on the reserves. This was the subject of a committee meeting in February 1975. The new counsel for the NFC, D'Arcy McCaffrey, warned the committee members that a united voice was essential, and that no deals be struck with Hydro on an individual or community basis. The NFC must be recognized as the sole voice of the northern people in the hydro issue. As Mike Stern of the NFC commented, "The Schreyer government must recognize that Indian communities are democracies in themselves."[149] But the Schreyer government still was not as yet willing to accept the delegated authority of the NFC. This fact was communicated to the NFC by Schreyer himself at a meeting in Thompson.[150] The Premier believed that some individuals or communities might wish to deal with the government directly, and the government would not force them to operate through the NFC.

The issue came to a head in the spring of 1975. McCaffrey, in a strongly worded letter to Steward Martin, stated, "Meaningful negotiations cannot, and will not, occur until there is an express recognition by the Government of Manitoba that the Northern Flood Committee is the sole negotiating agent for the constituent communities." The NFC rejected suggestions that its role be primarily that of a "watchdog," to stand by powerlessly while Hydro and the government proceeded "in violation of both the spirit and letter of legislation and treaties which protect the special rights of the Indian people of Canada."[151]

The Manitoba government, in the persona of none other than the Premier himself, responded to these assertions with a vengeance. In a letter, addressed "To Residents of Northern Manitoba," Schreyer quoted from McCaffrey's letter, and said: "No doubt the position put by Mr. McCaffrey will be of some concern to you, since you live in a democratic country and your representation is established by virtue of the democratic process through your elected representative in government. You no doubt have been of the opinion that you are entitled to settle your own damage claims, without preclearance from the Northern Flood Committee."[152] He then added, "You also have the option of appointing the Flood Committee to represent you and this right is recognized." Apparently this right was an individual one only, since the communities as wholes, through their own elected officials, had already appointed the NFC, a fact which the government failed to recognize.

Schreyer also pointed out that the Manitoba government believed it was proceeding legally with respect to the hydro project, and would not violate the legal rights of any group. Indeed, the government retained its position as protector of rights for all Manitobans, and expressed "no intention of transferring this responsibility to the Northern Flood Committee."[153]

THE PANEL OF PUBLIC ENQUIRY INTO NORTHERN HYDRO DEVELOPMENT

By 1975, South Indian Lake's legal position had substantially deteriorated, due in part, to legal stalling tactics by Manitoba Hydro, and in part to a resignment by the people to their fate. As the waters of Southern Indian Lake began rising, community members accelerated their attempts to get what they could from Hydro. What unity of purpose there had existed in the community was now dissolved. Despite the fact that the NFC continued to fight on their behalf, for many residents of South Indian Lake the battle was lost. Sensing victory, Premier Schreyer wrote a letter of appeasement to the "Residents of South Indian Lake" on 31 January 1975, in which he said, "There is no doubt that the hydro development will have some negative effects on your community, but it is also true that a number of benefits have been created." Failing to provide any specific details concerning these "negative effects," Schreyer went on to outline the "benefits" that the hydro project would bring to the community. These included: (a) "direct color TV broadcasts of improved quality"; (b) direct-dial telephone service; (c) unlimited electrical power, enabling the use of "many electrical appliances, such as stoves, refrigerators, and TVs"; (d) some job opportunities on clearing and construction work. In conclusion Schreyer wrote: "The Government has already indicated that it is committed to doing everything possible to ensure that people in Northern Manitoba have at least comparable options available to them after the diversion program as they had before."[154] The fact remains, however, that the benefits of the hydro project were largely structural and infrastructural; they would actually entail increasing expenditures on the part of the South Indian Lake residents. In contrast, the negative effects of the project threatened the viability of existing economic opportunities, and while the government was "committed" to providing "comparable options" to the people, nothing concrete had yet been put forward.

Attached to Schreyer's letter was a form, "Notice of Claim for Compensation," to be completed by those residents harmed by the project. It asked such questions as, "What was your loss?" "When did you suffer the loss?" and "Why do you think Manitoba Hydro caused your loss?" But few quantifiable losses had yet to be experienced by the people; these would come later and would be the subject of much debate between them and Manitoba Hydro. Besides, the concern of the residents at this time was with the loss of their way of life, and not just cabins, skidoos or fishing as separate entities. Very few people completed the compensation claim forms.

While the people of South Indian Lake were resigned to their fate, other groups were still fighting on their behalf. In the spring of 1974, an *ad hoc* group of clergymen had formed the Interchurch Task Force on Northern Flooding to support the efforts of the NFC.[155] The concept of a public hearing into Manitoba Hydro's activities emerged, especially since Hydro itself seemed unwilling to provide any substantial information on their plans. It was decided to hold these hearings in Winnipeg and Nelson House in September 1975. The public response was overwhelming.

A very large audience gathered in Winnipeg at the start of the hearings, and testimony was presented by a wide range of individuals. Walter Mink, a former Chief at Easterville, described to the audience the experience of his people and the effect of the Grand Rapids Dam on their way of life.[156] Other individuals, academics, professionals and members of the general public provided their views, and the testimony ranged from the very technical to the emotional.

One submission, presented by Mary Rance of the Sperling Citizen's Group, quoted parts of a letter sent to the group by Premier Schreyer, in response to their letter of concern over northern flooding. Dated 4 June 1975, Schreyer's letter portrayed his view of the NFC quite clearly: "Unfortunately, a group calling itself the Northern Flood Committee and purporting to be acting in the interests of the [Nelson House] band and several other bands has interposed itself and is making it difficult to arrive at a settlement."[157] Furthermore, wrote Schreyer, the NFC had become the "unwitting instrument" of the political opponents who hoped to stop the project and thereby seriously damage the credibility of the government. The attitude of the Manitoba government is clearly evident in this letter. Describing South Indian Lake as a community that was "slowly dying," Schreyer wrote that the government was "very concerned about the Indian's way of life, although not necessarily 'the Indian way of life.' "

The federal Department of Indian Affairs also offered a submission in which they refuted the province's argument that the 1966 Canada-Manitoba agreement implied federal support for the flooding of Indian lands. Under this agreement, Canada was to absorb the costs of building long-distance electrical transmission lines, while Manitoba was to construct the generating plants and related facilities. However, according to the federal government, this did not constitute federal permission to flood Indian lands, and the province was warned that they "must seek and obtain prior approval from the federal government before any flooding of such lands is legally permissable."[158]

Unfortunately, Manitoba Hydro was not represented at the enquiry, and in many respects the whole procedure became a public rally for the opponents of the project. Notably, there were no delegates from South Indian Lake at the sessions, and generally very few Native submissions were made. The enquiry was primarily a southern, non-Native exercise in solidarity with the northern Native peoples, and provided a release for those who felt the need to "do something." Not surprisingly, when the report was released, it was extremely critical of the hydro project. The treaty rights of the Indians were being unjustly threatened, the report argued, and these rights must remain intact at all costs. Yet the report stopped short of recommending abandonment of the project. Echoing the government's own argument, the report stated that too much money had already been spent on the project, most of which had been borrowed, and it would not be economically feasible to stop it now.[159]

THE NORTHERN FLOOD AGREEMENT:
A "CHARTER OF RIGHTS AND BENEFITS"

The Manitoba government was unmoved by the enquiry. Schreyer's letter, "To the Residents of Northern Manitoba," had effectively terminated all meaningful negotiations between the NFC and the provincial government. Letters between Schreyer and federal Minister of Indian Affairs Judd Buchanan blamed each other for the lack of progress in the negotiations.[160] The federal government developed a proposal which suggested the Manitoba government and the NFC go to arbitration, but this was rejected by the NFC. However, a subsequent federal proposal to appoint a mediator in the dispute was accepted.[161] It was not until early in 1976, with the appointment of a mediator, that the NFC was finally recognized by the province, and negotiations reconvened. However, the waters of Southern Indian Lake had already begun to rise behind the Missi Falls Dam, and Southern Indian Lake water was flowing south to the Nelson River. The South Indian Lake injunction had failed to make it to court, and the province successfully held off the NFC until it was too late for effective intervention. The NFC had little left with which to bargain, and had no choice but to acquiesce and negotiate an agreement.

The task of the mediator, Leon Mitchell, was not an easy one. The two sides had become firmly entrenched in their positions and had developed a genuine distaste for each other. Neither side was in the mood for congenial discussion. Since all objectivity had long since been lost, Mitchell was compelled to investigate the hydro issues thoroughly on his own. This he did through small-group meetings with the various parties involved, and through the commissioning of a study by a Winnipeg consulting firm. However, Manitoba Hydro, disagreeing with the retention of an external agency, refused to cooperate or provide any funding for the research. Hydro Chairman Leonard Bateman directed his staff as follows: "The Government's position is not to be involved with the . . . study. Hence, no staff are to provide information to this group without clearance from your office. The guideline to cover this is to give only that information which you would give to an ordinary citizen and that which we have available for the public."[162] Clearly and deliberately impeding Mitchell's attempts to obtain an accurate picture of the dispute, Hydro and the government may have been stalling in hopes that the mediation process would not be finalized until after the project had been completed. The NFC itself, and in particular the individual bands, also had difficulty providing input into the mediation process, particularly in response to the mediator's request for submission of community-based compensation proposals. The NFC's apparent lack of progress had even been criticized by the other Indian bands and members of the Manitoba Indian Brotherhood. Inexperience plagued all of the Native role players.[163] Nevertheless, Mitchell persevered.

The initial draft agreement developed by the NFC contained four basic provisions:

1 the substitution of provincial crown lands for flooded lands according to a formula of five acres for every one acre flooded;

2 the establishment of a development corporation to manage continuing compensation from royalties on hydro generation;

3 hunting and fishing rights in specified off-reserve areas;

4 the reimbursement of all costs of the NFC.[164]

The draft was submitted to the federal government in September 1976, but it inexplicably failed to act, even though it was a federal government proposal to mediate which led to the draft agreement. The delay caused the NFC to threaten to terminate the mediation process and resume legal action. The threat was not executed, however, when the mediator, after viewing the NFC proposal, developed and submitted his own. A new draft agreement was then completed in June 1977.[165]

The Manitoba government remained unrepentant right to the end. As the draft agreement was formulated, Schreyer informed Trudeau that Manitoba was willing to comply with its terms only because of the anticipated enormous costs of litigation, both financial and temporal. Manitoba maintained that Canada was in breach of the 1966 agreement, and that the federal government's funding of the NFC was delaying the project at great expense.[166] Furthermore, the Manitoba government stated that, if the agreement was not finalized by the end of July 1977, it would proceed to raise the water levels adjacent to the Nelson House reserve regardless.[167] The province was a reluctant and embittered partner to the agreement.

The draft agreement was signed on 31 July 1977. The Northern Flood Agreement, referred to as a "charter of rights and benefits" by then Minister of Indian Affairs Warren Allmand,[168] demonstrated some improvement over the Forebay Agreement, but fell short of securing the survival of the affected communities (in contrast to the James Bay and Northern Quebec Agreement). The major concessions won by the NFC were the right to receive proper compensation for damages caused by the hydro project, to be determined by an independent arbitrator if necessary, and the right to be consulted about future hydro developments. The agreement explicitly acknowledged the "uncertainty as to the effects of the Project, with respect not only to the project as it exists, . . . but also as it may develop in the future" and that "it is not possible to foresee all the adverse results of the Project nor to determine all those persons who may be affected by it."[169] Hence, the agreement would have no termination date; it would be in effect in perpetuity, or "for the lifetime of the Project."[170]

Some of the significant provisions of the Northern Flood Agreement were:

1 Any band whose land is affected by the Hydro project is to receive four acres of land for each affected acre, provided the selected land is unoccupied Crown land and "not required for public purposes."[171]

2 The necessary training for and employment of local residents on the hydro construction project.

3 The people of the affected communities are to be given first priority to all wildlife resources within their trapline zones, and in the rivers and lakes which were traditionally available to and used by them as a source of food supply, income-in-kind, and income.

4 "Manitoba has encouraged and will continue to encourage the residents of Reserves to achieve the maximum degree of self-sustenance in food supplies and to maximize the opportunity to earn income and income-in-kind from the wildlife resources and will therefore prohibit hunting, trapping, and fishing in the Resource Area by any non-resident of the Reserve." Further, members of affected communities should "expect that both themselves and their progeny should continue to be able to enjoy these benefits" of hunting, fishing, and trapping.[172]

5 Compensation for damages to fishing and trapping are to be negotiated, but individual compensation claims must be made within five years of the signing of the agreement. Hydro will retain the right to settle individual claims.

In signing the agreement, Canada acknowledged its "jurisdiction and responsibility for Indians and lands reserved for Indians." Furthermore, the federal government explicitly acknowledged its responsibility "in ensuring that the special rights of Indians, including those arising from Treaty 5, are adequately protected."[173] Yet, the parallels between the agreement and the treaties are striking. As Ken Young explained, "It [the agreement] is a treaty – a modern-day treaty."[174] The federal government had not seen fit to intercede to any real extent on the behalf of the treaty Indians when threatened by the hydro project, and of course South Indian Lake received virtually no support. In many ways, Young's comment was to foreshadow the effectiveness of the Northern Flood Agreement.[175]

As soon as the draft agreement had been initialed, dissension arose within the Manitoba government. Sidney Green, Minister of Mines and Natural Resources, objected specifically to the arbitration procedure, under which the government could be ordered to execute remedial measures or pay compensation to affected individuals. To Green, the government had been "sold down the river" by Chief

Negotiator Leonard Bateman, and he hoped to uncover "a procedure whereby with integrity we could repudiate this entire process."[176] Green was supported in his concerns by the Manitoba government, and when Canada and the NFC officially signed the Northern Flood Agreement the province refused. For his part, Bateman was bewildered, and no doubt hurt, that the government had rejected the agreement. According to Bateman, "Surely the Government should not authorize people to negotiate in good faith and sign for Manitoba when a reserved position is held by the Government."[177]

The Manitoba government's position on the Northern Flood Agreement did not change until after the provincial election in September 1977. The NDP government was defeated, and the new Conservative government led by Sterling Lyon signed a revised version of the draft agreement, along with the other parties, on 16 December 1977. The arbitration procedure objected to by Green was not altered substantially.[178]

While South Indian Lake is included under the Northern Flood Agreement, by virtue of the fact that many of the people are members of the Nelson House Band, there is no mention of the community in the agreement itself. Many South Indian Lake residents have interpreted this fact to mean that they are not included in the agreement, and have no recourse under the arbitration provision. According to Ken Young, South Indian Lake's inclusion under the agreement "is subject to interpretation."[179] An arbitration claim was submitted on behalf of the community in 1984, which would have clarified the issue, but it never reached the arbitrator. At least two other arbitration claims, one for trapping compensation and the other for fishing compensation, have been filed but have been settled through direct negotiation. South Indian Lake was the community predicted to be the most severely affected by the Churchill–Nelson River Project (and in fact it was); it is ironic that the exact status of the community under the Northern Flood Agreement remains a controversy. The payoff for having initiated and led the political struggle seems to have been slight.

THE COMMISSION OF INQUIRY INTO MANITOBA HYDRO

The storm which had been generated around the construction of the Churchill–Nelson River Hydro Project led to the establishment of a commission to investigate all aspects of the project about the same time as the Northern Flood Agreement was being finalized. The final report of the commission, commonly referred to as the Tritschler Report after the Commissioner, was published in 1979, and contained some start-ling revelations that did nothing less than provide vindication for all those who had fought the project.

With respect to impact assessment and compensation, the commission found that, as late as December 1972, neither Hydro nor the Manitoba government had a compensation scheme, and that the various government departments failed to cooperate in the areas of compensation and mitigation.[180] Hydro took the position that its responsibility was limited to structural repairs and replacements, that the social and environmental consequences of the project would not be significant, and assumed that the government would deal with the indirect effects of the project. The difficulties in arriving at a proper compensation agreement with the affected communities was due in part to this approach of Hydro. The report stated: "Hydro's difficulties with the mitigation aspects of CRD [Churchill River Diversion] illustrate how the failure to prepare a definitive assessment of all technical aspects of the diversion had serious detrimental effects on attempts to negotiate acceptable compensation arrangements with the citizens of Northern Manitoba directly affected by the scheme."[181] The commission also found that "Government and Hydro adopted a stance toward the native communities and the NFC of confrontation, hostility, and procrastination with, on more than one occasion, a lack of frankness."[182]

In a letter from the government's lawyer, Steward Martin, to the Manitoba Attorney-General's Office, dated 7 November 1977, the Commission also uncovered an admission that, contrary to the official position of the government, Manitoba Hydro was aware that it likely did not have the legal right to flood and thereby trespass on Indian lands by virtue of the 1966 Canada-Manitoba Agreement.[183] Martin's legal opinion in this context was apparently ignored.

The clear conflict of interest in which the government found itself was also reported by the commission:

The responsibility of Government in representing all interests of the Province, and the narrower responsibility of Hydro in fulfilling its mandate to supply power at the lowest cost are not always identical. In this case, Government became the advocate for Hydro and thus was unable to fulfill a meaningful role on behalf of the citizens of northern Manitoba affected by the activities of Hydro. This had much to do with the creation of the NFC. In future, Government should exercise its mandate on behalf of all the citizens of the Province to ensure that Hydro properly fulfills its responsibility.[184]

Finally, while providing vindication to the members of the affected communities, the Commissioner offered little else when he stated, "The Commission is well aware that what is done is done and cannot be reversed. We can, however, learn from history."[185] From the treaty experience, however, we know that the lessons of history tend not to be well learned.

AFTER THE FLOOD: NEGOTIATIONS AND COMPENSATION

Despite the existence of the Northern Flood Agreement, the people of South Indian Lake have largely steered their own course since the diversion project became operational. Indeed, the people are wholly unsure of the agreement and its effect upon them. While administratively the people have remained members of the Nelson House Indian Band, there exists some animosity between the two communities, at least politically. Recently, this animosity has led to the insistence by many South Indian Lake residents that a new band be formed, and that a new reserve be established at South Indian Lake.

One reality, however, which quickly came into force was Hydro's right under the Northern Flood Agreement to negotiate individual compensation deals with the communities. Bypassing the NFC whenever possible, Hydro has developed a variety of programs to compensate trappers and fishermen for lost production and damage caused to their operations by the hydro project. In these contexts, the political relationship between Hydro and South Indian Lake has continued.

As soon as the waters rose, the trappers and fishermen of South Indian Lake began to notice problems. They no longer recognized their lake, and were unsure of travel routes. Their favourite fishing locations had been obliterated, and parts of their traplines were submerged. As well, Hydro had bought and destroyed a large number of cabins around the lake, presumably because they were below the new lake level. It was now incumbent upon the people to re-establish themselves, rebuild their camps, and re-cut their trails. For its part, Hydro began to develop compensation programs to alleviate economic problems in the short run. From the start, however, it had been Hydro's position that permanent and final settlements be reached.

Manitoba Hydro implemented the Registered Trapline Program to provide such compensation. Relatively complex, the program was based on the notion that trappers should be compensated only for the differences in production they experienced as a result of the hydro

project. Using data from the previous ten-year period, a production pro-
file was developed for each trapper, and the extent of loss calculated
according to a variety of scenarios, for example: one hundred percent
total loss; permanent partial loss; partial loss through a transitional
period.[186] The program was to last for five years only, whereupon it
would be reviewed for each individual trapper. Compensation was paid
directly to individuals, although in the case of the South Indian Lake
community trapline (available to anyone who wished to trap), monies
were deposited into a community fund. By and large, trappers were
unhappy with Hydro's assessment of their production history, and the
fact that the assessment failed to include related factors such as
increasing transportation time and costs entailed in circumventing
unsafe sections of the lake while travelling to traplines. When, in 1982,
many trappers began to receive notice that their compensation would
be terminated, there was a great deal of dissatisfaction among them.

Manitoba Hydro also developed a program to compensate commercial fishermen for losses caused by the construction of the hydro project.
The Commercial Fishermen's Assistance Program was designed to
replace damaged equipment, such as nets and motors, and to provide
compensation payments for loss of production, particularly for white-
fish (which was the dominant and economically most important species in the Southern Indian Lake commercial fishery) over a five-year
period.[187] However, in contrast to the trappers' program, the fishermen's program entailed annual negotiations between Hydro and the
representatives of the South Indian Lake Fisherman's Association to
establish the exact amounts of compensation for each current fishing
season. While such a practice certainly allowed for greater community
input, it also proved to be time-consuming and acrimonious. As the
negotiating skills of the fishermen developed, their demands became
more refined and Hydro's opposition more steadfast. Frequently, many
meetings were required to hammer out the details of these agreements,
and it became an all-too-common occurrence that fishermen were setting out onto the lake at the beginning of the season without a firm
agreement in place. Each year's round of negotiations placed additional
strains on the representatives, and a collective sentiment for an agreement that would end such fruitless negotiations developed.[188]

Manitoba Hydro, too, was looking for a way to complete a final compensation program. Open-ended agreements were not to their liking,
and in at least this instance they received little criticism from the community. However, before negotiations could get under way, a claim

was submitted under the Northern Flood Agreement on behalf of South Indian Lake.

Since the five-year period of limitations on the Northern Flood Agreement was running out, NFC lawyer Ken Young had visited South Indian Lake and discussed the utility of submitting a claim while it was still possible. The community response was favourable, and the claim was filed on 8 March 1984, the last day in which the community could legally do so.[189] The claim was comprehensive, detailing a variety of adverse effects which the hydro project had had on the community, including: the creation of obstacles to navigation in the waterways; the loss of access to the shoreline and ice; the loss of domestic food; the loss of recreational and economic opportunities. Furthermore, in naming both the federal and provincial governments as defendants, the claim argued: "At all material times it has become necessary for the Government of Manitoba and the Government of Canada to ensure that damage to the interests, opportunities, lifestyles and assets of the Association and its members be compensated appropriately and justly, and the said Governments have failed to do so."[190] It is not likely that the community agreed to the claim solely to improve their bargaining position in the negotiations with Hydro for trapping and fishing compensation, although the action did have this effect to some extent. The claim was never pursued, a fact which Young asserts actually weakened their position in the negotiations.[191] Some problems developed between the community and Winnipeg lawyer Vic Savino, whom they had retained to represent them in compensation matters, and Savino was released. Subsequently, both the fishermen's and trappers' associations retained lawyer Don MacIvor from The Pas to pursue the issue, separate from the NFC.

Negotiations continued through 1983 and 1984, leading finally to the signing of compensation agreements in 1985. Under the trapping agreement, the South Indian Lake Trappers Association was to receive the sum of $1,017,835.62 "as full, final and complete compensation for all past, present and future loss and damages direct or indirect, with respect to or arising out of trapping activities and hunting activities in the Southern Indian Lake Registered Trapline Zone."[192] Similarly, the fishing agreement entailed the sum of $2,525,000 as compensation for damages to commercial fishing activity. In both cases, the finality of the settlement was clear, and a great amount of space was devoted to the absolving of Manitoba Hydro from any future liability. In a passage reminiscent of the "cede, release, surrender . . . forever" clause of the numbered treaties, these agreements stated: "The [Fisherman's]

Association . . . hereby releases and forever discharges Hydro of and from all actions, causes of action, suits, claims, demands, losses, costs, damages and expenses which they . . . have or may have at any time or times either before or after the execution of this Agreement, for or by reason on account of any loss or damage, or by virtue of any contractual right related to commercial fishing under the Northern Flood Agreement, which they . . . suffer or incur, caused by or resulting from any change in water quality in the level of Southern Indian Lake."[193] Similar passages are found throughout both the fishing and trapping agreements. The residents of South Indian Lake have gambled, hoping that the future damage of their lake and waterways will not be severe, that the commercial and domestic industries will recover, and that the water regime will stabilize. Their reward has been, on the surface, a significant amount of money, and freedom from the need for prolonged and stressful annual negotiations. It is the opinion of many observers that the community lost the gamble the minute the agreements were signed, and that a much better deal could have been negotiated through the NFC. While Hydro's commitment is clearly detailed, the position of the community remains dependent on a host of unknown factors. In the absence of detailed studies of the environmental effects of the project on Southern Indian Lake, and its economic effects on the community, hope as a factor looms much too large.

THE AUGMENTED FLOW DISPUTE

Soon after the fishing and trapping agreements were signed, the implications of their finality became evident. Manitoba Hydro had been operating the Churchill River Diversion on an interim licence, under which they were restricted to altering the level of Southern Indian Lake between 257.3 and 258.2 metres, with a maximum annual drawdown of 0.6 metres. However, soon after the diversion began operating, Hydro began requesting, and receiving, special permission to surpass these levels and increase the water flow through the South Bay diversion channel into the Nelson River system. The point of this was to ascertain the maximum flows which the project could feasibly handle, since this was an unknown fact at the time it was planned. Hydro's requests to exceed either or both the minimum and maximum elevations became such a routine event that it alarmed the South Indian Lake Community Council.

After extensive discussion, the community decided to oppose one such request in 1984. At a community meeting, it was resolved that compensation should be forthcoming from Manitoba Hydro for the damage and inconvenience that the augmented flow program was likely to cause.[194] The community based its argument on the belief that dangerous ice conditions would result from the program, and that, combined with the fluctuating water conditions, the utilization of the lake by both animals and people would be compromised.

An official letter of protest was sent to the Manitoba government in the spring of 1984, while the trapping and fishing agreements were still in their final negotiation stages.[195] Protests continued, and eventually the community went to the media and announced their intention to sue the province over the issue.[196] It was not until spring of 1985 that the community secured a meeting with Minister of Northern Affairs Harry Harapiak. It was agreed at this meeting that an investigation be undertaken of the consequences of the augmented flow program on the community, and to this end a board composed of delegates from the community, Manitoba Hydro and Northern Affairs was struck.

By the time the South Indian Lake Augmented Flow Study Board had its first meeting, in October 1985, the trapping and fishing agreements had been finalized (although the trapping agreement was being delayed for unrelated bureaucratic reasons).[197] Two facts became apparent at this time. First, since the compensation agreements had effectively been signed, Hydro was not willing to discuss the socioeconomic or environmental effects of the augmented flow program on either fishing or trapping, or the animal and fish species involved. The commercial and domestic aspects of these activities had been compensated for, and the agreement to that effect had stipulated that no subsequent action against Hydro was possible. Second, the lake levels stipulated in the compensation agreements were not the same as in the interim licence, but rather reflected those stated in the augmented flow program. In fact, soon after the compensation agreements were signed, Manitoba Hydro submitted a five-year operating plan to the provincial government, in which it detailed its intent to seek a permanent licence for the Churchill River Diversion in which the new lake elevation ranges would change from 257.3 and 258.2 to 256.8 and 258.5 metres. Furthermore, Hydro sought to have the 0.6-metre maximum annual drawdown limitation removed so that there would be no limit to which they could fluctuate water levels of Southern Indian Lake between the new minimum and maximum elevations. The residents who signed the compensation agreements, including the presidents of both the fisherman's and trappers associations, paid little attention to the elevations stipulated in the compensation agreements, assuming that the numbers represented existing levels as they experienced them. They were also unaware of Hydro's five-year plan.[198] Hence, the fishermen and trappers signed compensation agreements based on their experiences and losses associated with one water regime, only to discover that the agreements actually cover an altered water regime. For its part, the South Indian Lake Community Council was not party to the negotiations, and its members were surprised to learn the implications of the elevation figures stipulated in the compensation agreements. The ramifications of this were now clear: any impact assessment would be muted by the existence of the agreements.

In an effort to come to grips with the impact assessment issue, the Augmented Flow Study Board commissioned a study to determine the feasibility of conducting a post-project impact assessment of the Churchill River Diversion on the community of South Indian Lake. In its 1987 final report, Shawinigan Consultants Incorporated concluded that such a study was not feasible due to a lack of baseline or pre-project data. But the consultants did emphasize that "the perceived impacts caused by augmented flows pale in comparison with the apparent impacts caused by the CRD [Churchill River Diversion] itself."[199] In accepting the consultant's report, the South Indian Lake community called for the commencement of new negotiations to determine compensation for damages caused by both the diversion and the augmented flow program.[200] The initial response to this call by the Manitoba government, provided by the Minister of Energy, Jerry Storie, was to agree to talk to community representatives if they could specify what further compensation they wished and why it was necessary.[201] By February of 1988, no such talks had been initiated.

The people of South Indian Lake are exhausted from over fifteen years of concentrated negotiations. This exhaustion was clearly evident from the desire of some members of the community to sign final fishing and trapping compensation agreements, and it is likely that the full ramifications of these were not fully thought out. But their struggle is not yet over, and as the community mobilizes around the augmented flow issue a new fighting spirit is emerging. This new spirit is encapsulated in the view of the people that neither they, nor the hydro project, are going anywhere, and if a proper compensation agreement takes time to negotiate, then so be it.

For its part, Manitoba Hydro was clearly satisfied with the nature of the trapping and fishing agreements, and has recently indicated its intention, if possible, to renegotiate the Northern Flood Agreement in the hopes of reaching a final settlement with the bands involved.[202] This, of course, is clearly contradictory to the letter, spirit and intent of the agreement, and the NFC is not prepared, at this point, to acquiesce. Rather, their concern is that the agreement has not been implemented properly. In clear support for the contention that history repeats itself (and perhaps in support of Sidney Green's warning that certain ghosts from the past often come back to haunt us), the NFC has recently hired former federal Minister of Indian Affairs Jean Chrétien as their negotiator, in hopes that he might be able to secure fulfillment of the terms of the agreement.[203] It is not likely that the concerns of either the Northern Flood Committee or South Indian Lake will be alleviated in the near future.

Conclusion

6

*When we moved from our old settlement . . . this is the place that had been
chosen by us a hundred years ago by people who came into the country at that
time. We had been told at that time that we must give up our land and that we
could live at our old settlement as long as the sun shines, the grasses grow and
the rivers flow. But then a hundred years later people came into our land . . .
and told us that we would have to move . . . and that we must leave this land
that was to have been ours for as long as the sun shines, the rivers flow and the
grasses grow.*[1]

The treatment of Native people in the process of hydroelectric development in western Canada has direct parallels to their treatment by the
government of Canada in the negotiation of treaties and scrip almost
a century earlier. By what mechanism have these Native peoples been
forced to surrender their lands, their rivers and their rights?

TREATIES AND DAMS: FOR THE "COMMON GOOD"

Hydroelectric developments in western Canada have had a profound
effect on many Native communities. While very few pre-project impact
assessments have ever been conducted, the potential for negative
effects has always been acknowledged. In the cases of the three communities discussed in this book, only that of South Indian Lake was
the subject of a pre-project impact study, although it was actually completed after the major structures surrounding Southern Indian Lake
were completed. Yet, in all three cases, it was widely believed that some
negative effect would occur, a subject which was frequently the focus
of public debate. Post-project impact studies conducted have supported

the early fears of Native residents; it is clear that some serious damage has been done.[2] How, then, were the Manitoba and Saskatchewan governments, and their respective hydro utilities, Manitoba Hydro and the Saskatchewan Power Corporation, able to proceed with projects in which it was acknowledged that some damage to Native interests would occur? The answer, striking in its simplicity, was to appeal to the "public interest" over that of private, in this case Native, interests.

The link between historical and contemporary processes of Native land and resource alienation was perceptively made by J.E. Chamberlin in his work, *The Harrowing of Eden*. According to Chamberlin:

The idea of a [Native] usufructuary right (or a right of use and occupancy) of land, an idea which had been brought over from England with the Royal Proclamation of 1763, was obliterated not so much by treaties, though they were a crucial factor in the process, as by one of the most misunderstood of the engines of progress – the modern governmental state, with its righteous conviction and inordinate power to do anything at all, to anybody, if it is convinced or convinces itself that this is for the common good. . . . Such a sinister machine has long been a part of the life of the native peoples [of Canada and the United States]. . . . It was for the common good that the western lands were opened up for settlement, even as the eastern lands had been settled; it was for the common good that treaties were signed, and often broken, and that provision was made in these treaties for roads, way stations, trading houses and forts, which could be built at governmental whim on lands reserved for Indians; it was for the common good that rail and road links were established through Indian lands to link east and west; it was for the common good that Indian hunting and fishing rights, guaranteed by treaty or solemn promise, were revoked to make room for people, or things (such as dams) to serve people, or programs (such as conservationist schemes) to satisfy people; it was for the common good that the Indians were herded like cattle, treated like children, swatted like flies and quarantined like animals suspected of having rabies.[3]

In his dissenting comment on the *Report of the Panel of Public Enquiry into Northern Hydro Development* (1976) in Manitoba, Mel Watkins reiterated Chamberlin's views. According to Watkins,

Where it [the Report] errs is in its refusal seriously to analyze the most persistent argument used by developers, private and public, which is that large-scale resource projects serve the "public interest." The "Indian interest" is then disposed of either by saying, in effect, that it must regrettably be overridden, or by asserting that in some long-run sense the two interests are really identical. . . . The rhetoric of the developers must be exposed for the propaganda that it is, for it prevents us from seeing the fundamental issues which it manages to obfuscate. . . . The appeal to the public interest is a means to mask the possibility that some portion of the populace may be having their rights and interest gravely damaged. . . . The most profound issue that the appeal to the "public interest" raises . . . is whether, in a moral or ethical sense, "the greater good" can even be served if the interest of some people are ridden over roughshod.[4]

In their respective analyses, both Chamberlin and Watkins have much insight to offer us.

The arguments which the respective provincial governments presented to rationalize their hydro activities and other ongoing related developments clearly resembled the "common-good" perspective described by Chamberlin and Watkins. In the case of South Indian Lake, the "common good" of all the people of Manitoba, and their need for electricity, was continuously expressed by various Manitoba officials and even the Premier himself. In the case of Easterville and Cumberland House, the same rationale was also employed. Of course the Native residents were to receive "benefits" as a result of the projects, and were to be dealt with fairly. But this did not occur in a satisfactory manner, at least in the eyes of the residents of these communities. Hydro projects designed to serve southern provincial interests, and even to provide power for export, have largely failed to serve the interests of the northern Native people, the promises and "benefits" notwithstanding. For them, there has been, and remains, nothing common about the "common good."

The process of land and resource alienation through appeals to the "common good," as Chamberlin rightly points out, is not new to these Native people. The process, at least in its formal stages, began with the treaties and the issuing of scrip to the Indian and Métis inhabitants of the West over 100 years ago. The parallels between the treaty-making and scrip processes on the one hand, and the politics of hydro dam building on the other, are striking, and the parallels go far beyond the appeal to the "common good."

The Native inhabitants of western Canada were a non-issue in the eyes of the newly formed federal government in 1867. It was not until they became an issue, through the Métis threats of insurrection in 1869, or through the need to deal with their presence on land to be made available to settlers, that the government moved with any speed to negotiate with them. There was, quite simply, no desire to deal with the Indians and Métis until necessary, and this frequently meant after settlers began arriving and taking up Indian lands, and after the Métis had formed their own government and repudiated federal authority. Only with imminent development was the federal government willing to enter into treaties with the northern Indians. And then these were done quickly, with a minimum of negotiation. So too were hydro negotiations with Native communities commenced at the last moment and done quickly. While planning for these projects had been under way for many years, the Native residents of these communities were officially notified of the plans only just as construction was about to begin. Once officially contacted, in the cases of Easterville and South Indian Lake, it was made clear to the people that negotiations were to be opened and concluded quickly, and great lengths were taken to impress upon them that the projects were a *fait accompli.* Opposition, to both treaties and dams, would be fruitless.

In the late-nineteenth and early twentieth centuries, the treaty commissioners spent as little time as possible on site in the Northwest, and were in no way interested in learning about the people. "Negotiation" of the treaties generally meant that the government representatives presented a pre-formulated set of promises to the Indians, whereupon the Indians asked for clarifications, and haggled, and tried to have other promises included. Most of the Indians' requests were denied, although on occasion verbal promises were made (though rarely entered into the official text of the treaties). Prior to the construction of the hydro projects, government negotiators rarely visited the Native communities of Easterville and South Indian Lake, and there was little attempt to learn about the people prior to opening "negotiations." In both cases, pre-formulated compensation documents were presented; they were accepted with some minor revisions in the case of Easterville, and rejected in the case of South Indian Lake.

The compensation documents tabled at Easterville and South Indian Lake were very similar, and resembled Treaty Five in both text and intent. The Indians were requested to surrender reserve land (as in the case of Easterville) or to accept a compensation package as appeasement (as in the case of South Indian Lake). In return, promises were offered by the Manitoba government; these were usually commitments to build new towns. Like the treaties, these agreements addressed the concerns of the people for their future economic security, but in a vague, offhand way. The fishing and trapping compensation agreements signed in the 1980s by the people of South Indian Lake even resemble the "cede, release, surrender . . . forever" provisions of Treaty Five. In all, in both the treaties and subsequent hydro agreements, the Native people were asked to surrender their land, resources, or their interest in them, in the name of non-Native development, the "common good."

When it was deemed necessary by government to enter into treaties with the Indians, formal treaty commissions were convened. The commissions were impermanent bodies designed solely to treat with the Indians, and in some cases to issue scrip to the Métis. Once the treaties were signed, the commissioners returned home and went back to their previous vocations. The commissions were as readily dissolved as they were constituted. In dealing with the Indians and Métis at Easterville, the Manitoba government formed the Forebay Committee, and it bore a striking resemblence to a treaty commission. Quite clearly, the Forebay Committee's mandate was to enter into treaty with the Indians. While this mandate allowed it to exist for ten years, much longer than a treaty commission, it had virtually no power to enact any programs or even to fulfill the promises made in the agreement. From the Indians' point of view, it might just as well have been dissolved as soon as the agreement had been signed. For both the treaty commissions and the Forebay Committee, it was the federal and provincial governments respectively which took over responsibility for the implementation of the agreements.

Even though the Indians as a group were usually positive about the making of treaties, there was nevertheless always some opposition. The treaty commissioners were well aware of this fact, and while always hoping to obtain the signatures of all bands in a treaty area, they were clearly prepared to settle for less. In fact, in some cases, all bands in a treaty area were considered to have signed treaties if the majority of bands had done so. Securing adhesions was preferential, but the historical documents indicate that the federal government was prepared to enforce its legislation regardless. One strategy employed by the treaty commissioners to obtain the signatures of dissenting bands has been referred to as the "domino effect," whereby a few bands would be lured into signing by the immediate and obvious benefits of cash and presents, thereby breaking the resolve of the recalcitrant bands, who would soon follow suit. This process, perhaps more correctly known as "divide and conquer," was similarly employed in hydro negotiations. At South Indian Lake particularly, and for the Northern Flood Committee bands generally, Manitoba Hydro adopted such a tactic to obtain consent to compensation packages. It proved impossible for the local flood committee at South Indian Lake to maintain solidarity in the face of an increasing number of residents opting for individual compensation packages. The lure of ready cash was an effective tool for undermining the opposition. Where individuals, or bands such as Nelson House, refused to cooperate with Manitoba Hydro in accepting compensation, it was made known that flooding would occur anyway.

The years following the signing of the treaties and the hydro agreements have seen a great deal of debate and controversy. Many arguments have arisen concerning the wording of the treaties and the agreements. Some people have argued that the written versions do not reflect oral promises made in meetings and formal negotiations. For the Native people, the oral record of the treaty and hydro negotiations represents a record just as legitimate as the written version. Yet, the non-Natives might be accused of having loose tongues: certain government officials did indeed make oral promises which they were not authorized to make, and which they subsequently refuted, and which at any rate were never included in the written versions. In all cases the Indians were unable to communicate effectively in English, and translators were usually used. Were the terms and concepts of the English language adequately communicated to the people? Debate also still rages about the extent to which the federal and provincial governments have fulfilled the terms of the treaties and the hydro agreements, and the extent to which they have lived up to the spirit and intent of these pacts.

Construction of these hydro dams caused great difficulties for the Natives: the entire community of Chemawawin (Easterville) and half of South Indian Lake, for example, had to be relocated. The federal government has always felt it could move Native people around as it wished, particularly when their physical presence somehow interfered with development. The selection of reserve lands after the signing of the treaties, while allowing for Indian input, was carefully overseen by federal employees to ensure that no resources of value to the non-Native economy were included within reserve boundaries. Indians inhabiting areas of potential wealth were moved, as in the case of Grand Rapids in 1875. When the need to relocate Chemawawin arose, the Indians were allowed only token input into the site selection procedure, and were, in effect, baited into selection of the economically and physically depressed Easterville site.

The situation of the Métis in the nineteenth century, and subsequently in the mid-twentieth century, was anomalous. The federal government seems always to have held the view that the Métis were, really, non-Natives and were to be treated as such, with no special services or programs, and no special consideration. While it is true that some Métis were allowed to become treaty Indians, such conversion was not extensive, and of course the federal government had some success in subsequently reversing the process. The Métis in the late nineteenth century were to be treated as individuals, not as collectivities, as were the Indians. Hence, there were no treaties, no agreements, no promises; there was only scrip.[5] And, as many scholars have documented, the federal government failed to protect the Métis lands from the alienation process. Only the threat of Métis violence (some would say the threat of the Métis arming themselves to protect and defend their interests), led to serious consideration by the federal government of Métis grievances. But exclusive of the Métis who were involved at Red River in 1869/70, and those at Batoche in 1885, the concerns of most Métis (i.e., the "quiet" ones) were simply not a priority. This is especially true of the northern Métis, whose petitions for scrip were largely ignored until the Indians had signed treaties.

The subordination of Métis rights and claims to those of the Indians, so evident in the nineteenth and early twentieth centuries, is also characteristic of the hydro era. The Métis of Easterville and South Indian Lake were at no time considered separate from the Indians. The Métis were allowed all of the "benefits" of compensation agreements signed with the Indians, but were not allowed to negotiate or sign their own agreements. That the Métis would receive anything was entirely contingent upon the prior acceptance by the Indians of the compensation agreements. The manner in which Cumberland House was dealt with, and continues to be dealt with, underscores this fact. With no treaty Indians initially located in the immediate downstream impact area, there was no need for federal intervention on their behalf, and no need for the Province of Saskatchewan to be concerned about illegally abrogating Indian rights.[6] Métis rights existed only as general rights as citizens of the province, and these proved to be of little significance. The province failed to discuss the hydro project with them, and has subsequently failed to deal adequately with their concerns in the post-project era. Indeed, it is difficult to believe that these Métis were accorded even general rights as provincial citizens in light of the great attention paid by the Saskatchewan government to non-Native residents in the impact area. The Métis, in all three communities, truly were a "forgotten people."

During the treaty negotiations, "advisors" were frequently provided for the Indians to assist them in understanding the agreements. These were rarely uninterested third parties, but rather were individuals in the employ of the treaty commissioners, or otherwise with ulterior motives which certainly prohibited their contribution as unbiased advisors. Of course, no lawyers were provided to the Indians, even though the treaties were considered by the federal government to be legal documents. No negotiations ensued with the

Métis of Cumberland House before the Squaw Rapids Dam was constructed, and no lawyer was provided for the Indians at Chemawawin during their negotiation of the Forebay Agreement. At Chemawawin, federal and provincial government employees were made available as advisors in a move similar to that of the treaties years earlier. In the case of South Indian Lake, where legal representation was made available, the provincial government proved to be uncooperative and the federal government unsupportive.

The federal government, and the provincial governments of Manitoba and Saskatchewan, have, over the years, found themselves in conflict-of-interest situations in their dealings with Native people. Neither level of government has extricated itself from such situations with grace, and Native people have suffered as a result. In hydro development, the provincial governments, through their own power corporations, have subordinated the rights of their Métis and non-status Indian citizens to that of their southern, predominantly non-Native citizens. Indeed, little consideration was even paid to the Natives' rights in all three communities. The provinces were more concerned with the legality of their projects and their effects vis-a-vis the treaty status Indians. Fear of federal government intervention on behalf of these people, as well as the possibility of legal action, seems to have provoked this concern. The provinces had little to fear from the Métis and non-status Indians; they would not likely interfere, and the federal government would not intervene on their behalf. Yet, the federal government always seemed unable to support fully the rights of even the treaty status Indians for whom they were responsible. When pushed by the provincial governments, the federal government invariably backed down, since natural resource development was a provincial prerogative. And the federal government usually found ways to moderate their interventions: the Métis and non-status Indians of Cumberland House and the communities of Easterville and South Indian Lake were not within federal jurisdiction; South Indian Lake was not a reserve; funding of the Northern Flood Committee was stipulated to be used for negotiation purposes only, not for legal action.

Since the signing of the treaties and hydro agreements, Indian and Métis communities and organizations have hired professional advisors, usually lawyers, to aid them in their disputes with the two levels of government. Issues surrounding the legality and fulfillment of the treaties have recently become issues for renegotiation, and occasionally litigation, particularly in the context of the federal government's specific claims policy developed in 1973. In the case of hydro development, all three Native communities have hired lawyers and researchers to support their claims, yet all three have met with only marginal success. At this point, despite injunction applications, the filing of statements of claim, and the real threat of litigation, no substantive action has made it to court. The increasing sophistication on the part of the Native communities, as well as the actions of their lawyers, has been countered by the increasing sophistication of the provincial governments and their utilities to undermine opposition to their plans and to keep compensation to a minimum. Lawyers have been no more successful in the contemporary era than they likely would have been in the treaty negotiations of yesteryear.

HOW COMMON IS THE "COMMON GOOD"?

It is a common perception that hydroelectric developments, similar to other power projects (such as nuclear and thermal), are undertaken when domestic power requirements warrant. Demands for increased power come from the private sector, both individual and industrial consumers, but it is the public sector that must facilitate power developments. The role of government, therefore, is to enact legislation to allow for power developments and, in many cases, actually undertake the developments itself through crown power corporations. The hydro potential of Canadian rivers is viewed as a common property resource to be developed for the benefit of all provincial residents, and in a wider context, all Canadians. While private industry is an important consumer, industry alone cannot be relied upon to produce power on terms beneficial to the people in general (although specific industries are occasionally allowed to develop hydroelectric projects to provide for the power needs of its operations in remote areas). Generally, the benefits to accrue to provincial citizens from hydroelectric power development are expressed in terms of reduced or comparatively low utility rates. While these power developments initially require an enormous capital outlay, provincial utilities frequently point out that, in the long run, hydroelectric power is renewable, relatively inexpensive, and safe in comparison to either thermal or nuclear power. Each of the three projects discussed in this book, the Squaw Rapids, Grand Rapids and the Churchill–Nelson River projects, were presented to the public as projects for their "common good." Indeed, the "common good" ideology has been an important feature of most major hydroelectric developments in Canada. But a closer look at these developments would likely reveal that they were proposed and constructed for reasons other than simply the production of cheap power for domestic consumption. Politics, and the machinations of politicians, have frequently become so intertwined with hydroelectric power projects that the improvement of political fortunes, rather than the production of power for the "common good," has been the real goal of provincial governments.

Recently, various provincial governments and their power corporations have announced and/or commenced a new era of hydro dam construction, and have done so for reasons which are blatantly political. Of specific note are developments in Quebec, Manitoba and British Columbia. While the late 1970s saw a significant public backlash against megaprojects, documented in the Mackenzie Valley Pipeline Inquiry and Thomas Berger's monumental report,[7] the 1980s has witnessed a new interest in megaprojects by provincial governments hoping to shore up sagging economic conditions and improve their political fortunes.

The paramount role of politics in hydroelectric development is perhaps exemplified in the pronouncements of Premier Robert Bourassa, Quebec's newly resurrected political magus. As part of his campaign to re-acquire the premiership in 1985, he wrote a book entitled *Power From the North,*[8] in which he laid the cornerstone for phase two of the James Bay Project, a $25 billion scheme that would add an additional 8,000 megawatts of power to the province's energy supply.[9] Yet, Quebec currently has a surplus of power for domestic purposes. The success of Bourassa's scheme, therefore, is predicated on the firm sale of surplus power to neighbouring markets, including Ontario, but concentrating on the northeastern United States. It is believed that the project will create up to 130,000 person-years of employment commencing in the late 1980s, which, combined with the income that Bourassa believes would be generated from power sales, would make Quebec once again a "have" province. Such a scenario would also ensure the future of the Quebec Liberal Party, and Bourassa as Premier for many years to come. The people of Quebec were so convinced that Bourassa would bring prosperity to the province, through his hydroelectric scheme and some of his other plans, that they swept him to power in late 1985.

Manitoba's NDP Premier, Howard Pawley, recently experienced the political benefits of hydroelectric dam construction. The Limestone Generating Station on the Nelson River, part of the second phase of the Churchill–Nelson River Hydro Project, was rushed into construction in early 1985 in a bid to improve the NDP's political fortunes in an upcoming election. At a cost of almost $2 billion, the power plant will produce some 1,300 megawatts of power when completed.[10] However, like Quebec, Manitoba already has a surplus of electrical power, and it is apparent that Limestone's entire production capacity is targeted for export, to Ontario and Saskatchewan, and to the mid-northern United States. Indeed, it was the premature announcement of a $3 billion, twelve-year contract with Minneapolis-based Northern States Power Corporation which accelerated the construction schedule of the planned project. Subsequently, the Manitoba government was forced to admit that this contract was in fact not firm when announced during the 1986 election campaign, and that the deal was in jeopardy.[11] Yet, with some 1,300 workers on-site at Limestone in mid-1986, it represented the largest construction project in Canada,[12] and Pawley was re-elected with a majority government. Plans are now under way to begin construction of the Conawapa Generating Station on the Nelson River, at a cost of $3 billion.

In British Columbia, prior to his resignation, Premier Bill Bennett and his Social Credit government also found the key to political success in hydro dam construction. By 1982, over one-third of the employees of B.C. Hydro had been laid off because of Bennett's austerity program. But, with his political popularity sinking, Bennett recalled an old political trick once used by his father, W.A.C. Bennett, and announced construction of the Revelstoke Dam. Completed in 1985 at a cost of $2 billion, the Revelstoke Dam's power was totally superfluous to domestic consumption requirements. But its employment creation was a boon to the province, and was so politically successful that Bennett was able to announce at its official opening that "the days of dams, their construction and their contribution to the B.C. economy, rather than being over, never looked brighter."[13] The province was not prepared to stop with construction of the Revelstoke Dam. Looking south to that power-hungry giant, the state of California, in 1985 Bennett proposed that a new power dam be constructed on the Peace River. Known as Site C, this dam will cost over $3 billion and will produce 500 megawatts of power, none of which is likely to be consumed domestically.[14] Although Bennett has stepped down, his successor, William Vander Zalm, has obviously reaped the political benefits of the Revelstoke Dam; he was swept to power in the 1986 provincial election.

In order to finance these megaprojects, all three provinces have had to borrow extensively, primarily from American sources. In recent years, as the value of the Canadian dollar has declined relative to its

American counterpart, the provinces' debt loads have increased substantially. It has been estimated that among the three provinces the debt is approximately $30 billion, and that half of the current revenues being generated by their hydro plants is channelled toward paying this debt.[15] As a result, the public utilities have been forced to increase rates, thereby passing off part of the debt on the very consumers who had been convinced they would benefit from the projects.[16] Hydro power, while still relatively inexpensive in relation to nuclear and thermal power, has seen its reputation severely tainted by blatant political manipulation. The "common good" more and more looks like "the good of the party" in power.

The processes functioning 100 years ago, best exemplified by treaties and scrip, whereby non-Natives acquired ownership of the land and resources of western Canada, clearly resurfaced once again in the contemporary era of hydroelectric development. Realizing a desire for a particular resource, in this case water power, the provincial governments (often aided by the federal government) devised ways to deal with Native opposition to their power projects which have remarkable parallels to the treaty and scrip era. I would not argue that these governments consciously resurrected the nineteenth-century methods of dealing with Native title and interest in the land and resources. Rather, I would argue that the parallels that do exist between the treaty and scrip era on the one hand, and the hydroelectric era on the other, demonstrate a continuity in the manner in which government has handled Native issues for over 100 years.

The original treaties are still considered by the Indians to have immense symbolic importance as the expression of their relationship to the federal government on a nation-to-nation basis. In agreeing with the federal government that the treaties would remain in force for "as long as the rivers run," the Indians believed they were securing their future as self-governing nations within the Canadian polity. But since the days of treaty and scrip, the struggle to achieve this status has been difficult and frustrating for Native people. Could it be that the era of hydro development, which has seen mighty rivers dammed, represents the symbolic, final comment of the federal and provincial governments concerning the validity of the treaties? Is it possible that the new "treaties," the compensation and mitigation pacts which have arisen out of the hydro disputes, are worth no more than their nineteenth-century counterparts? Unless the philosophy of government toward

Native people changes dramatically, for some the hydro era may indeed come to represent the twilight of Native rights in Canada.

APPENDIX 1

Treaty No. Five

TREATY NO. 5 BETWEEN
HER MAJESTY THE QUEEN AND THE
SAULTEAUX AND SWAMPY CREE TRIBES OF INDIANS
AT BEREN'S RIVER AND NORWAY HOUSE
WITH ADHESIONS

ARTICLES OF A TREATY *made and concluded at Beren's River the 20th day of September, and at Norway House the 24th day of September, in the year of Our Lord one thousand eight hundred and seventy-five, between "Her Most Gracious Majesty the Queen" of Great Britain and Ireland, by Her Commissioners the Honourable Alexander Morris, Lieutenant-Governor of the Province of Manitoba and the North-west Territories, and the Honourable James McKay, of the one part, and the Saulteaux and Swampy Cree tribes of Indians, inhabitants of the country within the limits hereinafter defined and described, by their Chiefs, chosen and named as hereinafter mentioned, of the other part.*

WHEREAS, the Indians inhabiting the said country have, pursuant to an appointment made by the said Commissioners, been convened at meetings at Beren's River and Norway House to deliberate upon certain matters of interest to Her Most Gracious Majesty, of the one part, and the said Indians of the other.

AND WHEREAS the said Indians have been notified and informed by Her Majesty's said Commissioners that it is the desire of Her Majesty to open up for settlement, immigration and such other purposes as to Her Majesty may seem meet, a tract of country bounded and described as hereinafter mentioned, and to obtain the consent thereto of Her Indian subjects inhabiting the said tract, and to make a treaty and arrange with them, so that there may be peace and good will between them and Her Majesty, and that they may know and be assured of what allowance they are to count upon and receive from Her Majesty's bounty and benevolence.

AND WHEREAS the Indians of said tract, duly convened in council as aforesaid, and being requested by Her Majesty's said Commissioners to name certain Chiefs and Headmen who should be authorized on their behalf to conduct such negotiations and sign any treaty to be founded thereon, and to become responsible to Her Majesty for the faithful performance by their respective bands of such obligations as shall be assumed by them the said Indians, have thereupon named the following persons for that purpose, that is to say:

For the Indians within the Beren's River region and their several bands: Nah-wee-kee-sick-quah-yash, Chief; Kah-nah-wah-kee-wee-nin and Nah-kee-quan-nay-yash, Councillors, and Pee-wah-roo-wee-nin, of Poplar River, Councillor; for the Indians within the Norway House region and their several bands: David Rundle, Chief, James Cochrane, Harry Constatag and Charles Pisequinip, Councillors; and Ta-pas-ta-num, or Donald William Sinclair Ross, Chief, James Garrioch and Proud McKay, Councillors.

AND THEREUPON, in open council, the different bands having presented their Chiefs to the said Commissioners as the Chiefs and Headmen for the purposes aforesaid of the respective Bands of Indians inhabiting the said district hereinafter described.

AND WHEREAS the said Commissioners then and there received and acknowledged the persons so presented as Chiefs and Headmen, for the purposes aforesaid, of the respective Bands of Indians inhabiting the said district hereinafter described.

AND WHEREAS the said Commissioners have proceeded to negotiate a treaty with the said Indians, and the same has been finally agreed upon and concluded as follows, that is to say:

The Saulteaux and Swampy Cree Tribes of Indians and all other the Indians inhabiting the district hereinafter described and defined, do hereby cede, release, surrender and yield up to the Government of the Dominion of Canada, for Her Majesty the Queen and Her successors for ever, all their rights, titles and privileges whatsoever to the lands included within the following limits, that is to say:

Commencing at the north corner or junction of Treaties Nos. 1 and 3; thence easterly along the boundary of Treaty No. 3 to the "Height of Land," at the northeast corner of the said treaty limits, a point dividing the waters of the Albany and Winnipeg Rivers; thence due north along the said "Height of Land" to a point intersected by the 53° of north latitude; and thence north-westerly to "Favourable Lake"; thence following the east shore of said lake to its northern limit; thence north-westerly to the north end of Lake Winnipegoosis; thence westerly to the "Height of Land" called "Robinson's Portage"; thence north-westerly to the east end of "Cross Lake"; thence north-westerly crossing "Foxes Lake"; thence north-westerly to the north end of "Split Lake"; thence south-westerly to "Pipestone Lake," on "Burntwood River"; thence south-westerly to the western point of "John Scott's Lake"; thence south-westerly to the north shore of "Beaver Lake"; thence south-westerly to the west end of "Cumberland Lake"; thence due south to the "Saskatchewan River"; thence due south to the north-west corner of the northern limits of Treaty No. 4, including all territory within the said limits, and all islands on all lakes within the said limits, as above described; and it being also understood that in all cases where lakes form the treaty limits, ten miles from the shore of the lake should be included in the treaty.

And also all their rights, titles and privileges whatsoever to all other lands wherever situated in the North-west Territories or in any other Province or portion of Her Majesty's dominions situated and being within the Dominion of Canada;

The tract comprised within the lines above described, embracing an area of one hundred thousand square miles, be the same more or less;

To have and to hold the same to Her Majesty the Queen, and Her successors forever;

And Her Majesty the Queen hereby agrees and undertakes to lay aside reserves for farming lands, due respect being had to lands at present cultivated by the said Indians, and other reserves for the benefit of the said Indians, to be administered and dealt with for them by Her Majesty's Government of the Dominion of Canada, provided all such reserves shall not exceed in all one hundred and sixty acres for each family of five, or in that proportion for larger or smaller families — in manner following, that is to say: For the Band of "Saulteaux, in the Beren's River" region, now settled or who may within two years settle therein, a reserve commencing at the outlet of Beren's River into Lake Winnipeg, and extending along the shores of said lake, and up said river and into the interior behind said lake and river, so as to comprehend one hundred and sixty acres for each family of five, a reasonable addition being, however, to be made by Her Majesty to the extent of the said reserve for the inclusion in the tract so reserved of swamp, but reserving the free navigation of the said lake and river, and free access to the shores and waters thereof, for Her Majesty and all Her subjects, and expecting thereout such land as may have been granted to or stipulated to be held by the "Hudson Bay Company," and also such land as Her Majesty or Her successors, may in Her good pleasure, see fit to grant to the Mission established at or near Beren's River by the Methodist Church of Canada, for a church, school-house, parsonage, burial ground and farm, or other mission purposes; and to the Indians residing at Poplar River, falling into Lake Winnipeg north of Beren's River, a reserve not exceeding one hundred and sixty acres to each family of five, respecting, as much as possible, their present improvements:

And inasmuch as a number of the Indians now residing in and about Norway House of the band of whom David Rundle is Chief are desirous of removing to a locality where they can cultivate the soil, Her Majesty the Queen hereby agrees to lay aside a reserve on the west side of Lake Winnipeg, in the vicinity of Fisher River, so as to give one hundred acres to each family of five, or in that proportion for larger or smaller families, who shall remove to the said locality within "three years," it being estimated that ninety families or thereabout will remove within the said period, and that a reserve will be laid aside for that or the actual number; and it is further agreed that those of the band who remain in the vicinity of "Norway House" shall retain for their own use their present gardens, buildings and improvements, until the same be departed with by the Queen's Government, with their consent first had and obtained, for their individual benefit, if any value can be realized therefor:

And with regard to the Band of Wood Indians, of whom Ta-pas-ta-num, or Donald William Sinclair Ross, is Chief, a reserve at Otter Island, on the west side of Cross Lake, of one hundred and sixty acres for each family of five or in that proportion for smaller families — reserving, however, to Her Majesty, Her successors and Her subjects the free navigation of all lakes and rivers and free access to the shores thereof; Provided, however, that Her Majesty reserves the right to deal with any settlers within the bounds of any lands reserved for any band as She shall deem fit, and also that the aforesaid reserves of land or any interest therein may be sold or otherwise disposed of by Her Majesty's Government for the use and benefit of the said Indians entitled thereto, with their consent first had and obtained.

And with a view to show the satisfaction of Her Majesty with the behaviour and good conduct of Her Indians, She hereby, through Her Commissioners, makes them a present of five dollars for each man, woman and child belonging to the bands here represented, in extinguishment of all claims heretofore preferred.

And further, Her Majesty agrees to maintain schools for instruction in such reserves hereby made as to Her Government of the Dominion of Canada may seem advisable, whenever the Indians of the reserve shall desire it.

Her Majesty further agrees with Her said Indians, that within the boundary of Indian reserves, until otherwise determined by Her Government of the Dominion of Canada, no intoxicating liquor shall be allowed to be introduced or sold, and all laws now in force, or hereafter to be enacted, to preserve Her Indian subjects inhabiting the reserves, or living elsewhere within Her North-west Territories, from the evil influence of the use of intoxicating liquors, shall be strictly enforced.

Her Majesty further agrees with Her said Indians, that they, the said Indians, shall have right to pursue their avocations of hunting and fishing throughout the tract surrendered as hereinbefore described, subject to such regulations as may from time to time be made by Her Government of Her Dominion of Canada, and saving and excepting such tracts as may from time to time be required or taken up for settlement, mining, lumbering or other purposes, by Her said Government of the Dominion of Canada, or by any of the subjects thereof duly authorized therefor by the said Government.

It is further agreed between Her Majesty and Her said Indians that such sections of the reserves above indicated as may at any time be required for public works or buildings, of what nature soever, may be appropriated for that purpose by Her Majesty's Government of the Dominion of Canada, due compensation being made for the value of any improvements thereon.

And further, that Her Majesty's Commissioners shall, as soon as possible after the execution of this treaty, cause to be taken an accurate census of all the Indians inhabiting the tract above described, distributing them in families, and shall in every year ensuing the date hereof, at some period in each year to be duly notified to the Indians, and at a place or places to be appointed for that purpose within the territory ceded, pay to each Indian person the sum of five dollars per head yearly.

It is further agreed between Her Majesty and the said Indians that the sum of five hundred dollars per annum shall be yearly and every year expended by Her Majesty in the purchase of ammunition, and twine for nets, for the use of the said Indians, in manner following, that is to say: in the reasonable discretion as regards the distribution thereof among the Indians inhabiting the several reserves or otherwise included therein of Her Majesty's Indian Agent having the supervision of this treaty.

It is further agreed between Her Majesty and the said Indians that the following articles shall be supplied to any band of the said Indians who are now cultivating the soil, or who shall hereafter commence to cultivate the land, that is to say: "Two hoes for every family actually cultivating; also one spade per family as aforesaid; one plough for every ten families as aforesaid; five harrows for every twenty families as aforesaid; one scythe for every family as aforesaid, and also one axe; — and also one cross-cut saw, one hand-saw, one pit-saw, the necessary files, one grindstone, and one auger for each band; and also for each Chief, for the use of his band, one chest of ordinary carpenter's tools; also for each band enough of wheat, barley, potatoes and oats to plant the land actually broken up for cultivation by such band; also for each band one yoke of oxen, one bull and four cows — all the aforesaid articles to be given once for all for the encouragement of the practice of agriculture among the Indians.

It is further agreed between Her Majesty and the said Indians that each Chief duly recognized as such shall receive an annual salary of twenty-five dollars per annum, and each subordinate officer, not exceeding three for each band, shall receive fifteen dollars per annum; and each such Chief and subordinate officer as aforesaid shall also receive, once every three years, a suitable suit of clothing; and each Chief shall receive, in recognition of the closing of the treaty, a suitable flag and medal.

And the undersigned Chiefs, on their own behalf and on behalf of all other Indians inhabiting the tract within ceded, do hereby solemnly promise and engage to strictly observe this treaty, and also to conduct and behave themselves as good and loyal subjects of Her Majesty the Queen. They promise and engage that they will, in all respects, obey and abide by the law, and they will maintain peace and good order between each other, and also between themselves and other Tribes of Indians, and between themselves and others of Her Majesty's subjects, whether Indians or whites, now inhabiting or hereafter to inhabit any part of the said ceded tracts, and that they will not molest the person or property of any inhabitant of such ceded tracts, or the property of Her Majesty the Queen, or interfere with or trouble any person passing or travelling through the said tracts, or any part thereof; and that they will aid and assist the officers of Her Majesty in bringing to justice and punishment any Indian offending against the stipulations of this treaty, or infringing the laws in force in the country so ceded.

IN WITNESS WHEREOF, Her Majesty's said Commissioners and the said Indian Chiefs have hereunto subscribed and set their hands at "Beren's River" this twentieth day of September, A.D. 1875, and at Norway House on the twenty-fourth day of the month and year herein first above named.

Signed by the Chiefs within named in presence of the following witnesses, the same having been first read and explained by the Honourable James McKay: Thos. Howard, A.G. Jackes, M.D., Christine Morris, E.C. Morris, Elizabeth Young, William McKay, John McKay, Egerton Ryerson Young.

Alex. Morris, L.G. [L.S.]; James McKay, [L.S.]; Nah-wee-kee-sick-quah-yash, otherwise, Jacob Berens, Chief, his mark X ; Kah-nah-wah-kee-wee-nin, otherwise, Antoine Gouin, his mark X ; Nah-kee-quan-nay-yash, his mark X ; Pee-wahroo-wee-nin, his mark X ; Councillors.

Signed at Norway House by the Chiefs and Councillors hereunto subscribing in the presence of the undersigned witnesses, the same having been first read and explained by the Honourable James McKay: Rodk. Ross, John H. Ruttan, Methodist Minister, O. Grinder, Methodist Min., D.C. McTavish, Alex Sinclair,

L.C. McTavish, Christine V.K. Morris, E.C. Morris, A.G. Jackes, M.D., Thos. Howard.

Alex. Morris, L.G., [L.S.]; James McKay, [L.S.]; David Rundle, Chief; James Cochrane, his mark X ; Harry Constatag, his mark X ; Charles Pisequinip, his mark X ; Councillors. Ta-pas-ta-num, or, Donald William Sinclair Ross, Chief, his mark X ; George Garriock; Proud McKay, his mark X ; Councillors.

ADHESION TO TREATY 5
BY SPLIT LAKE AND NELSON HOUSE

We, the undersigned Chiefs and Headmen, on behalf of ourselves and the other members of the Split Lake and Nelson House Bands of Indians, having had communication of the Treaty with certain Bands of Saulteaux and Swampy Cree Indians, known as Treaty No. 5, hereby in consideration of the provisions of the said Treaty being extended to us, it being understood and agreed that the said provisions shall not be retroactive, transfer, surrender, and relinquish to His Majesty the King, his heirs and successors, to and for the use of the Government of Canada, all our right, title and privileges whatsoever, which we have or enjoy in the territory described in the said Treaty, and every part thereof, to have and to hold to the use of His Majesty the King, and his heirs and successors forever.

And we also hereby transfer, surrender and relinquish to His Majesty the King, His heirs and successors, to and for the use of the Government of the Dominion of Canada, all our right, title and interest whatsoever which we and the said Bands which we represent hold and enjoy, or have held and enjoyed, of, in and to the territory within the following limits: All that portion of the North West Territories of Canada comprised within the following limits, that is to say; commencing where the sixtieth parallel of latitude intersects the water's edge of the West shore of Hudson Bay, thence West along the said parallel to the North East corner of the Province of Saskatchewan, thence south along the East boundary of the said Province to the Northerly limit of the Indian treaty number Five, thence North Easterly, then South Easterly, then South Westerly and again South Easterly following the northerly limit of the said Treaty number Five to the intersection of a line drawn from the North East corner of the Province of Manitoba, North Fifty-five degrees East; thence on the said line produced fifty miles; thence North twenty-five degrees East one hundred and eighty miles more or less to a point situated due South of Cape Tatnam, thence due North ninety-eight miles more or less to the said Cape Tatnam; thence South Westerly and then Northerly following the water's edge of the West shore of Hudson Bay to the point of commencement, together with all the foreshores, and Islands adjacent to the said described tract of land, and containing approximately an area of one hundred and thirty-three thousand four hundred (133,400) square miles.

And also, all our right, title and interest whatsoever to all other lands wherever situated, whether within the limits of any other treaty heretofore made, or hereafter to be made with the Indians, and whether the said lands are situated in the North West Territories or elsewhere in His Majesty's Dominions, to have and to hold the same unto and for the use of His Majesty, the King, His heirs and successors forever.

And we hereby agree to accept the several benefits, payments and reserves promised to and accepted by the Indians adhering to the said Treaty No. 5. And we solemnly engage to abide by, carry out and fulfil all the stipulations, obligations and conditions therein contained on the part of the Chiefs and Indians therein named to be observed and performed, and we agree in all things to conform to the articles of the said treaty, as if we ourselves and the Bands which we represent had been originally contracting parties thereto and had attached our signatures to the said treaty.

And his Majesty hereby agrees to set apart Reserves of land of a like proportionate area to those mentioned in the original Treaty No. 5.

And his Majesty further hereby agrees to provide a grant proportionate to that mentioned in the original treaty to be yearly and every year expended by His Majesty in the purchase of ammunition and twine for nets for the use of the said Indians; and to further increase this annual grant in lieu of other supplies provided by the said treaty when this action is shown to be in the interests of the Indians.

And his Majesty further agrees to pay to each Indian a gratuity of Five Dollars in cash, once for all, in addition to the Five Dollars annuity promised by the Treaty in order to show the satisfaction of His Majesty with the behaviour and good conduct of his Indians and in extinguishment of all their past claims.

IN WITNESS WHEREOF, His Majesty's Special Commissioner and the Chiefs and Councillors of the Bands hereby giving their adhesion to the said treaty have hereunto subscribed and set their hands at Split Lake this Twenty-sixth day of June in the year of our Lord one thousand nine hundred and eight.

Signed by the parties hereto in the presence of the undersigned witnesses, the same having been first explained to the Indians by John Semmens, Commissioner; W.J. Grant, M.D., Medical Officer; R.J. Spencer, Clerk; H. McKay, Commissioner; G.J. Wardner, Constable; H.C. McLeod; H.B. Coy; J.M. Thomas, C.F.

Wm. Keche-kesik, Charles Morris, Albert Spence [*Names in Cree characters*].

IN WITNESS WHEREOF, His Majesty's Special Commissioner and the Chiefs and Councillors of the Bands hereby giving their adhesion to the said treaty have hereunto subscribed and set their hands at Nelson House this thirtieth day of July in the year of our Lord one thousand nine hundred and eight.

Signed by the parties hereto in the presence of the undersigned witnesses, the same having been first explained to the Indians by John Semmens, Commissioner; W.J. Grant, M.D., Medical Officer; R.J. Spencer, Clerk; H. McKay, Commissioner; G.J. Wardner, Constable; Fred A. Semmens; G.D. Butler, S/Sergt. R.N.W.M. Police; Charles George Fox, Missionary-Anglican; Geo Thos. Vincent; Alexander Flett; William Isbester; F.A. Semmens.

Peter Moose, Chief; Murdoch Hart, Councillor; James Spence, Councillor [Names in Cree characters].

APPENDIX 2

The Forebay Agreement

Province of Manitoba
Department of Mines and Natural Resources
Deputy Minister's Office
Winnipeg 1

June 7, 1962

Chief Donald Easter,
Chemahawin Indian Band,
Cedar Lake, via The Pas,
The Pas, Manitoba.

Dear Chief Easter:

On April 18, 1962, I wrote you a letter in which I advised you that I was authorized by the Province of Manitoba and Manitoba Hydro to make a number of commitments and offers, which I outlined in that letter. After you received this letter and studied it with the Chemahawin Committee, in consultation with Mr. Bell and Mr. Wells, you proposed certain changes and additions. On June 5 and 6, 1962, we discussed my letter and the changes and additions you proposed and reached agreement on the commitments and offers which are mutually accepted. This letter, therefore, will supersede my letter of April 18, 1962, and contains the revised offers and commitments to which I now commit the Province of Manitoba and Manitoba Hydro. I am authorized by the Province of Manitoba and Manitoba Hydro to make the following commitments and offers.

Item 1. Housing and Outbuildings

We will:

(a) Provide families living in houses at Chemahawin with a new or reconditioned home and pit toilet and in cases where barns, warehouses, garages and other out-buildings were with the houses at the old location these will be provided at the new location, houses to be based on the present size of the family unit and subject to the surrender of the present buildings to the Government. All new and reconditioned houses provided will be wired for electricity.

(b) Provide houses of a size, standard and design similar to plans Nos. 1, 2, 3, 4 and 6 shown in the book "Canadian Indian Homes" issued by the Indian Affairs Branch. The size of houses provided will be on the basis of the following family units:

Plan 1	up to 3 people	16' x 24'	4 rooms
Plan 2	4	20' x 24'	4 "
Plan 3	6	24' x 26'	5 "
Plan 6	over 6	24' x 30'	4 down, 2 up

Note: Plans to be modified to eliminate basements and substitute Selkirk metal chimneys instead of masonry chimneys.

(c) Move the people, their belongings and their livestock to the new site and compensate each adult at normal daily rates of pay for a reasonable time (minimum of 10 days) in preparing for the move, the move and getting settled at the new site.

(d) Pay compensation for isolated serviceable buildings as may be affected by the raising of the water, such as fishing and trapping cabins below elevation 848, on a basis of (1) moving the building, or (2) replacing it with a serviceable building, with the owner's concurrence, or (3) paying the owner a fair replacement price.

(e) Newly-Weds: The Forebay Committee will assist those married couples who reside on the Chemahawin Indian Reserve or in the Cedar Lake Métis Settlement who, at the time of the move to the new settlement, reside with parents, relatives or friends in the following manner: (Note: Any agreement between Indians and Indian Affairs in respect to housing is outside this agreement.) (1) The Forebay Committee will assist those married couples who reside on the Chemahawin Indian Reserve who at the time of the move to the new site reside with parents, relatives or friends by a payment towards the cost of a new home of $20.00 for each month these married couples lived in this manner after January 1, 1960, until the rehousing program of the Forebay Committee at the new site has been completed. (2) In the case of Métis in this category. Supply a new or reconditioned house as under Item 1(b) and transfer title to the house and lot when full payment has been made, through a 10% deduction of all wages paid him by Manitoba and a one cent per pound deduction from all fish he delivers to a buyer.

Item 2. Schools

A new school will be constructed on Provincial Crown Land to meet the needs of the residents in accordance with the agreed upon town plan, between the Indian and Métis settlements, and provided with playground and room for future expansion.

Item 3. Timber

We shall establish a forest management unit as outlined on Map 1 attached. The Grand Rapids west portion of which, on a sustained yield basis, it is estimated can produce 5,180 cords plus 650,000 f.b.m. of all species.

On this forest management unit we will:

(a) reserve timber adjacent to Cedar Lake Settlement to insure that requirements for fuelwood will be available on Crown lands and Indian Reserves to meet the continuing needs of the settlement;

(b) confine cutting in this area to the sustained capacity of the area;

(c) will not within this forest management area make available timber sales for more than 1-1/2 million f.b.m. sawtimber or 3,000 cords of pulpwood, or equivalent, unless larger sales are agreed to by the Indian Affairs Branch. In all timber sales conditions in the above-mentioned forest management area, the following clause will be inserted: "Preference will be given to the employment of local labour, which, if such labour is available, shall at no time comprise less than 75% of the labour force."

Item 4. Harbour and Dock Facilities

We will provide a suitable harbour or dock or both, at Cedar Lake, built in accordance with a design and specification being prepared by the Federal Department of Public Works (Harbours and Rivers) who are acting as our consulting engineers for this provision.

Item 5. Town Planning and Community Development

(a) We will, in consultation with the Band, draft a plan of Cedar Lake Settlement, partially on and partially off a new Indian Reserve, to be used to insure orderly development of the settlement.

(b) In respect to Community Development guidance, we will make this service available but cannot commit the Government to stating in what manner this will be arranged for.

(c) It is anticipated that many community improvements will be required, such as minor roads, air strip, minor dykes and dams, community pastures and gardens and electric power, the need for some of these may not be evident for some years. The Committee therefore agrees, until ten (10) years after the Hydro plant is put into operation, to provide community improvements felt to be in the best interest of the residents of Cedar Lake Settlement. We say this because we do not feel that any of these items should be decided upon now, as there may be better ways to spend the money available to strengthen your economy.

Item 6. Roads

A gravelled, all-weather road will be constructed prior to break-up 1964 from P.T.H. #6 to the harbour at Cedar Lake.

Item 7. Public Utilities

We will drill wells in sufficient number to adequately serve the new settlement. If suitable wells cannot be made available, then other suitable water supply will be provided. Wells will be constructed in accordance with Public Health regulations and be provided with high standard quality hand pumps or faucets and with shelters, if recommended.

Item 8. Supply Facilities

The approved plan for the new Cedar Lake Settlement will be zoned for residential, commercial and industrial use. We recommend that retail outlets shall be provided for on the Indian Reserve and undertake to place a reservation against vacant provincial land within a five (5) mile radius of the Cedar Lake Settlement against occupancy except after consultation with the Indian Affairs Branch.

Item 9. Recreation

We will turn over to the community our prefabricated building and move it on to a suitable site after it has served our needs in 1965. Sports grounds will be developed in connection with the new townsite.

Item 10. Cemeteries

The wishes of the Bishop of Brandon will be met in respect to the closing down of the Chemahawin cemeteries and the laying out of a new Anglican cemetery. Roman Catholic or other cemeteries, if needed, will be laid out and all will be made accessible by an all-weather road from the settlement.

Item 11. Hay and Pasture

It is anticipated that some hay and grazing will be available on shorelines on Collins Island and the mainland where clearing to 844' is done. We shall clear and sow to tame grass an area or areas sufficient to meet the balance of the hay and grazing needs of the people of Cedar Lake, based on the highest number of livestock owned by the people during the 5-year period prior to the spring of 1964, or if necessary and mutually agreed upon, we shall develop wagon trail access to wild hay lands. At any time that hay is in short supply, during the period that hay lands are being located or developed, the Forebay Committee will assist in the cost of meeting the hay requirements.

Item 12. Hunting, Trapping and Fishing

We shall continue our scientific and engineering studies and investigations in order to assure maximum economic development of the interior and fringe areas of the forebay for wildlife propagation. In connection with fishing we shall continue to:

(a) allow fishing for family use without charge, as in the past;

(b) give first preference for permits and licences to fishermen of Cedar Lake Settlement for commercial fishing in Cedar Lake, based on an economic operation;

(c) take necessary steps to maintain the commercial fishery on Cedar Lake, if forebay conditions reduce the population of desirable fish species, including a fish rearing plant if this is recommended by our biologists;

(d) In respect to hunting and trapping in the forebay and under R.T.L., some adjustments will be needed. In general, spring trapping in the forebay will be adversely affected. To compensate for this the Saskeram area west of The Pas is being improved and we are investigating improving Areas B, C and D, both sides of the Summerberry River. We anticipate that in future most of the spring trappers from The Pas can be accommodated on the Saskeram and the trappers from Cedar, Cormorant and Moose Lakes on Areas A, B, C and D in the forebay. Actual results will have to be observed before definite commitments can be made. In respect to R.T.L. we shall arrange meetings between individuals and communities for any adjustments requested. We have no plans to change the hunting arrangements now in effect. The request for changes in the R.T.L. boundaries made by the residents of Cedar Lake have been noted and we shall arrange for negotiations on these changes with the other communities affected.

Item 13. Industries

On behalf of the Government of Manitoba, we agree to take every step possible to maintain the income of the people of Chemahawin at the new site, with the advice and cooperation of Indian Affairs. To achieve this and to endeavour to improve the economy, we will undertake studies to determine what economic developments should take place and how any mutually agreed upon developments can be brought about.

Item 14. Health

A semi-modern nursing station will be built.

Item 15.

Land will be set aside to provide adequate nuisance grounds and community gardens, if the latter is requested and available, and truck access to these sites will be provided.

Item 16.

We will employ local labour, at prevailing wage rates for 'public works' listed in the Fair Wage schedule of the Province of Manitoba, as far as possible for house and other construction in the forebay, including work let under contract.

Item 17.

We will hand clear the mainland shoreline at the new settlement to elevation 844 for a distance of approximately four (4) miles southward from McKenzie Portage and that portion of Collins Island lying below elevation 844, if requested to do so by the residents of Cedar Lake Settlement.

Item 18.

We will:

(a) exchange all of the Chemahawin Indian Reserve (5,813 acres, more or less) for vacant provincial land lying above elevation 848' in one or more blocks on the basis of 2 acres of new reserve for 1 acre of the old; or

(b) make available vacant provincial land for a portion of the old on the basis of (a) and pay into Band Funds an amount of $6.00 per acre for the balance;

(c) in respect to any Indian lands acquired, retain the right to future rights-of-way for public works across such land. Manitoba agrees that the acreage contained in such rights-of-way will be replaced by an equal acreage to be mutually selected. In respect to the lands being retained in Block 32A, Manitoba will be relieved of all future liability.

(d) We neglected to discuss the matter of mineral rights owned by you under the present reserves and by Manitoba under reserves to be selected. It would be very serious if our negotiations over mineral rights delayed the completion of our dealings and I therefore recommend that we shall negotiate the mineral rights as soon as possible but that we agree in the meantime that if we can't agree by negotiation, the matter be brought to arbitration and that both parties agree now that the decision of the arbitration will be binding on both parties.

(e) survey the boundaries of the new reserve, more or less on the 848' contour where the new boundary lies along the shore of Cedar Lake, at provincial cost.

Item 19.

Grant conveyance of title of residential lots within the townsite, without charge to Métis on Crown lands, where new or reconditioned houses are provided by 1964.

Item 20. Economic Developments

(a) The Forebay Committee will pay $20,000 into the Band funds of the Cedar Lake Band.

(b) The Committee undertakes to have economic studies made to assist the future economy of the Cedar Lake Settlement and in consultation with Indian Affairs and a local advisory committee, on which the residents of Cedar Lake will be represented, will finance and institute programs which are considered to be sound.

The period this offer is effective will terminate on April 1, 1974.

On the basis of the foregoing undertakings, the Forebay Committee requests the Cedar Lake Band to pass a resolution accepting this offer for the exchange of land for the Cedar Lake Reserve lands required for forebay purposes, it being understood however, that the Cedar Lake Band will exclude from this exchange those portions of Indian Reserve Block 32A lying above elevation 848 contour. It is agreed that the band will choose a block of reserve comprising 2,000 acres more or less in Township 48, Ranges 16 and 17, W.P.M., part of which will comprise the new Cedar Lake townsite, the balance of the land to be acquired in exchange will be within the Grand Rapids West Forest Management Area to obtain suitable timber and hayland as mutually agreed upon.

Yours very truly,

S.W. Schortinghuis,
Chairman, Grand Rapids Forebay
Administration Committee

BAND COUNCIL RESOLUTION

Department of Citizenship and Immigration
Indian Affairs Branch
Band Council Resolution

The Council of the Chemawawin Band of Indians, in The Pas Indian Agency, in the Province of Manitoba at a meeting, held at Chemawawin Reserve this Fourteenth day of June A.D. 1962

DO HEREBY RESOLVE: in accordance with our Band Council Resolution of June 6th, 1962 wherein we agreed to transfer certain Reserve Lands to the Province of Manitoba under the terms and conditions outlined in Mr. S.W. Schortinghuis' letter of April 18th, 1962 and the amendments thereto of June 5th, 1962, attached hereto the original of a duly revised and amended letter of Mr. Schortinghuis dated June 7th, 1962 addressed Chief Donald Easter of our Band, countersigned by us, and which we agree to accept as the final and binding agreement between the Chemawawin Band and the Province of Manitoba providing the following amendments to Mr. Schortinghuis' letter of June 7th, 1962 are made and agreed to by the Province of Manitoba:-

1. Item 5, subsection (c) - Add, at the end of the second sentence, the words, "and after consultation with the residents of Cedar Lake."

2. Item 18, subsection (b) - To be deleted in its entirety.

3. Item 18, subsection (d) - To be deleted as the matter of mineral rights are beyond our understanding and ability to negotiate, and substitute the following:- "The negotiation of the mineral rights under Chemawawin Reserve Lands and under Provincial Crown Lands to be selected for Reserve Lands is placed in the hands of the Indian Affairs Branch who will act on behalf of the Chemawawin Band.

4. Item 18, subsection (e) - To be deleted and the following substituted: "The manner of survey of the boundaries of the Reserve Lands to be retained in Reserve No. 32A and new Reserve Lands to be obtained will be at the discretion of the Surveyor General of Canada."

"Robert Mink"	"Donald Easter"	"William Captain"
(Councillor)	(Chief)	(Councillor)

ORDER OF PRIVY COUNCIL

P.C. 1962-1617
Canada
Privy Council
At the Government House at Ottawa
Thursday, the 15th day of November, 1962

Present:

His Excellency

The Governor General in Council:

WHEREAS the Minister of Mines and Natural Resources for the Province of Manitoba has applied for the Indian Reserve lands described in the attached Schedule, required for a large hydro electric power development on the Saskatchewan River at Grand Rapids, which necessitates the flooding of a large area of land, including these Reserve lands held for three separate Bands of Indians, namely Chemahawin, Moose Lake and The Pas;

AND WHEREAS the flooding of the Reserve and other lands makes it necessary to relocate the whole of the Chemahawin Band and a number of families of the Moose Lake Band, while none of The Pas Indians are disturbed; but the general economy of all three Bands is adversely affected through the loss of trapping areas, fishing waters, forestry products and haylands, which form their principal means of livelihood;

AND WHEREAS an agreement has been reached between the Province and the Chemahawin and Moose Lake Bands of Indians on the terms for payment of compensation, and this agreement has been detailed in an exchange of letters between the said Minister and the Minister of Citizenship and Immigration dated October 1, 1962 and October 16, 1962 respectively, which agreement makes provision for the resettlement of the Indians and, among other things, provides for an exchange of land on the basis of one acre of Indian Reserve land for two acres of Provincial Crown land (mines and minerals are to be exchanged on an acre-for-acre basis), along with an immediate cash payment of Twenty Thousand ($20,000) Dollars to the Chemahawin Band and Ten Thousand ($10,000) Dollars to the Moose Lake Band;

AND WHEREAS the Council of the Chemahawin Band of Indians, by resolution dated June 14, 1962, and the Council of the Moose Lake Band of Indians, by resolution dated June 12, 1962, approved and confirmed their said respective agreements with the Province of Manitoba.

THEREFORE, His Excellency the Governor General in Council, on the recommendation of the Minister of Citizenship and Immigration, pursuant to Section 35 of the Indian Act, is pleased hereby to consent to the taking of the land described as Parcels One and Two in the Schedule hereto, subject to the terms and conditions set out in the said exchange of letters, the administration and control thereof to be transferred to Her Majesty in right of the Province of Manitoba upon: (a) payment by the Province of the sum of Thirty Thousand ($30,000) Dollars; (b) conveyance by the Province to Her Majesty in right of Canada of an area of land acceptable to the said Indians, containing twice the acreage of the said two parcels, together with mines and minerals underlying one-half of the total area so to be conveyed by the Province, and subject to the reversion of that portion of the said Parcel One in Block A which is not flooded, together with all mines and minerals underlying the same, for the use and benefit of the Chemahawin Band of Indians.

Certified to be a true copy.

"R.B. Bryce"
Clerk of the Privy Council.

APPENDIX 3

Manitoba Hydro's 1969 Compensation Proposal for South Indian Lake

Manitoba Hydro's 1969 Compensation Proposal For South Indian Lake (as read at the Public Hearing on Manitoba Hydro's Proposal for the Churchill River Diversion, South Indian Lake, 7 January 1969, by the Assistant General Manager of Manitoba Hydro, Kris Kristjanson).

Manitoba recognizes a responsibility to compensate the residents of Southern Indian Lake [sic] who are displaced or otherwise suffer damage through the raising of the level of South Indian Lake [sic]. The following areas of responsibility are recognized:

First we would be prepared to move or replace with equivalent structures the houses and related outbuildings, the stores, buildings, churches and related buildings and schools at or to the location selected for the new community. Wherever necessary new homes would be built to a standard at least comparable to the standards of homes being built in northern settlements by the Department of Indian Affairs in such communities as Split Lake. Now I would like to emphasize at this point that when the people of this community, through their relocation committee and through their legal counsel, have decided where they wish to move we would be prepared to discuss the arrangement that would best meet the needs of the people of this community within the framework of this general statement.

Manitoba Hydro would also be prepared to provide new docking facilities at the new site.

We would be prepared to replace or pay for the fish camps belonging to the residents of Southern Indian Lake [sic] and Granville Lake which will be flooded.

We would also be prepared to clear the area for the new site and provide access from the lake to the new fish camps.

Manitoba Hydro would pay the cost of moving the people that would be displaced by the raising of the water levels, and their personal effects.

You will remember that when we were here on April 21st to 22nd someone I think asked what consideration we would give to the graves. At that time we said that we would give every consideration to whatever the people of this community decided is the right and proper thing to do. We are prepared to move and/or suitably mark existing graves which will be affected by the raising of the water levels. Here again I would like to emphasize that we would want to work out arrangements that are suitable to the people of this community.

In addition to these responsibilities Manitoba Hydro is prepared to work with other appropriate government agencies to provide electric service to the new community – on the standards which now apply in other comparable communities like Island Lake.

We are prepared to share with other appropriate government agencies to the extent of $60,000 the cost of constructing a floating fish plant to be used on Southern Indian Lake. Some people have talked about a fish plant which could be on floats and operated by diesel power with a freezing plant so that you could catch the fish, clean it, fillet it, quick freeze it and package it ready for marketing and as I say Manitoba Hydro is willing to pay up to $60,000 towards the cost of that.

We are also prepared to work with other appropriate government agencies providing training programmes for the people that work at Missi Falls or Notigi Falls.

We are also prepared to work with other agencies or appropriate government agencies to provide Adult Education.

We are also willing to provide under mutually satisfactory arrangements, a boat equipped with an electronic depth and fish detector. That boat can be made available now.

Now let me again say that Manitoba Hydro is very anxious to work with members of the Relocation Committee and the legal counsel for the people of this community to work out a fair and reasonable settlement for the people of this community. Thank you very much.

Bibliography

Bartlett, Richard H. "Indian and Native Rights in Uranium Development in Northern Saskatchewan." *Saskatchewan Law Review* 45, no. 1 (1980): 13–51.
_____. "Indian Water Rights on the Prairies." *Manitoba Law Journal* 11, no. 1 (1980): 59–90.
Berger, Thomas R. *Northern Frontier, Northern Homeland. The Report of the Mackenzie Valley Pipeline Inquiry.* 2 vols. Ottawa: Supply and Services, 1977.
Bourassa, Robert. *Power from the North.* New York: Simon and Schuster, 1986.
Brody, Hugh. *Maps and Dreams: Indians and the British Columbia Frontier.* 1981. Reprint. Harmondsworth, England: Pelican, 1983.
Brokensha, David, and Thayer Scudder. "Resettlement." In *Dams in Africa*, edited by N. Rubin and W. Warren, 20–62. New York: A.M. Kelly, 1968.
Brown, George, and Ron Maguire. "Indian Treaties in Historical Perspective." In *Native People in Canada: Contemporary Conflicts*, edited by James S. Frideres, 34–80. Scarborough: Prentice-Hall, 1983.
Canada. *Treaty No. 11 (June 27, 1921) and Adhesion (July 17, 1922) with Reports, etc.* Ottawa: Queen's Printer, 1957.
_____. *Copy of Treaty No. 6 between Her Majesty the Queen and the Plain and Wood Cree Indians and Other Tribes of Indians at Fort Carlton, Fort Pitt and Battle River, with Adhesions.* Ottawa: Queen's Printer, 1964.
_____. *The James Bay Treaty. Treaty No. 9.* Ottawa: Queen's Printer, 1964.
_____. *Treaty No. 8, Made June 21, 1899, and Adhesions, Reports, etc.* Ottawa: Queen's Printer, 1966.
_____. *Treaty No. 10 and Reports of Commissioners.* Ottawa: Queen's Printer, 1966.
_____. *Treaty No. 5 between Her Majesty the Queen and the Saulteaux and Swampy Cree Tribes of Indians at Beren's River and Norway House, with Adhesions.* Ottawa: Queen's Printer, 1969.
_____. Department of Regional Economic Expansion. Prairie Farm Rehabilitation Administration. *Cumberland Lake Water Level Control Study,* 1977.
Chamberlin, J.E. *The Harrowing of Eden: White Attitudes toward North American Natives.* Toronto: Fitzhenry and Whiteside, 1975.

Chambers, Robert. *The Volta Resettlement Experience.* New York: Praeger, 1970.

Charest, Paul. "Hydroelectric Dam Construction and the Foraging Activities of Eastern Quebec Montagnais." In *Politics and History in Band Societies,* edited by Eleanor Leacock and Richard Lee, 413–426. Cambridge: Cambridge University Press, 1982.

_____. "Les Barrages hydro-électrique en territoire montagnais et leurs effets sur les communautes amérindiennes." *Recherches amérindiennes au Québec* 9, no. 4 (1980): 323–337.

Churchill River Board of Inquiry. *Report.* Saskatoon: Churchill River Board of Inquiry, 1978.

Coates, K.S., and W.R. Morrison. "More Than a Matter of Blood: The Federal Government, the Churches and the Mixed Blood Populations of the Yukon and the Mackenzie River Valley, 1890–1950." In *1885 and After: Native Society in Transition,* edited by F. Laurie Barron and James B. Waldram, 253–277. Regina: Canadian Plains Research Center, 1986.

_____. *Treaty Research Report: Treaty Five.* Ottawa: Treaties and Historical Research Centre, Indian and Northern Affairs Canada, forthcoming.

Collinson, J.D. "Social and Economic Impact of the Nelson River Hydro Development (with Emphasis on South Indian Lake)." In *Lake Winnipeg, Churchill and Nelson Rivers Study Board,* Social and Economic Studies, vol. 2-C, Technical Report Appendix 8.

Colson, Elizabeth. *The Social Consequences of Resettlement: The Impact of the Kariba Resettlement upon the Gwembe Tonga.* Manchester: Manchester University Press, 1971.

Committee on Saskatchewan River Delta Problems. *Resources, Development and Problems of the Saskatchewan River Delta.* Regina: Committee on Saskatchewan River Delta Problems, 1972.

Cumming, Peter A., and Neil H. Mickenberg. *Native Rights in Canada.* 2nd ed. Toronto: General Publishing, 1972.

Damas and Smith Consultants Ltd. *Cumberland House Development Plan.* Winnipeg: Damas and Smith, 1980.

Daniel, Richard. "The Spirit and Terms of Treaty Eight." In *The Spirit of the Alberta Indian Treaties,* edited by Richard Price, 47–100. Montreal: Institute for Research on Public Policy, 1979.

Daugherty, W.E. *Treaty Research Report: Treaty One and Treaty Two.* Ottawa: Treaties and Historical Research Centre, Indian and Northern Affairs, 1983.

Diamond, Billy. "Aboriginal Rights: The James Bay Experience." In *The Quest for Justice: Aboriginal Peoples and Aboriginal Rights,* edited by Menno Boldt and J. Anthony Long, 265–285. Toronto: University of Toronto Press, 1985.

Duckworth, H.E. *Reconnaissance Study of the Effect on Human and Natural Resources of the Churchill River Diversion Plans.* Winnipeg: 1967.

Federation of Saskatchewan Indians. *Aski-Puko (The Land Alone).* A report on the expected effects of the proposed hydro-electric installation at Wintego Rapids upon the Cree of the Peter Ballantyne and Lac la Ronge bands. Regina: Federation of Saskatchewan Indians, 1976.

Feit, Harvey. "Political Articulations of Hunters to the State: Means of Resisting Threats to Subsistence Production in the James Bay and Northern Quebec Agreement." *Etudes/Inuit/Studies* 3, no. 2 (1979): 37–52.

_____. "Negotiating Recognition of Aboriginal Rights: History, Strategies and

Reactions to the James Bay and Northern Quebec Agreement." *Canadian Journal of Anthropology* 1, no. 2 (1980): 159–172.

————. "The Future of Hunters within Nation-States: Anthropology and the James Bay Cree." In *Politics and History in Band Societies*, edited by Eleanor Leacock and Richard Lee, 373–411. Cambridge: Cambridge University Press, 1982.

Flanagan, Thomas. *Riel and the Rebellion: 1885 Reconsidered.* Saskatoon: Western Producer Prairie Books, 1983.

Foster, John E. "The Métis: The People and the Term." *Prairie Forum* 3 (1978): 79–90.

Frank, André Gunder. *Lumpenbourgeoisie: Lumpendevelopment. Dependence, Class and Politics in Latin America.* New York: Monthly Review Press, 1972.

Fumoleau, René. *As Long as the Land Shall Last.* Toronto: McClelland and Stewart, 1973.

Gill, Don, and Alan Cooke. "Hydroelectric Developments in Northern Canada: A Comparison with the Churchill River Project in Saskatchewan." *Musk-Ox* 15 (1975): 35–56.

Gillespie, Beryl C. "Major Fauna in the Traditional Economy." In *Handbook of North American Indians, Vol. 6: Subarctic,* edited by June Helm, 15–18. Washington, DC: Smithsonian Institution, 1981.

Gorrie, Peter. "Harnessing the Mighty Slave." *Maclean's* 95, no. 36 (1982): 14.

Hanson, A., and A. Oliver-Smith, eds. *Involuntary Migration and Resettlement: The Problems and Responses of Dislocated People.* Boulder, CO: Westview Press, 1982.

Hartt, Mr. Justice E.P. *Royal Commission on the Northern Environment – Issues Report.* Toronto: Royal Commission on the Northern Environment, 1978.

Harvey, Michael. *Impacts of Hydro Projects on Indian Lands in Western Canada: Indian Strategies.* Ottawa: Indian and Northern Affairs Canada, 1984.

Hatt, Ken. "The Northwest Scrip Commissions as Federal Policy – Some Initial Findings." *Canadian Journal of Native Studies* 3, no. 1 (1983): 117–149.

————. "The North-West Rebellion Scrip Commissions, 1885–1889." In *1885 and After: Native Society in Transition,* edited by F. Laurie Barron and James B. Waldram, 189–204. Regina: Canadian Plains Research Center, 1986.

Helm, June. "Introduction." In *Handbook of North American Indians, Vol. 6: Subarctic,* edited by June Helm, 1–4. Washington, DC: Smithsonian Institution, 1981.

Henry, Chief John. "It is No Longer Possible to Be an Indian." *Maclean's* 84, no. 6 (1971): 47–48.

Hickling-Johnston Management Consultants. *Interventions in Support of Indian and Inuit People.* Ottawa: DIAND, 1979.

Jacobson, Solomon J. *Social Adjustment to a Public Power Project: An Analysis of the Resettlement of the Chemawawin Bands.* Report prepared for the Federal-Provincial Coordinating Committee on Indian and Métis Affairs, 1966.

Keeper, Joe. *A Short Report on Cedar Lake.* Unpublished report, 1963.

Kew, J.E.M. *Cumberland House in 1960.* Saskatoon: Institute for Northern Studies, 1962.

Lagassé, Jean H. *The People of Indian Ancestry in Manitoba.* 3 vols. Winnipeg: Manitoba Department of Agriculture and Immigration, 1959.

_____. "Community Development in Manitoba." *Human Organization* 20 (1961): 232–237.

Lake Winnipeg, Churchill and Nelson Rivers Study Board. *The Chemahawin Relocation.* Social and Economic Studies, vol. 2, app. 8, appendix H (1974): 220–252.

Landa, Michael J. "Easterville: A Case Study in the Relocation of a Manitoba Native Community." Thesis, University of Manitoba, 1969.

Mailhot, P.R., and D.N. Sprague, "Persistent Settlers: The Dispersal and Resettlement of the Red River Métis, 1870–1885." *Canadian Ethnic Studies* 17, no. 2 (1985): 1–30.

Manitoba. *Northern Flood Agreement.* Winnipeg: 1977.

Manitoba Hydro. *Manitoba Power: The Hydro Advantage.* Winnipeg: Manitoba Hydro, n.d.

_____. *Grand Rapids.* Winnipeg: Manitoba Hydro, n.d.

_____. Property Department. *Registered Trapline Program.* Winnipeg: Manitoba Hydro, 1975.

_____. Property Department. *Commercial Fishermen's Assistance Program.* Winnipeg: Manitoba Hydro, 1978.

Manuel, George. *Aboriginal People of Canada and Their Environment.* Ottawa: National Indian Brotherhood, 1973.

Matthiasson, John S. "Caught in the Middle: Two Cree Communities and the Southern Indian Lake Hydro Power Controversy." *International Congress of Americanists* 11 (1972): 593–601.

McLean, Donald. "1885: Métis Rebellion or Government Conspiracy." In *1885 and After: Native Society in Transition,* edited by F. Laurie Barron and James B. Waldram, 79–104. Regina: Canadian Plains Research Center, 1986.

_____. *1885: Métis Rebellion or Government Conspiracy?* Winnipeg: Pemmican, 1985.

McNab, David T. "Métis Participation in the Treaty-Making Process in Ontario: A Reconnaissance." *Native Studies Review* 1, no. 2 (1985): 57–79.

Michael, B.E. *Effect of Limitations to the Squaw Rapids Discharge on the Operation of the Saskatchewan Power Corporation System.* Regina: Saskatchewan Power Corporation, 1976.

Morris, Alexander. *The Treaties of Canada with the Indians.* 1880. Reprint. Toronto: Coles Publishing Co., 1979.

Morton, W.L. *Manitoba: A History,* 2nd ed. Toronto: University of Toronto Press, 1967.

Mulgrew, Ian. "Land of Power and Glory." *Report on Business Magazine* (March 1986): 37–40.

Muller, R.A., and P.J. George. *Evaluating the Environmental Impact of Hydroelectric Development in Northern Ontario: A Preliminary Report.* Hamilton: Program for Technology Assessment in Subarctic Ontario, McMaster University, 1982.

Newbury, Robert W., and Gerald Malaher. *The Destruction of Manitoba's Last Great River.* Ottawa: Canadian Nature Federation, 1973.

Newbury, Robert W. "Return to the Rivers of Discovery of Western Canada." *Landscape Planning* 6 (1979): 237–248.

Nicholls, W.G. *Aishihik: The Politics of Hydro Planning in the Yukon.* Ottawa: Canadian Arctic Resources Committee, 1981.

Nichols, Mark. "Selling Canadian Power to the States." *Maclean's* 99, no. 7 (1986): 10–12.

Paine, Robert, ed. *Patrons and Brokers in the Eastern Arctic.* St. John's, Newfoundland: Institute of Social and Economic Research, Memorial University of Newfoundland, 1971.

Panel of Public Enquiry Into Northern Hydro Development. *Report.* Appendix A. Transcript of Hearings, 22 Sept. 1975. Winnipeg, 1975.

Peterson, Jacqueline, and Jennifer S.H. Brown, eds. *The New Peoples: Being and Becoming Métis in North America.* Winnipeg: University of Manitoba Press, 1985.

Poppe, Roger. "Where Will all the Natives Go?" *Western Canadian Journal of Anthropology* 2, no. 1 (1970): 164–175.

Purich, Donald. *Our Land: Native Rights in Canada.* Toronto: Lorimer, 1986.

Raby, S. "Indian Treaty No. 5 and The Pas Agency, Saskatchewan, NWT." *Saskatchewan History* 25, no. 3 (1972): 92–114.

Ray, Arthur J. *Indians in the Fur Trade: Their Role as Hunters, Trappers and Middlemen in the Lands Southwest of Hudson Bay, 1660–1870.* Toronto: University of Toronto Press, 1974.

Reid, Dale. "Identity and Adaptation to Community and Economic Change among the Southend Cree." Thesis, University of Saskatchewan, 1984.

Richardson, Boyce. *Strangers Devour the Land.* 1975. Reprint. Toronto: Macmillan, 1977.

Salisbury, Richard F. *A Homeland for the Cree: Regional Development in James Bay, 1971–1981.* Kingston and Montreal: McGill-Queens University Press, 1986.

Sanders, Douglas E. *Native People in Areas of Internal National Expansion: Indians and Inuit in Canada.* Copenhagen: International Workgroup for Indigenous Affairs, No. 14, 1973.

Saskatchewan. Department of Tourism and Renewable Resources. *Cumberland House Historic Park.* Regina: Department of Tourism and Renewable Resources, n.d.

Saskatchewan Power Corporation. *The Squaw Rapids Story.* Regina: Saskatchewan Power Corporation, n.d.

Sealey, D. Bruce, "Statutory Land Rights of the Manitoba Métis." In *The Other Natives, Vol. 2,* edited by A.S. Lussier and D.B. Sealey, 1–30. Winnipeg: Manitoba Métis Federation, 1978.

Shawinigan Consultants Inc. "Augmented Flows at Southern Indian Lake. An Analysis of the Water Regime and the Feasibility of an Environmental Impact Assessment." Final report to Manitoba Department of Northern Affairs. Winnipeg: 1987.

Shkilnyk, Anastasia M. *A Poison Stronger than Love: The Destruction of an Ojibwa Community.* New Haven: Yale University Press, 1985.

Shouldice, Michael. "A Discussion of the Political Framework of Resource Development in Relation to Native People. The Nelson River Hydroelectric Project: A Case Study." Thesis, University of Manitoba, 1976.

Smith, Doug. "The Shaping of Limestone." *Maclean's* 99, no. 32 (1986): 34–36.

Smith, James G.E. "Preliminary Notes on the Rocky Cree of Reindeer Lake." In *Contributions to Canadian Ethnology,* Mercury Series Paper No. 31, 171–185. Ottawa: National Museum of Man, 1975.

_____. "Leadership among the Indians of the Northern Woodlands." In *Currents in Anthropology: Essays in Honour of Sol Tax,* edited by Robert Hinshaw, 305–324. The Hague: Mouton, 1979.

_____. "Chipewyan, Cree and Inuit Relations West of Hudson Bay, 1714–1955." *Ethnohistory* 28, no. 2 (1981): 133–156.

_____. "Western Woods Cree." In *Handbook of North American Indians, Vol. 6: Subarctic,* edited by June Helm, 256–270. Washington, DC: Smithsonian Institution, 1981.

Sprague, D.N. "The Manitoba Land Question, 1870–1882." *Journal of Canadian Studies* 15, no. 3 (1980): 74–84.

Stanley, George F.G. *The Birth of Western Canada: A History of the Riel Rebellions.* Toronto: University of Toronto Press, 1961.

Taylor, John L. "Two Views on the Meaning of Treaties Six and Seven." In *The Spirit of the Alberta Indian Treaties,* edited by Richard Price, 9–45. Montreal: Institute for Research on Public Policy, 1979.

_____. "An Historical Introduction to Métis Claims in Canada." *Canadian Journal of Native Studies* 3, no. 1 (1983): 151–181.

Tobias, John L. "Canada's Subjugation of the Plains Cree, 1979–1885." Canadian *Historical Review* 64, no. 4 (1983): 519–548.

_____. "The Origins of the Treaty Rights Movement in Saskatchewan." In *1885 and After: Native Society in Transition,* edited by F. Laurie Barron and James B. Waldram, 241–252. Regina: Canadian Plains Research Center, 1986.

Tough, Frank. "Changes to the Native Economy of Northern Manitoba in the Post-Treaty Period: 1870–1900." *Native Studies Review* 1, no. 1 (1984): 40–66.

de Tremaudan, A.-H. *Hold High Your Heads: History of the Métis Nation in Western Canada.* Winnipeg: Pemmican Publications, 1982.

Tritschler, G. *Commission of Inquiry into Manitoba Hydro.* Final report. Winnipeg: 1979.

Troyer, Warner. *No Safe Place.* Toronto: Clarke, Irwin and Co., 1977.

Van Ginkel Associates, in association with Hedlin, Menzies and Associates. *Transition in the North: The Churchill River Diversion and the People of South Indian Lake.* Winnipeg: Manitoba Development Authority, 1967.

Waldram, James B. "Relocation and Social Change in a Manitoba Native Community." Thesis, University of Manitoba, 1980.

_____. "Relocation and Political Change in a Manitoba Native Community." *Canadian Journal of Anthropology* 1, no. 2 (1980): 173–178.

_____. "The Impact of Hydroelectric Development upon a Northern Manitoba Native Community." Dissertation, University of Connecticut, 1983.

_____. "Manitoba's Hydro Employment Program for Native Northerners." *Native Studies Review* 1, no. 2 (1985): 47–56.

_____. "The 'Other Side': Ethnostatus Distinctions in Western Subarctic Native Communities." In *1885 and After: Native Society in Transition,* edited by F. Laurie Barron and James B. Waldram, 279–295. Regina: Canadian Plains Research Center, 1986.

Weaver, Sally M. "Federal Policy-Making for Métis and Non-Status Indians in the Context of Native Policy." *Canadian Ethnic Studies* 17, no. 2 (1985): 80–102.

Weitz, J. *Grand Rapids Forebay Land Exchange.* Draft. Ottawa: Department of Indian Affairs, 1978.

White, Clinton O. *Power for a Province: A History of Saskatchewan Power.* Regina: Canadian Plains Research Center, 1976.

Willard, J.R., W.W. Sawchyn, D.A. Meyer, J.E. Polson and D. Russell. *Environmental Implications of the Proposed Water Level Control Program for Cumberland Lake.* Saskatoon: Saskatchewan Research Council, 1978.

Wolford, Jim. "Aishihik River – An Unfortunate Precedent," *Northern Perspectives* 1, no. 5 (1973): 2.

Wright, James V. "Cree Culture History in the Southern Indian Lake Region." In *Contributions to Anthropology VII: Archaeology, Bulletin 232,* 1–31. Ottawa: National Museum of Canada, 1968.

Zlotkin, Norman K., and Donald R. Colborne. "Internal Canadian Imperialism and the Native People." In *Imperialism, Nationalism and Canada,* edited by Craig Herron, 170–171. Toronto: New Hogtown Press, 1977.

Zlotkin, Norman K. "Post-Confederation Treaties." In *Aboriginal Peoples and the Law: Indian, Métis and Inuit Rights in Canada,* edited by Brad Morse, 272–407. Ottawa: Carleton University Press, 1985.

Notes

CHAPTER 1

1 *Easterville Brief.* Presented at meeting with Manitoba Hydro, 30 Sept. 1975.
2 Personal interview with Cumberland House resident, 14 July 1984.
3 Throughout this book, the term *Native* will be employed to describe *Indians* and *Métis* collectively. Where necessary, specific references to these groups and others (such as *non-status Indians*) will be made.
4 André Gunder Frank, *Lumpenbourgeoisie: Lumpendevelopment. Dependence, Class and Politics in Latin America* (New York: Monthly Review Press, 1972), preface.
5 Leroy Little Bear, "The Aboriginal Conception of Water Rights," Aboriginal Water Rights Workshop, Native Law Centre, Saskatoon, 2 Oct. 1986.
6 See: Richard H. Bartlett, "Indian Water Rights on the Prairies," *Manitoba Law Journal* 11, no. 1 (1980): 59–90.
7 Among other effects, hydro projects have frequently disrupted the water regimes of rivers and lakes, making travel in both summer and winter more unpredictable and dangerous. Deaths from motor boat collisions with floating debris, or from snowmobile accidents on thin ice, have been recorded.
8 In other countries, particularly those of the Third World, hydro projects have necessitated the relocation of entire regions of people. See: David Brokensha and Thayer Scudder, "Resettlement," in *Dams in Africa,* ed. N. Rubin and W. Warren (New York: A.M. Kelly, 1968), 20–62; Robert Chambers, *The Volta Resettlement Experience* (New York: Praeger, 1970); Elizabeth Colson, *The Social Consequences of Resettlement: The Impact of the Kariba Resettlement upon the Gwembe Tonga* (Manchester: Manchester University Press, 1971); and, A. Hanson and A. Oliver-Smith, eds., *Involuntary Migration and Resettlement: The Problems and Responses of Dislocated People* (Boulder, CO: Westview Press, 1982).
9 *Alumni Journal,* University of Manitoba, n.d.
10 Manitoba Hydro, *Manitoba Power: The Hydro Advantage* (Winnipeg: Manitoba Hydro, n.d.).

11 South Indian Lake, in Manitoba, is a case in point. When the community was relocated as a result of the Churchill River Diversion, new housing was provided. The houses were poorly built and insulated, with installed electric heaters, and inappropriate for wood heating. As a result, people are now forced to pay monthly power bills that frequently exceed $250. Prior to the relocation, they had no electricity, and of course no power bills.

12 Douglas E. Sanders, *Native People in Areas of Internal National Expansion: Indians and Inuit in Canada* (Copenhagen: International Workgroup for Indigenous Affairs, no. 14, 1973), 10–14.

13 Billy Diamond, "Aboriginal Rights: The James Bay Experience," in *The Quest for Justice: Aboriginal Peoples and Aboriginal Rights*, ed. Menno Boldt and J. Anthony Long (Toronto: University of Toronto Press, 1985), 267.

14 Boyce Richardson, *Strangers Devour the Land* (1975; reprint, Toronto: Macmillan, 1977), 301.

15 Harvey Feit has written extensively on the Cree experience in the formation of the James Bay and Northern Quebec Agreement. See: "Political Articulations of Hunters to the State: Means of Resisting Threats to Subsistence Production in the James Bay and Northern Quebec Agreement," *Etudes/Inuit/Studies* 3, no. 2 (1979): 37–52; "Negotiating Recognition of Aboriginal Rights: History, Strategies and Reactions to the James Bay and Northern Quebec Agreement," *Canadian Journal of Anthropology* 1, no. 2 (1980): 159–172; "The Future of Hunters within Nation-States: Anthropology and the James Bay Cree," in *Politics and History in Band Societies*, ed. Eleanor Leacock and Richard Lee (Cambridge: Cambridge University Press, 1982), 373–411. See also: Richard F. Salisbury, *A Homeland for the Cree: Regional Development in James Bay 1971–1981* (Kingston and Montreal: McGill-Queens University Press, 1986.

16 Paul Charest, "Hydroelectric Dam Construction and the Foraging Activities of Eastern Quebec Montagnais," in *Politics and History in Band Societies*, ed. Eleanor Leacock and Richard Lee (Cambridge University Press, 1982), 413–426; "Les Barrages hydro-électrique en territoire montagnais et leurs effets sur les communautes amérindiennes," *Recherches amérindiennes au Québec* 9, no. 4 (1980): 323–337.

17 For a comprehensive discussion of the methylmercury poisoning issue, see: Warner Troyer, *No Safe Place* (Toronto: Clarke, Irwin and Co., 1977); Anastasia M. Shkilnyk, *A Poison Stronger than Love: The Destruction of an Ojibwa Community* (New Haven: Yale University Press, 1985).

18 Justice E.P. Hartt, *Royal Commission on the Northern Environment – Issues Report* (Toronto: Royal Commission on the Northern Environment, 1978), 133–137.

19 Ibid., 136; Norman K. Zlotkin and Donald R. Colborne, "Internal Canadian Imperialism and the Native People," in *Imperialism, Nationalism and Canada*, ed. Craig Herron (Toronto: New Hogtown Press, 1977), 170–171; Peter Usher, personal communication, 27 Feb. 1987.

20 Shkilnyk, *A Poison Stronger than Love,* 137; Chief John Henry, "It Is No Longer Possible to Be an Indian," *Maclean's* 84, no. 6 (1971): 47–48.

21 R.A. Muller and P.J. George, *Evaluating the Environmental Impact of Hydroelectric Development in Northern Ontario: A Preliminary Report* (Hamilton:

Program for Technology Assessment in Subarctic Ontario, McMaster University, 1982), 2–3.

22 See: James B. Waldram, "Relocation and Social Change in a Manitoba Native Community" (Thesis, University of Manitoba, 1980); also, Chapter 4 of this volume.

23 See: James B. Waldram, "The Impact of Hydroelectric Development upon a Northern Manitoba Native Community" (Dissertation, University of Connecticut, 1983); also, Chapter 5 of this volume.

24 Doug Smith, "The Shaping of Limestone," *Maclean's* 99, no. 32 (1986): 34–35.

25 For a critique of the Limestone hiring policy, see: James B. Waldram, "Manitoba's Hydro Employment Program for Native Northerners," *Native Studies Review* 1, no. 2 (1985): 47–56.

26 Dale Reid, "Identity and Adaptation to Community and Economic Change among the Southend Cree" (Thesis, University of Saskatchewan, 1984), 33.

27 Richard H. Bartlett, "Indian and Native Rights in Uranium Development in Northern Saskatchewan," *Saskatchewan Law Review* 45, no. 1 (1980): 39–40.

28 *New Breed Journal*, Dec. 1983, 9–10.

29 Reid, "Identity and Adaptation," 366–375.

30 Don Gill and Alan Cooke, "Hydroelectric Developments in Northern Canada: A Comparison with the Churchill River Project in Saskatchewan," *Musk-Ox* 15 (1975): 35–56.

31 Now known as the Federation of Saskatchewan Indian Nations, they produced an excellent report conveying the Indian view of the proposed dam in specific, and northern development in general. See: FSI, *Aski-Puko (The Land Alone)* (Regina: FSI, 1976); Churchill River Board of Inquiry, *Report* (Saskatoon: Churchill River Board of Inquiry, 1978).

32 *Saskatoon Star-Phoenix,* 8 Aug. 1986.

33 Sanders, *Native People in Areas of Internal National Expansion,* 10; George Manuel, *Aboriginal People of Canada and Their Environment* (Ottawa: National Indian Brotherhood, 1973), 8.

34 Roger Poppe, "Where Will all the Natives Go?" *Western Canadian Journal of Anthropology* 2, no. 1 (1970): 166.

35 *Saskatoon Star-Phoenix,* 25 April 1985.

36 Peter Gorrie, "Harnessing the Mighty Slave," *Maclean's* 95, no. 36 (1982): 14.

37 Michael Harvey, *Impacts of Hydro Projects on Indian Lands in Western Canada: Indian Strategies* (Ottawa: Indian and Northern Affairs Canada, 1984): 26.

38 Ibid., 31–32.

39 Ibid., 29. Specific Claim for Compensation Filed by Cheslatta Indian Band to the Office of Native Claims, 21 April 1984.

40 Specific Claim, Letter of Transmittal, 1.

41 *Globe and Mail,* 4 Nov. 1985.

42 Gill and Cooke, "Hydroelectric Developments in Northern Canada, 53.

43 Hugh Brody, *Maps and Dreams: Indians and the British Columbia Frontier* (1981; reprint, Harmondsworth, England: Pelican, 1983), 134.

44 Ibid.

45 Harvey, *Impacts of Hydro Projects,* 23.

46 Statement of Claim No. 4955, in the Supreme Court of British Columbia, 16 Oct. 1970; Sanders, *Native People in Areas of Internal National Expansion,* 10.

47 Harvey, *Impacts of Hydro Projects,* 25.
48 Gill and Cooke, "Hydroelectric Developments in Northern Canada," 53.
49 Jim Wolford, "Aishihik River – An Unfortunate Precedent," *Northern Perspectives* 1, no. 5 (1973): 2.
50 W.G. Nicholls, *Aishihik: The Politics of Hydro Planning in the Yukon* (Ottawa: Canadian Arctic Resources Committee, 1981), 84.

CHAPTER 2

1 A.G. Jackes, Secretary to the Treaty Six Commission, quoting Lieutenant-Governor Alexander Morris at Fort Carlton treaty signing with the Plains Cree, 18 Aug. 1876; cited in Alexander Morris, *The Treaties of Canada with the Indians* (1880; reprint, Toronto: Coles Publishing Co., 1979), 202.
2 June Helm, "Introduction," in *Handbook of North American Indians, Vol. 6: Subarctic,* ed. June Helm (Washington, DC: Smithsonian Institution, 1981), 1.
3 Ibid.
4 Beryl C. Gillespie, "Major Fauna in the Traditional Economy," in *Handbook of North American Indians, Vol. 6: Subarctic,* ed. June Helm (Washington, DC: Smithsonian Institution, 1981), 16.
5 The Northern Ojibwa now refer to themselves as the *Anicinabe;* the Montagnais refer to themselves as the *Attikamek*; and the Naskapi refer to themselves as the *Innu.*
6 James G.E. Smith, "Western Woods Cree," in *Handbook of North American Indians, Vol. 6: Subarctic,* ed. June Helm (Washington, DC: Smithsonian Institution, 1981), 256.
7 Ibid., 259.
8 James G.E. Smith, "Leadership among the Indians of the Northern Woodlands," in *Currents in Anthropology: Essays in Honour of Sol Tax,* ed. Robert Hinshaw (The Hague: Mouton, 1979), 305.
9 James G.E. Smith, "Western Woods Cree," 259.
10 Arthur J. Ray, *Indians in the Fur Trade: Their Role as Hunters, Trappers and Middlemen in the Lands Southwest of Hudson Bay, 1660–1870* (Toronto: University of Toronto Press, 1974), 139–141.
11 For a discussion of the patron-broker-client relationship as it developed and operates among northern Indians and Inuit, see the various papers in: Robert Paine, ed., *Patrons and Brokers in the Eastern Arctic* (St. John's, Newfoundland: Institute of Social and Economic Research, Memorial University of Newfoundland, 1971).
12 René Fumoleau, *As Long as the Land Shall Last* (Toronto: McClelland and Stewart, 1973), 8.
13 For a good discussion of these early treaties, see: George Brown and Ron Maguire, "Indian Treaties in Historical Perspective," in *Native People in Canada: Contemporary Conflicts,* ed. James S. Frideres (Scarborough: Prentice-Hall, 1983), 34–80.
14 Peter A. Cumming and Neil H. Mickenberg, *Native Rights in Canada,* 2nd ed. (Toronto: General Publishing, 1972), 30.
15 "Excerpts from the Royal Proclamation of 1763," in Peter A. Cumming and Neil H. Mickenberg, *Native Rights in Canada,* 2nd ed. (Toronto: General Publishing, 1972), 291–292.

16 Ibid.
17 Cumming and Mickenberg, *Native Rights in Canada*, 149.
18 Brown and Maguire, "Indian Treaties in Historical Perspective," 58.
19 Norman K. Zlotkin, "Post-Confederation Treaties," in *Aboriginal Peoples and the Law: Indian, Métis and Inuit Rights in Canada*, ed. Brad Morse (Ottawa: Carleton University Press, 1985), 273.
20 Morris, *The Treaties of Canada*, 17.
21 Ibid., 16.
22 Zlotkin, "Post-Confederation Treaties," 273.
23 John L. Tobias, "Canada's Subjugation of the Plains Cree, 1879–1885," *Canadian Historical Review* 64, no. 4 (1983): 520.
24 Ken Hatt, "The Northwest Scrip Commissions as Federal Policy – Some Initial Findings," *Canadian Journal of Native Studies* 3, no. 1 (1983): 119; see also, Donald McLean, "1885: Métis Rebellion or Government Conspiracy," in *1885 and After: Native Society in Transition*, ed. F. Laurie Barron and James B. Waldram (Regina: Canadian Plains Research Center, 1986), 79–104.
25 See: George F.G. Stanley, *The Birth of Western Canada: A History of the Riel Rebellions* (Toronto: University of Toronto Press, 1961); A.-H. de Tremaudan, *Hold High Your Heads: History of the Métis Nation in Western Canada* (Winnipeg: Pemmican Publications, 1982). Although many historians and others have often referred to the events of 1869/70 as a "rebellion," there has been some suggestion that Riel's actions were perfectly legal. See: Donald Purich, *Our Land: Native Rights in Canada* (Toronto: Lorimer, 1986), 161.
26 Morris, *The Treaties of Canada*, 170.
27 Cumming and Mickenberg, *Native Rights in Canada*, 149.
28 Ibid., 123.
29 Brown and Maguire, "Indian Treaties in Historical Perspective," 66.
30 John L. Taylor, "Two Views on the Meaning of Treaties Six and Seven," in *The Spirit of the Alberta Indian Treaties*, ed. Richard Price (Montreal: Institute for Research on Public Policy, 1979), 15.
31 Zlotkin, "Post-Confederation Treaties," 275.
32 W.E. Daugherty, *Treaty Research Report: Treaty One and Treaty Two* (Ottawa: Treaties and Historical Research Centre, Indian and Northern Affairs, 1983), 10.
33 Morris, *The Treaties of Canada*, 29.
34 See: ibid., 126–127.
35 Ibid., 45.
36 Ibid.
37 Ibid., 59.
38 Ibid., 61.
39 Ibid.
40 Ibid., 62.
41 Brown and Maguire, "Indian Treaties in Historical Perspective," 70.
42 Morris, *The Treaties of Canada*, 81–82, 83, 119–120.
43 Ibid., 86.
44 Canada, *Copy of Treaty No. 6 between Her Majesty the Queen and the Plain and Wood Cree Indians and Other Tribes of Indians at Fort Carlton, Fort Pitt and Battle River with Adhesions* (Ottawa: Queen's Printer, 1964), 4.
45 Morris, *The Treaties of Canada*, 176.

46 Ibid., 177.
47 Ibid., 184.
48 Taylor, "Two Views," 19.
49 Federation of Saskatchewan Indians (FSI), *Aski-Puko (The Land Alone)*. A report on the expected effects of the proposed hydro-electric installation at Wintego Rapids upon the Cree of the Peter Ballantyne and Lac la Ronge bands (Regina: FSI, 1976), 54.
50 Morris, *The Treaties of Canada*, 245–246.
51 Ibid., 257.
52 Richard Daniel, "The Spirit and Terms of Treaty Eight," in *The Spirit of the Alberta Indian Treaties*, ed. Richard Price (Montreal: Institute for Research on Public Policy, 1979), 56–58.
53 Fumoleau, *As Long as the Land Shall Last*, 41.
54 Daniel, "The Spirit and Terms of Treaty Eight," 58.
55 Ibid., 76.
56 Ibid., 79.
57 Canada, *Treaty No. 8, Made June 21, 1899, and Adhesions, Reports, etc.* (Ottawa: Queen's Printer, 1966), 12.
58 Fumoleau, *As Long as the Land Shall Last*, 79.
59 Daniel, "The Spirit and Terms of Treaty Eight," 75.
60 Fumoleau, *As Long as the Land Shall Last*, 79.
61 Ibid., 73.
62 Zlotkin, "Post-Confederation Treaties," 281.
63 Ibid.
64 Canada, *The James Bay Treaty. Treaty No. 9.* (Ottawa: Queen's Printer, 1964), 5.
65 *James Bay Treaty*, 27, 11.
66 Canada, *Treaty No. 10 and Reports of Commissioners* (Ottawa: Queen's Printer, 1966), 7.
67 Fumoleau, *As Long as the Land Shall Last*, 19; see also, 153.
68 Canada, *Treaty No. 11 (June 27, 1921) and Adhesion (July 17, 1922) with Reports, etc.* (Ottawa: Queen's Printer, 1957), 3.
69 Fumoleau, *As Long as the Land Shall Last*, 210–211.
70 Ibid., 212.
71 Alexander Morris, 22 Aug. 1873; as quoted in Frank Tough, "Changes to the Native Economy of Northern Manitoba in the Post-Treaty Period: 1870–1900," *Native Studies Review* 1, no. 1 (1984): 41.
72 Public Archives of Manitoba, MG12, B1, LB/J, Alexander Morris Papers. Letter by Alexander Morris, 31 May 1875.
73 Morris, *The Treaties of Canada*, 144.
74 K.S. Coates and W.R. Morrison, *Treaty Research Report: Treaty Five* (Ottawa: Treaties and Historical Research Centre, Indian and Northern Affairs Canada, forthcoming), 18.
75 Ibid., 21.
76 Ibid., 28.
77 Morris, *The Treaties of Canada*, 145.
78 Ibid., 160.
79 Ibid., 162.
80 Coates and Morrison, *Treaty Research Report*, 38–40.

81 S. Raby, "Indian Treaty No. 5 and The Pas Agency, Saskatchewan, NWT," *Saskatchewan History* 25, no. 3 (1972): 99–100.

82 Tough, "Changes to the Native Economy," 44.

83 Coates and Morrison, *Treaty Research Report*, 45.

84 Ibid., 53, 59–60.

85 Tough, "Changes to the Native Economy," 45.

86 Canada, *Treaty No. 5 between Her Majesty the Queen and the Saulteaux and Swampy Cree Tribes of Indians at Beren's River and Norway House with Adhesions* (Ottawa: Queen's Printer, 1969), 4.

87 *Treaty No. 5,* 5–6.

88 Ibid., 4, 10.

89 Tough, "Changes to the Native Economy," 45.

90 Coates and Morrison, *Treaty Research Report*, 67.

91 FSI, *Aski-Puko*, 61.

92 Taylor, "Two Views," 42, 44.

93 Daniel, "The Spirit and Terms of Treaty Eight," 95.

94 Fumoleau, *As Long as the Land Shall Last*, 79.

95 Zlotkin, "Post-Confederation Treaties," 275.

96 John L. Tobias, "The Origins of the Treaty Rights Movement in Saskatchewan," in *1885 and After: Native Society in Transition*, ed. F. Laurie Barron and James B. Waldram (Regina: Canadian Plains Research Center, 1986), 241.

97 FSI, *Aski-Puko*, 76.

98 For a good discussion of the development of the Métis and other mixed-blood peoples, see: John E. Foster, "The Métis: The People and the Term," *Prairie Forum* 3 (1978): 79–90; and Jacqueline Peterson and Jennifer S.H. Brown, eds., *The New Peoples: Being and Becoming Métis in North America* (Winnipeg: University of Manitoba Press, 1985).

99 David T. McNab, "Métis Participation in the Treaty-Making Process in Ontario: A Reconnaissance," *Native Studies Review* 1, no. 2 (1985): 62–63.

100 John L. Taylor, "An Historical Introduction to Métis Claims in Canada," *Canadian Journal of Native Studies* 3, no. 1 (1983): 153.

101 See: Stanley, *The Birth of Western Canada*. Stanley offers the orthodox history of the "Red River Rebellion." See the other references in this section for more current interpretations, and in particular the work of Sprague. Much has been written about this event, and the reader is directed to this literature for a more extensive discussion. For our purposes here, it is only necessary to discuss the basic causes of the incident and, more important, its consequences.

102 Manitoba Act, S. 31, S.C. 1870, c. 3; as cited in Cumming and Mickenberg, *Native Rights in Canada*, 200.

103 D. Bruce Sealey, "Statutory Land Rights of the Manitoba Métis," in *The Other Natives, Vol. 2*, ed. A.S. Lussier and D.B. Sealey (Winnipeg: Manitoba Métis Federation, 1978), 2–3.

104 Purich, *Our Land*, 165.

105 See: D.N. Sprague, "The Manitoba Land Question, 1870–1882," *Journal of Canadian Studies* 15, no. 3 (1980): 77.

106 P.R. Mailhot and D.N. Sprague, "Persistent Settlers: The Dispersal and Reset-

tlement of the Red River Métis, 1870–1885," *Canadian Ethnic Studies* 17, no. 2 (1985): 7.

107 Sealey, "Statutory Land Rights," 15–16.

108 Ibid., 21–22.

109 Taylor, "An Historical Introduction," 153.

110 Mailhot and Sprague, "Persistent Settlers," 3.

111 Purich, *Our Land*, 7.

112 John A. Macdonald, as quoted in Thomas Flanagan, *Riel and the Rebellion: 1885 Reconsidered* (Saskatoon: Western Producer Prairie Books, 1983), 62.

113 Sprague, "The Manitoba Land Question," 79.

114 McNab, "Métis Participation," 66.

115 Ken Hatt, "The North-West Rebellion Scrip Commissions, 1885–1889," in *1885 and After: Native Society in Transition*, ed. F. Laurie Barron and James B. Waldram (Regina: Canadian Plains Research Center, 1986), 200.

116 See, for instance: Daniel, "The Spirit and Terms of Treaty Eight," 76, for Treaty Eight.

117 Hatt, "The North-West Rebellion Scrip Commissions, 1885–1889," 199.

118 Ibid.

119 K.S. Coates and W.R. Morrison, "More Than a Matter of Blood: The Federal Government, the Churches and the Mixed Blood Populations of the Yukon and the Mackenzie River Valley, 1890–1950," in *1885 and After: Native Society in Transition*, ed. F. Laurie Barron and James B. Waldram (Regina: Canadian Plains Research Center), 259.

120 Hatt, "The North-West Rebellion Scrip Commissions, 1885–1889," 197.

121 Raby, "Indian Treaty No. 5," 101–102.

122 Cumming and Mickenberg, *Native Rights in Canada*, 203. Of course, the Indian Act for many years provided a mechanism for "de-Indianizing" both Indians and Métis who had taken treaty, at least in terms of legal recognition of Indian status. This was through the enfranchisement process, whereby a person legally registered as an Indian for purposes of the Indian Act could voluntarily, or arbitrarily, lose such status.

123 Taylor, "An Historical Introduction," 166.

124 For a treatment of this conspiracy theory, see: Donald McLean, "1885: Métis Rebellion or Government Conspiracy?" in *1885 and After: Native Society in Transition*, ed. F. Laurie Barron and James B. Waldram (Regina: Canadian Plains Research Center, 1986), 79–104; and, *1885: Métis Rebellion or Government Conspiracy?* (Winnipeg: Pemmican, 1985), 139.

125 Section 35 (1) of the Constitution Act, 1981, recognizes and affirms "the existing aboriginal and treaty rights of the aboriginal peoples of Canada," while Section 35(2) describes these "aboriginal peoples" as "Indian, Inuit and Métis peoples." It is likely that both federal and provincial governments will need to develop more coherent policies to deal with the Métis. For a discussion of recent federal policy regarding the Métis, see: Sally M. Weaver, "Federal Policy-Making for Métis and Non-Status Indians in the Context of Native Policy," *Canadian Ethnic Studies* 17, no. 2 (1985): 80–102.

CHAPTER 3

1 Churchill River Board of Inquiry. Minutes. Cumberland House, Saskatche-

wan, 19 Jan. 1978, 22.

2 June Helm, "Introduction," in *Handbook of North American Indians. Vol. 6: Subarctic,* ed. June Helm (Washington: Smithsonian Institution, 1981), 1–4.

3 Saskatchewan Department of Tourism and Renewable Resources, *Cumberland House Historic Park* (Regina: Department of Tourism and Renewable Resources, n.d.), 5.

4 J.E.M. Kew, *Cumberland House in 1960* (Saskatoon: Institute for Northern Studies, 1962), 5.

5 Ibid.

6 Alexander Morris, *The Treaties of Canada with the Indians* (1862; reprint, Toronto: Coles, 1979), 162–163.

7 Kew, *Cumberland House in 1960,* 7.

8 *Saskatchewan News,* 2 Oct. 1962.

9 Saskatchewan Power Corporation (SPC), *1955 Annual Report* (Regina: 1955).

10 SPC, *1956 Annual Report* (Regina: SPC, 1956).

11 Ibid., 4.

12 *Regina Leader-Post,* 25 Sept. 1959.

13 SPC, *1961 Annual Report* (Regina: SPC, 1961), 2.

14 W.S. Lloyd, Official Opening of the Squaw Rapids Hydro-Electric Power Station, Squaw Rapids, Saskatchewan, 15 June 1963, 8.

15 *Regina Leader-Post,* 4 Oct. 1962.

16 *The Commonwealth,* 26 June 1963.

17 Lloyd, Official Opening, 2.

18 Ibid., 6.

19 Ibid., 8.

20 *Regina Leader-Post,* 8 March 1960.

21 *Saskatchewan News,* 2 Oct. 1962. Paradoxically, insufficient shoreline clearing in Tobin Lake prior to the filling of the reservoir resulted in a major problem with floating debris, and a major clean-up expense.

22 *The Commonwealth,* 26 June 1963. To the contrary, the Cumberland House water supply has become increasingly unreliable. Sudden releases of water from the Squaw Rapids Dam have washed away fish nets, boats and docks, and have stranded people; the ice in winter has become dangerous and in some cases impassable; and low summer water levels in the Cumberland House region have rendered water travel difficult and sometimes impossible.

23 SPC, *The Squaw Rapids Story* (Regina: SPC, n.d.), 3.

24 *The Commonwealth,* 26 June 1963.

25 Saskatchewan Archives Board (SAB), 470. Department of Natural Resources, Deputy Minister's Papers. Memorandum, J.W. Churchman, Deputy Minister, Department of Natural Resources, to Messers. R. Young, W. Parks, E. Couldwell, B. Matheson and M. Miller, 23 Oct. 1958.

26 Ibid.

27 Ibid., R–369. Saskatchewan Power Management Advisory Committee. Minutes, 29 March 1960.

28 Ibid., R78–129. Squaw Rapids Hydro Electric Liaison Committee. Minutes, 25 Jan. 1960, 29 Feb. 1960.

29 Ibid., SR/00 (94). Letter, Crippen-Wright Engineering Ltd. to SPC (attention Mr. E.R. Smith), 17 May 1960.

30 Ibid., R78–129. Squaw Rapids Hydro Electric Liaison Committee. Minutes, 26 Jan. 1962.

31 Ibid., 15 June 1962.

32 Ibid., 23 Nov. 1962.

33 Ibid., SR/00(94). Letter, E.B. Campbell to C.E. Smith, Chairman, Squaw Rapids Liaison Committee, 13 Dec. 1962.

34 Ibid., SR/00(97). Letter, D.W. Pratt, Secretary, Squaw Rapids Hydro Electric Liaison Committee, to R.W. Tomlinson, Property and Claims, SPC, 15 Jan. 1963.

35 Interviews conducted by the author with Cumberland House residents, June through August, 1984. Actual names cannot be disclosed for reasons of confidentiality.

36 Interviews, 1984.

37 Ibid.

38 *Regina Leader-Post*, 16 Oct. 1962

39 Ibid., 8 March 1963.

40 Ibid.

41 SAB, R78–129. Saskatchewan Power Management Advisory Committee. Minutes, 27 Nov. 1962.

42 Ibid., 15 May 1963.

43 Ibid.

44 Presumably, the Les Voyageurs claim was settled out of court, although the author has been unable to uncover any documentation to confirm this.

45 SAB, NB 1/5–426, Department of Natural Resources, Deputy Minister's Papers. Letter, Gordon Fosseneuve, Joseph Carrière and J.B. Settee of the Cumberland House Ratepayers Association, to the Hon. E. Kramer, Minister of Natural Resources, 20 April 1963.

46 Ibid., NR 1/5–426, Department of Natural Resources, Deputy Minister's Papers. Memorandum, W.S. Lloyd, Natural Resources, to the Hon. E. Kramer, Minister of Natural Resources, 2 May 1963; Memorandum, Office of the Director of Northern Affairs, to J.W. Churchman, Deputy Minister of Natural Resources, 16 Sept. 1963; Memorandum, E. Kramer, Minister of Natural Resources, to the Treasury Board, 26 Sept. 1963.

47 Ibid. Letter, David Goulet, President of the Cumberland House Fishermen's Co-op, to the Hon. J. Cuelenaere, Minister of Natural Resources, 13 July 1964.

48 Ibid. Letter, the Hon. J. Cuelenaere, Minister of Natural Resources, to David Goulet, President of the Cumberland House Fishermen's Co-op, 15 Sept. 1964.

49 Ibid. Memorandum, G.R. Bowerman, Fisheries Supervisor, Department of Natural Resources, to the Chief of the Resource Program, Department of Natural Resources, 4 Aug. 1964.

50 Ibid. Memorandum, Director of Wildlife, Office of the Wildlife Branch, Department of Natural Resources, to the Office of the Chief of Resource Programs, 13 Aug. 1964.

51 Ibid. Report of the Cumberland House Wood Products Co-operative Limited, 1963-64.

52 Committee on Saskatchewan River Delta Problems, *Resources, Development and Problems of the Saskatchewan River Delta* (Regina: 1972).

53 *Saskatoon Star-Phoenix*, 4 Mar. 1976.

54 Ibid., 17 May 1976.

55 Canada. Department of Regional Economic Expansion, Prairie Farm Rehabilitation Administration, *Cumberland Lake Water Level Control Study – Engineering Report*, 1977.

56 J.R. Willard et al., *Environmental Implications of the Proposed Water Level Control Program for Cumberland Lake*. Report C-78-1 (Saskatoon: Saskatchewan Research Council, 1978).

57 B.E. Michael, *Effect of Limitations to the Squaw Rapids Discharge on the Operation of the Saskatchewan Power Corporation System* (Regina: SPC, 1976).

58 Clinton O. White, *Power for a Province: A History of Saskatchewan Power*, Canadian Plains Studies No. 5 (Regina: Canadian Plains Research Center, 1976), 334.

59 Churchill River Board of Inquiry. *Report* (Saskatoon: June 1978), xviii.

60 *Prince Albert Herald*, 3 Nov. 1973; cited in White, *Power for a Province*, 333–334.

61 *Regina Leader-Post*, 19 Nov. 1977.

62 Churchill River Board of Inquiry. Minutes. Cumberland House, Saskatchewan, 19 Jan. 1978, 22.

63 Ibid., 65–66.

64 Federation of Saskatchewan Indians (FSI), *Aski-Puko (The Land Alone)* (Regina: FSI, 1976).

65 Damas and Smith Consultants Ltd., *Cumberland House Development Plan* (Winnipeg: Damas and Smith, 1980).

66 *Prince Albert Herald*, 12 Jan. 1980, 17 Jan. 1980.

67 *Saskatoon Star-Phoenix*, 5 Feb. 1980.

68 Letter, Cumberland House Local Resource Allocation Committee to the Hon. Jerry Hammersmith, Minister of Northern Saskatchewan, 28 Jan. 1980.

69 Minutes, Strategy Meeting of the Cumberland House LCA and the Local Resource Allocation Committee, 17 July 1980.

70 Letter, Don Murphy to Cumberland House LCA and Local Resource Allocation Committee, 17 July 1980.

71 *Prince Albert Herald*, 28 Aug. 1980.

72 Undated and unsigned photocopy.

73 *Prince Albert Herald*, 24 Sept. 1980.

74 Minutes, Meeting of Cumberland House LCA, 17 Jan. 1983.

75 Minutes, SPC and Trapper's Committee Meeting, 25 April 1983.

76 Letter, O.W. Hanson, Senior Vice-President, SPC, to Winston McKay, Mayor of Cumberland House, 13 May 1983.

77 Letter, Winston McKay to Sheilagh McGee, of *The Fifth Estate*, 26 Oct. 1983.

78 Ibid.

79 Statement of Claim. In the Court of Queen's Bench, Judicial Centre of Prince Albert, Q.B. No. 1442.

80 Ibid.

81 *Prince Albert Herald*, 26 May 1983.

82 Although the federal Department of Indian Affairs was involved in the negotiations surrounding the construction of the Grand Rapids Dam further downstream in Manitoba, wherein the Chemawawin Indian Band was forced to relocate (see Chapter 4), there is no record of federal involvement on behalf of the Cumberland House Indians. Apparently, almost all records held by the Department of Indian Affairs for the band which cover the late 1950s and early

1960s have been destroyed. It is impossible to believe that Indian Affairs employees would not have at least superficially investigated the project, given the parallel development in Manitoba. The exact nature and extent of their involvement has never been fully revealed.

83 *Saskatoon Star-Phoenix*, 21 Sept. 1984.

84 Ibid., 30 Nov. 1985.

85 Telephone interview with Robert Haynes, solicitor for the SPC, Regina, 6 Aug. 1986.

86 *Saskatoon Star-Phoenix*, 20 Aug. 1986.

87 Ibid., 5 Aug. 1987.

88 Ibid., 31 Aug. 1987.

89 Ibid., 15 Oct. 1987.

CHAPTER 4

1 Anonymous Easterville resident, Aug. 1979.

2 See: James B. Waldram, "Relocation and Political Change in a Manitoba Native Community," *Canadian Journal of Anthropology* 1, no. 2 (1980): 173–178; and, "The 'Other Side': Ethnostatus Distinctions in Western Subarctic Native Communities," in *1885 and After: Native Society in Transition*, ed. F. Laurie Barron and James B. Waldram (Regina: Canadian Plains Research Center, 1986), 279–295. The former article details the specific political problems that have developed in Easterville since the relocation from Chemawawin, with particular emphasis on the political rift which has developed between the Indian band council and the Métis community council. The latter article discusses the problems which have developed in the subarctic for Native people who find their own cultural definitions of themselves being submerged by the political and legal definitions being applied increasingly to them by the non-Native community.

3 James B. Waldram, "Relocation and Social Change among the Swampy Cree and Métis of Easterville, Manitoba" (Thesis, University of Manitoba, 1980).

4 W.L. Morton, *Manitoba: A History*, 2nd ed. (Toronto: University of Toronto Press, 1967), 33.

5 Michael J. Landa, "Easterville: A Case Study in the Relocation of a Manitoba Native Community" (Thesis, University of Manitoba, 1969), 32.

6 Alternative spellings are: Chemahawin; Chemuhowin; Cimahawin. The literature also often refers to the settlement as Cedar Lake.

7 Alexander Morris, *The Treaties of Canada with the Indians* (1880; reprint, Toronto: Coles, 1979), 161.

8 Morris, *The Treaties of Canada*, 61.

9 Ibid.

10 Ibid., 65.

11 Treaty and Aboriginal Rights Research Centre, Winnipeg. Information on file, 13 April 1986.

12 Personal interview with Armand Pouliot, The Pas, 8 Sept. 1979.

13 Ibid.

14 Pouliot was neither doctor nor law-enforcement agent in the official sense. In the true tradition of the northern fur trader, he stocked a supply of basic medicines, and received some direction from physicians in The Pas via his two-

way radio (the only one in the community). He also acted to control the flow of liquor into the community, seizing brewing supplies or organizing occasional raids by the RCMP. Personal interview with Armand Pouliot, The Pas, 8 Sept. 1979.

15 *Winnipeg Tribune*, 15 Nov. 1965.

16 Public Archives of Canada (PAC), RG10, v. 7989, file 578/19-4-1, pt. 1. Consolidated Extracts. File 128/29–12.

17 Manitoba Hydro, *Grand Rapids* (Winnipeg: Manitoba Hydro, n.d.), 2–3.

18 Martin Loney, *Grand Rapids Forebay* (draft, n.d.), 5. (On file at Northern Flood Committee, Winnipeg).

19 PAC, RG10, v. 7989, file 578/19-4-1, pt. 1. Memorandum, H.M. Jones, Director, Indian Affairs Branch, to A.G. Leslie, Regional Superintendent, Indian Affairs, Winnipeg, 1 Aug. 1960.

20 Ibid. Memorandum of Understanding made this 26th day of October, 1960, between Manitoba Hydro-Electric Board and Manitoba Department of Mines and Natural Resources.

21 In fact, the expiry date for the committee's obligation to undertake economic studies and to finance community programs was set as 1 April 1974.

22 Van Ginkel Associates, in association with Hedlin, Menzies and Associates, *Transition in the North: The Churchill River Diversion and the People of South Indian Lake* (Winnipeg: Manitoba Development Authority, 1967), 51.

23 Solomon G. Jacobson, *Social Adjustment to a Public Power Project: An Analysis of the Resettlement of the Chemawawin Bands.* Report prepared for the Federal-Provincial Coordinating Committee on Indian and Métis Affairs, Nov. 1966, 8.

24 Lake Winnipeg, Churchill and Nelson Rivers Study Board (LWCNRSB), *The Chemahawin Relocation.* Social and Economic Studies, vol. 2, app. 8, appendix H, 1974, 220.

25 PAC, RG10, v. 7989, file 578/19-4-1, pt. 1. Memorandum, A.G. Leslie to Indian Affairs Branch, Ottawa, 27 Dec. 1960.

26 The Indian Act, R.S., c. 149, s. 37–41.

27 Ibid., s. 35.

28 PAC, RG10, v. 7989, file 578/19-4-1, pt. 1. Letter, A.G. Leslie to S.W. Schortinghuis, Assistant Deputy Minister, Department of Mines and Natural Resources, 20 Dec. 1960. Schortinghuis was also the first Chairman of the Forebay Committee.

29 Ibid. Operation Grand Rapids. Divisional Chiefs Meeting, 7 Oct. 1960.

30 Ibid. Memorandum, A.G. Leslie to Indian Affairs, Ottawa, 22 Sept. 1960.

31 Ibid. Memorandum, Chief Reserves and Trusts to Director, Indian Affairs Branch, 27 Sept. 1960.

32 While the option of leaving the Cedar Lake region entirely was provided, the residents overwhelmingly voiced their desire to remain along the shores of the lake they knew so well. It is believed that only two families chose to leave at the time of relocation.

33 PAC, RG10, v. 7989, file 578/19-4-1, pt. 1. Memorandum, A.G. Leslie to Indian Affairs Branch, Ottawa, 10 Aug. 1960.

34 Interestingly, an unsigned memorandum to the Deputy Minister of Indian Affairs, sent in late 1961, contained the following comment about Chemawawin (cited in Loney, *Grand Rapids Forebay*, 45–46): "After visiting their

reserve and observing the hay lands and excellent location in relation to trapping and hunting grounds one readily concludes that their forefathers did a far superior job of land selection than it has been possible to do; . . . they have the choicest spot in the whole area."

35 PAC, RG10, v. 7989, file 578/19-4-1, pt. 1. Memorandum, H.M. Jones to A.G. Leslie, 1 Aug. 1960.

36 Personal interview with Walter Mink, Easterville, 10 Aug. 1979.

37 Jacobson, *Social Adjustment to a Public Power Project*, 29.

38 *Easterville Brief.* Presented at meeting with Manitoba Hydro, 30 Sept. 1975, 1.

39 Report of the Panel of Public Enquiry Into Northern Hydro Development. Appendix A. Transcript of Hearings, 22 Sept. 1975, 106–107.

40 LWCNRSB, 235.

41 "Chemawawin Meeting – Concerning the Move," 20 May 1961. In LWCNRSB, 238.

42 Personal interview with Joe Keeper, Winnipeg, 30 May 1979. Keeper was a community development officer first stationed in Chemawawin in 1962.

43 Personal interview with Walter Mink, Easterville, 10 Aug. 1979.

44 "Chemawawin Meeting – The Meeting of Decision," 3 June 1961. In LWCNRSB, 238.

45 Personal interview with Walter Mink, Easterville, 10 Aug. 1979.

46 In a letter describing the deconsecration of St. Alban's Church in Chemawawin, and the consecration of a new Anglican church in Easterville, E.S.W. Cole, the priest-in-charge, described Easterville as "a mammoth rockery" which, "by a white man's standards is not the best place for a new village." (PAM MG7B9, 13 Aug. 1964, Diocese of Brandon). This view contrasts sharply with that provided in a public relations document published by Manitoba Hydro soon after the relocation. In this document, the new townsite was described as follows: "The neat new homes and buildings erected under supervision were constructed to standards established by the Indian Affairs Branch of the Government of Canada. These replace the sadly overcrowded mud-caulked unpeeled log quarters they formerly occupied. A street sign designates the main street as Cedar Lake Road. Roads throughout the community are broad. The brightly painted homes, nestled in a background of evergreens and birches, convey the impression of a lakeside summer resort. Water wells have been drilled and a new wharf for commercial purposes has been constructed. A new way of life is unfolding for these people" (Manitoba Hydro, "Grand Rapids – Power Development by Manitoba Hydro," n.d.). Subsequent public relations documents on the Grand Rapids Dam have made progressively less mention of the Easterville townsite.

47 Personal interview with Walter Mink, Easterville, 10 Aug. 1979.

48 Personal interview with Gordon George, Easterville, 8 Aug. 1979.

49 Memorandum, J.R. Bell to A.G. Leslie, 26 June 1961; cited in Lonie, *Grand Rapids Forebay*, 47.

50 Minutes, Grand Rapids Forebay Committee Meeting, Chemawawin, 22 March 1962.

51 As Pouliot stated: "Maybe they were afraid I'd throw water on it or something." Personal interview with Armand Pouliot, The Pas, 8 Sept. 1979.

52 Jean H. Lagassé, *The People of Indian Ancestry in Manitoba*, 3 vols. (Winni-

peg: Manitoba Department of Agriculture and Immigration, 1959). For a review of Lagassé's community development philosophy, see: Jean H. Lagassé, "Community Development in Manitoba," *Human Organization* 20 (1961): 232–237.

53 Memorandum, Jean H. Lagassé, Director, Community Development Services, to the Hon. J.A. Christianson, Minister of Welfare, 4 Sept. 1962, 2.

54 Minutes, Grand Rapids Forebay Meeting, 26 Aug. 1963.

55 Personal interview with Joe Keeper, Winnipeg, 30 May 1979, 6 June 1986.

56 Memorandum, Lagassé to Christianson, 4 Sept. 1962, 1.

57 Joe Keeper, *A Short Report on Cedar Lake* (unpublished report, 1963), 12. This report represents the only attempt to develop a socioeconomic data base to assist in planning the relocation of the people of Chemawawin.

58 Letter, Lagassé to Christianson, 4 Sept. 1962.

59 Memorandum, Joe Keeper to F.R. Langin, Supervisor of Field Services, 19 Feb. 1963.

60 Ibid., 2? Feb 1963 (date obscured on copy).

61 For instance, it was believed that the army would come in and forcibly move the people if they did not quickly settle. Personal interview with Joe Keeper, Winnipeg, 30 May 1979.

62 Loney, *Grand Rapids Forebay*, 51.

63 Memorandum, J.R. Bell to A.G. Leslie, 21 Jan. 1961; cited in Loney, *Grand Rapids Forebay*, 45.

64 Memorandum, A.G. Leslie to Department of Indian Affairs, Ottawa, 7 Dec. 1962; cited in Loney, *Grand Rapids Forebay*, 57.

65 Letter, Premier Duff Roblin to Chief Donald Easter, 21 Aug. 1964; cited in Loney, *Grand Rapids Forebay*, 60.

66 Letter, Chemawawin Band to Premier Duff Roblin, 3 Mar. 1963; cited in Loney, *Grand Rapids Forebay*, 60.

67 Personal interview with Armand Pouliot, The Pas, 8 Sept. 1979.

68 Memorandum, J.I. Keeper to F.R. Langin, 11 Oct. 1962.

69 Ibid., 19 Feb. 1963.

70 Personal interview with Walter Mink, Easterville, 10 Aug. 1979.

71 Memorandum, J.I. Keeper to F.R. Langin, 10 April 1963.

72 PAC, RG10, v. 7989, file 578/19-4-1, pt. 1. Letter, A.G. Leslie to S.W. Schortinghuis, 20 Dec. 1960.

73 Ibid. Memorandum, Special Assistant to The Director, Indian Affairs Branch, Ottawa, 13 Oct. 1960.

74 Ibid. Letter, H.M. Jones to S.W. Schortinghuis, 28 Dec. 1960.

75 Ibid., Memorandum, A.G. Leslie to R.F. Battle, Director, Indian Affairs Branch, 4 Feb. 1964.

76 Letter, Manitoba Deputy Minister of Mines and Natural Resources to the Deputy Minister of Citizenship and Immigration, 15 July 1964; cited in Loney, *Grand Rapids Forebay*, 61.

77 PAC, RG10, v. 7989, file 578/19-4-1, pt. 2. Statement of Duties – Mr. J.R. Bell.

78 Personal interview with Armand Pouliot, The Pas, 8 Sept. 1979.

79 Ibid.

80 Memorandum, Joe Keeper to F.R. Langin, 11 Oct. 1962.

81 Letter, Henry Wilson, Tribal Chief, Swampy Cree Tribal Council, to Ken Young, 17 March 1978.

82 Personal interview with Gordon George, Easterville, 8 Aug. 1979.
83 *Grand Rapids Settlement: Moose Lake and Chemahawin – Preliminary Report*, n.d.
84 Personal interview with Gordon George, Easterville, 8 Aug. 1979.
85 J. Weitz, *Grand Rapids Forebay Land Exchange* (draft) (Ottawa: Department of Indian Affairs, 1978), 1.
86 LWCNRSB, 224.
87 Ibid., 224–225.
88 PAC, RG10, v. 7989, file 578/30-44-31A, vol. 2. Memorandum, A.G. Leslie to R.F. Battle, 4 Feb. 1964.
89 Letter, Donald Easter, William Captain, Robert Mink [Chemawawin Indian Band] and Wilson Easter, Walter Mink and McLeod George [Local Forebay Committee] to S.W. Schortinghuis, 24 Jan. 1964. Reproduced in LWCNRSB, 230–231.
90 LWCNRSB, 227.
91 Memorandum, J.I. Keeper to F.R. Langin, 20 Nov. 1962.
92 Letter, R.M. Connelly to J. McGilp, Director, Community Affairs Branch, Department of Indian Affairs, Ottawa, 5 Nov. 1970.
93 Letter, S.W. Schortinghuis to Chief Donald Easter, 7 June 1962. Also referenced as: Schedule A, Order-in-Council 1566/63. This letter is more commonly known as the Letter of Intent or the Forebay Agreement.
94 Personal interview with Joe Keeper, Winnipeg, 30 May 1979.
95 Unfortunately, the harmonious political relations between the Indians and Métis did not last. For a discussion of the post-relocation political turmoil in Easterville, see: Waldram, "Relocation and Political Change," 173–178.
96 Testimony by Harvey Pollock before the sitting of the Standing Committee of Public Utilities and Natural Resources, Winnipeg, 21 May 1969.
97 PAC, RG10, v. 7989, file 578/30-44-31A, vol. 2. Memorandum, A.G. Leslie to R.F. Battle, 4 Feb. 1964.
98 Letter, S.W. Schortinghuis to Chief Donald Easter, 7 June 1962.
99 Department of Citizenship and Immigration, Indian Affairs Branch, Band Council Resolution Passed by Chemawawin Indian Band, 14 June 1962.
100 P.C. 1962–1617. Passed in Ottawa 15 Nov. 1962.
101 Minutes, Grand Rapids Forebay Committee Meeting, 22 July 1968.
102 *Winnipeg Tribune*, 12 Nov. 1968.
103 Letter, Harvey Pollock to Stanley C. Knapp, Department of Indian Affairs, 8 Jan. 1969.
104 Personal interview with Harvey Pollock, Winnipeg, 5 June 1986.
105 *Winnipeg Tribune*, 12 Nov. 1968
106 Testimony by Harvey Pollock, sitting of the Standing Committee of Public Utilities and Natural Resources, Winnipeg, 21 May 1969.
107 *Winnipeg Tribune*, 12 Nov. 1968.
108 Letter, J.D. Raichura to Harvey Pollock, 3 Feb. 1969.
109 Statement of Claim. Queen's Bench No. 1530/70. Winnipeg.
110 Minutes, Grand Rapids Forebay Committee Meeting, 14 Sept. 1970; Letter, H. Krentz, Senior Resource Officer, Department of Indian Affairs, to R.M. Connelly, Manitoba Regional Director, Department of Indian Affairs, 23 Oct. 1970.
111 Statement of Defence. Court of Queen's Bench 1530/70. Winnipeg.

112 The Forebay Committee itself was apparently hampered by its lack of legal status. Wrote Soloman G. Jacobson, in his 1966 report (page 9): "The lack of clear legal authority further complicated the existence of the committee to take an effective stand on any issue . . . no doubt the vague legal authority of the Forebay Committee increased the difficulty of federal-provincial co-operation." The Forebay Committee, for its part, was very critical of Jacobson's report, with the Chairman of the committee, S.W. Schortinghuis, stating that it "bristles with mis-information and in numerous cases with deliberate misinterpretation of the facts." Letter, S.W. Schortinghuis to members of the Grand Rapids Forebay Administration Committee, 8 Dec. 1966.

113 Statement of Defence, 2.

114 Memorandum, R.M. Connelly to J. McGilp, 5 Nov. 1970.

115 Personal interview with Harvey Pollock, 5 June 1986.

116 See: Landa, "Easterville: A Case Study," for an anthropological account of community disintegration in Easterville following the relocation.

117 Personal interview with Easterville Band Council, Chief Percy Mink, and councillors Riley Easter and Alpheus Brass, Easterville, 25 July 1979.

118 Memorandum, Sidney Green, Minister, Manitoba Department of Mines, Resources and Environmental Management, to R. McBryde, Manitoba Minister of Northern Affairs, and Len Bateman, Chairman, Manitoba Hydro, 9 Feb. 1975.

119 The Chemawawin Indian Band was also granted title to minerals on a one-to-one acre exchange basis, meaning they could claim title to the mineral resources on 5,813 acres, the total amount of reserve land surrendered by them.

120 Testimony by Walter Mink. Report of the Panel of Public Enquiry Into Northern Hydro Development. Appendix A. Transcript of Hearings, 22 Sept. 1975, 109.

121 Personal interview with Easterville Band Council, Chief Percy Mink, and councillors Riley Easter and Alpheus Brass, Easterville, 25 July 1979.

122 Letter, Henry Wilson to "All SCTC Chiefs," 1 Dec. 1977.

123 J.M. Weitz, *Grand Rapids Forebay Land Exchange* (draft) (Ottawa: Department of Indian Affairs, 1978).

124 Apparently, this funding was not without strings attached. Funds were to be used for negotiation with the Manitoba government and Manitoba Hydro, and not for legal action. Personal interview with Ken Young, Winnipeg, 13 Aug. 1986.

125 Letter, Ken Young to Arthur Kroeger, Deputy Minister, Department of Indian and Northern Affairs, 27 June 1979. Section 28 of the Indian Act current at that time read as follows: "28.(1) Subject to subsection (2), a deed, lease, contract, instrument, document or agreement of any kind whether written or oral, by which a band or a member of a band purports to permit a person other than a member of that band to occupy or use a reserve or to reside or otherwise exercise any rights on a reserve is void. (2) The Minister may by permit in writing authorize any person for a period not exceeding one year, or with the consent of the council of the band for any longer period, to occupy or use a reserve or to reside or otherwise exercise rights on a reserve" (R.S., c. 149, s. 28; 1956, c. 40, s. 10.)

126 Letter, Ken Young to Arthur Kroeger, Deputy Minister, Department of Indian and Northern Affairs, 27 June 1979.

127 Letter, Ken Young to J. Weitz, Indian and Inuit Affairs, 2 Aug. 1978.

128 Although the Province had applied in 1979 to have the Chemawawin claim struck for want of prosecution, the claim remained active. E.H. Hobbs and Associates, *Special Forebay Committee Strategic Planning Workshop* (Winnipeg: 1984), 6.

129 Personal interview with Ken Young, Winnipeg, 13 Aug. 1986.

130 Letter, Young to Weitz, 2 Aug. 1978.

131 Personal interview with Ken Young, Winnipeg, 13 Aug. 1986.

132 *Grand Rapids Forebay* (unpublished information paper). Northern Flood Committee files.

133 In the Guerin case, the Supreme Court of Canada found in favour of the plaintiff, a member of the Musqueum Band of British Columbia, that the federal government abrogated its fiduciary or trust relationship to the Indians when it failed to safeguard the band's interests in a surrender of reserve land (Guerin et al., v. R and National Indian Brotherhood, [1984] 6 W.W.R. 481 [S.C.C.]).

134 Letter, Minister of Indian Affairs, to Hon. Al Mackling, Minister of Natural Resources, and Chief Russell Tobacco, Chairman, Special Forebay Committee, 23 Dec. 1983.

135 Ibid.

136 Personal interview with Ken Young, 13 Aug. 1986.

137 *The New Nation*, Feb. 1981.

138 *Easterville Brief*, 1.

CHAPTER 5

1 Rosie Dumas, South Indian Lake. Minutes, Meeting with Lawyer, 29 Jan. 1974.

2 John S. Matthiasson, "Caught in the Middle: Two Cree Communities and the Southern Indian Lake Hydro Power Controversy," *International Congress of Americanists* 11 (1972): 593–601; Douglas E. Sanders, *Native People in Areas of Internal National Expansion: Indians and Inuit in Canada* (Copenhagen: International Work Group for Indigenous Affairs, No. 14, 1973), 14–16.

3 James G.E. Smith, "Preliminary Notes on the Rocky Cree of Reindeer Lake," in *Contributions to Canadian Ethnology*, Mercury Series Paper No. 31 (Ottawa: National Museum of Man, 1975), 171–185.

4 James B. Waldram, "The Impact of Hydroelectric Development upon a Northern Manitoba Native Community" (Dissertation, University of Connecticut, 1983).

5 *Winnipeg Free Press*, 30 Aug. 1972. See also: James V. Wright, "Cree Culture History in the Southern Indian Lake Region," in *Contributions to Anthropology VII: Archaeology*, Bulletin 232 (Ottawa: National Museum of Canada, 1968), 1–31.

6 James G.E. Smith, "Chipewyan, Cree and Inuit Relations West of Hudson Bay, 1714–1955," *Ethnohistory* 28, no. 2 (1981): 133–156.

7 J.D. Collinson, "Social and Economic Impact of the Nelson River Hydro Development (with Emphasis on South Indian Lake)," in *Lake Winnipeg,*

Churchill and Nelson Rivers Study Board, Social and Economic Studies Vol. 2-C, Technical Report Appendix 8, 59.

8 Personal interview with Charlie Dysart, South Indian Lake, 9 July 1981.

9 Collinson, "Social and Economic Impact," 59.

10 Ibid.

11 Michael Shouldice, "A Discussion of the Political Framework of Resource Development in Relation to Native People. The Nelson River Hydroelectric Project: A Case Study" (Thesis, University of Manitoba, 1976), 75.

12 The paradox of this situation is that, after the project had been constructed, the debacle surrounding it would provoke one judicial inquirer to note that, hopefully, we had all *now* learned from the past!

13 Personal interview with Harold Buchwald, Winnipeg, 9 June 1986.

14 *Winnipeg Tribune,* 15 Nov. 1965.

15 Ibid., 13 April 1965.

16 Ibid., 15 Feb. 1969.

17 Robert W. Newbury, "Return to the Rivers of Discovery of Western Canada," *Landscape Planning* 6 (1979): 244.

18 Shouldice, "A Discussion of the Political Framework," 77.

19 H.E. Duckworth, *Reconnaissance Study of the Effect on Human and Natural Resources of the Churchill River Diversion Plans* (Winnipeg: 1967). This report was also known as the Duckworth Report.

20 Ibid., 6.

21 Public Archives of Manitoba (PAM), Malaher Papers, P591. Robert Newbury and Gerald Malaher, *The Destruction of Manitoba's Last Great River* (Ottawa: Canadian Nature Federation, 1973), 11.

22 Shouldice, "A Discussion of the Political Framework," 78.

23 Van Ginkel Associates, in association with Hedlin, Menzies and Associates, *Transition in the North. The Churchill River Diversion and the People of South Indian Lake* (Winnipeg: Manitoba Development Authority, 1967.)

24 Van Ginkel, covering letter to *Transition in the North.*

25 Transcript of press conference by Harry Enns, 20 Jan. 1968.

26 Nelson Agency, Manitoba Development Authority, *South Indian Lake. The Position at mid-August 1968,* 1968, 10.

27 Transcript of Proceedings at a Meeting Held at South Indian Lake, on Monday 22 April 1968, 1.

28 Ibid., 5.

29 Ibid., 10.

30 Ibid., 3.

31 Ibid., 6.

32 Ibid., Sunday 28 April 1968.

33 Ibid., Friday 14 June 1968, 5.

34 Personal interview with Harold Buchwald, Winnipeg, 9 June 1986.

35 Letter, Yude Henteleff to the author, 18 Nov. 1986. According to Henteleff, the information provided by the people was so detailed that, at the conclusion of the first hearing in South Indian Lake, Manitoba Hydro's Assistant General Manager, Kris Kristjanson, questioned whether the information had even come from the people.

36 Transcript of Proceedings at a Meeting Held at South Indian Lake, on Fri-

day 14 June 1968, 5. Even the Deputy Minister of Mines and Natural Resources stated this. At the Winnipeg hearings into Hydro's license application, Winston Mair stated that "the project at Southern Indian Lake will almost double the water area. It will more than double in volume and hence, theoretically, the fish population should double" (Minutes of the South Indian Lake Public Hearing, Winnipeg, 27–29 Jan. 1969, 161).

37 Transcript of Proceedings at a Meeting Held at South Indian Lake, on Friday 14 June 1968, 5.

38 Personal interview with Yude Henteleff, Winnipeg, 9 June 1986.

39 *Winnipeg Free Press*, 19 June 1968.

40 Letter, Buchwald, Henteleff and Zitzerman, to the Director, Water Control and Conservation, 5 July 1968.

41 Memorandum, Henteleff to Buchwald, 2 Dec. 1968.

42 Ibid.

43 Letter, C. Booy, A.M. Lansdowne, J.S. Matthiasson, R.W. Newbury, J.M. Walker, to The Hon. H.J. Enns, Minister of Mines and Natural Resources, 19 Dec. 1965.

44 Ibid.

45 Personal interview with Yude Henteleff, Winnipeg, 9 June 1986.

46 Transcript of Proceedings, Public Hearing on Manitoba Hydro's Proposal for the Churchill River Diversion. South Indian Lake, 7 Jan. 1969, 21–23.

47 Transcript of Proceedings, Public Hearing on Manitoba Hydro's Proposal for the Churchill River Diversion. South Indian Lake, 7 Jan. 1969.

48 *Winnipeg Free Press*, 20 Jan. 1969.

49 Shouldice, "A Discussion of the Political Framework," 88.

50 *Winnipeg Tribune*, 25 Jan. 1969.

51 Minutes of the South Indian Lake Public Hearing, Winnipeg, 27–29 Jan. 1969, 31.

52 Ibid., 40, 41, 252.

53 Ibid., 87, 106.

54 Position Statement on Behalf of (1) The South Indian Lake Community (2) The Pickerel Narrows Community, with Respect to the Application by Manitoba Hydro Electric Board to Divert Water From the Churchill River into the Nelson River and to Store Water on the Rat River, Southern Indian Lake and Granville Lake, 27 Jan. 1969. Pickerel Narrows, otherwise known as Granville Lake, was a tiny community located to the west of South Indian Lake. The residents were members of the Mathias Colomb Indian Band at Pukatawagan. The community was not active in the political struggle against the project, and quickly became forgotten as the media and the public focused on South Indian Lake.

55 Minutes of the South Indian Lake Public Hearing, Winnipeg, 27–29 Jan. 1969, 145.

56 Memorandum, Henteleff to Buchwald, 5 Feb. 1969.

57 Letter, Henteleff to Isabel Moose, Bill Anderson, Bob Dysart, Basil Colomb, and Noah Soulier, South Indian Lake, 31 March 1969. There was some confusion at the hearings concerning who in fact was the chairman. Two individuals appeared to be acting in that capacity.

58 *Winnipeg Free Press*, 3 May 1969.

59 Open letter to Premier Weir, from the Residents of South Indian Lake, 12 May 1969.
60 *Winnipeg Tribune*, 20 May 1969.
61 Sitting of Standing Committee of Public Utilities and Natural Resources, 22 May 1969, 55–77.
62 Ibid., 82.
63 Sitting of Standing Committee of Public Utilities and Natural Resources, 22 May 1969, 86.
64 *Winnipeg Free Press*, 27 May 1969.
65 *Manitoban*, Special Supplement, Nov. 1974, 5.
66 Ibid.
67 Hansard. Legislative Assembly of Manitoba, 15 Sept. 1969, 733.
68 *Winnipeg Free Press*, 16 Sept. 1969.
69 Ibid.
70 Shouldice, "A Discussion of the Political Framework," 125.
71 Letter, Premier Edward Schreyer to Buchwald, 12 May 1972.
72 Statement by the Chairman of Manitoba Hydro to the Standing Committee of the Legislature on Public Utilities and Natural Resources, 25 May 1972.
73 Letter, Buchwald to Murdo Dysart, 2 June 1972.
74 Statement of Counsel for the South Indian Lake Community with Respect to the Manitoba Hydro Proposal of May 25, 1972, 5 June 1972.
75 Letter, Buchwald and Henteleff to Schreyer, 5 June 1972.
76 Letter, Schreyer to Buchwald and Henteleff, 14 June 1972.
77 Minutes, Meeting at South Indian Lake, 15 June 1972.
78 Press release, Department of Mines, Resources and Environmental Management, 7 Dec. 1972, 2.
79 Memorandum, Henteleff and Buchwald to Members of the Town Council and Members of the Flood Committee of South Indian Lake, 18 Dec. 1972.
80 Letter, Henteleff to the author, 18 Nov. 1986.
81 Statement of Claim No. 2785/72, Court of Queen's Bench, Winnipeg.
82 Personal interview with Harold Buchwald, Winnipeg, 9 June 1986; personal interview with Yude Henteleff, Winnipeg, 9 June 1986.
83 Letter, Charlie Dysart, South Indian Lake, to Henteleff, 1 Dec. 1972.
84 Letter, Steward Martin to Edward Schreyer, Sidney Green and J.F. Funnel, 20 July 1973; cited in G. Tritschler, *Commission of Inquiry into Manitoba Hydro* (Winnipeg: 1979), 215.
85 Letter, Henteleff to the Hon. Jean Chrétien, Minister of Indian Affairs and Northern Development, 21 Feb. 1973.
86 Letter, Henteleff to James Richardson, 14 March 1973.
87 Letter, Henteleff to Chrétien, 14 March 1973.
88 Letter, Henteleff to Keith Taylor, 21 March 1973.
89 Letter, Taylor to Henteleff, 27 March 1973. Throughout 1973 and 1974, Henteleff communicated periodically with James O'Reilly, the lawyer representing the James Bay Cree in their negotiations with the Quebec government over hydro plans in the northern part of that province. The primary subject of discussion was the similarities and differences between the two cases, particularly in the area of Indian rights. Legal strategies were also discussed. However, because they were both exploring new legal ground, and because the context of each case was significantly different (the James Bay Cree never

having signed treaties surrendering their aboriginal rights), the two lawyers were unable to utilize each other to any great extent. Henry Spence, Chairman of the Northern Flood Committee, also communicated with O'Reilly, and even travelled to Quebec to gain first-hand knowledge of the situation there.

90 Letter, Jack Davis, Minister of the Environment, to Sidney Green, Manitoba Minister of Mines, Resources and Environmental Management, 3 April 1973.

91 Letter, Chrétien to Henteleff, 11 April 1973.

92 Memorandum, C.I. Fairholm, Acting Director, Policy, Planning and Research, DIAND, to W.C. Thomas, Manitoba Regional Director, Indian and Eskimo Affairs Program, DIAND, 31 May 1973.

93 Letter, Henteleff to Robert E. Dysart, South Indian Lake, 12 July 1973.

94 Letter, Henteleff to James O'Reilly, 12 March 1974; Letter, Henteleff to Robert E. Dysart, South Indian Lake, 12 July 1973.

95 Letter, Chrétien to Henteleff, 18 July 1973.

96 Letter, Henteleff to Chrétien, 20 July 1973; Letter, Chrétien to Henteleff, 26 Sept. 1973; Letter, Tommy Thomas, Acting Mayor, South Indian Lake, to Chrétien, 24 Sept. 1973.

97 Letter, Henteleff to Chrétien, 9 Oct. 1973.

98 Personal interview with Yude Henteleff, Winnipeg, 9 June 1986.

99 *Manitoban*, Special Supplement, Nov. 1974, 5.

100 Letter, Rev. John McFarlane to an unidentified colleague, undated.

101 Letter, Henteleff to Chrétien, 23 Nov. 1973.

102 In contrast, the lawyers for South Indian Lake argued that the continuation of construction of the project before the impact studies had been completed was a violation of the spirit of the same agreement.

103 Letter, Taylor to Chrétien, 26 Nov. 1973.

104 Letter, Chrétien to Henteleff, 10 April 1974.

105 This fact was put rather bluntly by Jock Gibb, on behalf of the Manitoba Commissioner of Northern Affairs, in a letter to Yude Henteleff (6 Dec. 1973): "We can pay you on a basis that your service to our Department is for compensation advice only. We can not pay for 'fight flooding' advice."

106 Letter, Taylor to Chrétien, 7 Feb. 1974.

107 Letter, Henteleff to Taylor, 4 March 1974.

108 Letter, Mayor Basil Colomb, South Indian Lake, to Schreyer, 16 Jan. 1976; Minutes, Meeting with Lawyer, South Indian Lake, 29 Jan. 1974; personal interview with Noah Soulier, South Indian Lake, 30 Jan. 1982; personal interview with Isabel Moose, South Indian Lake, 14 March 1982; personal interview with Charlie Dysart, South Indian Lake, 9 July 1981.

109 Letter, South Indian Lake Mayor and Council to Premier Edward Schreyer, n.d.

110 Telegram, from the People of South Indian Lake to Premier Schreyer, 30 Jan. 1974.

111 Letter, Schreyer to Mayor Basil Colomb and Councillors, South Indian Lake, 7 Feb. 1974.

112 Letter, Henteleff to Colomb, 12 Feb. 1974.

113 *South Indian Lake Newsletter*, n.d.

114 Letter, Schreyer to Basil Colomb and Councillors, South Indian Lake, 11 April 1974; cited in *South Indian Lake Newsletter*, n.d.

115 *South Indian Lake Newsletter*, n.d.

116 Letter, Robert E. Dysart to Buchwald, 9 April 1974. On 25 February, 1974, Henteleff articulated these concerns in a letter to Schreyer, noting that the government seemed to be of the view that its position, especially regarding possible future legal action, would be greatly compromised if Buchwald and Henteleff were allowed to act as advisors to the community (Letter, Henteleff to Schreyer, 25 Feb. 1974).

117 Letter, Henteleff to Colomb, 26 March 1974.

118 Letter, Henteleff to Buchwald, 12 July 1974.

119 Letter, Henteleff to Basil Colomb, the Community of South Indian Lake, and all our Plaintiffs, 23 Aug. 1974.

120 Resolution on Churchill River Diversion, by Chiefs and Representatives of Northern Manitoba, 2 Feb. 1973.

121 Minutes, Flood Committee Meeting, 2 March 1974.

122 Personal interview with Yude Henteleff, Winnipeg, 9 June 1986.

123 Letter, Henry Spence, Chief of Nelson House Indian Band, to Chiefs and Councils of Cross Lake, Norway House, York Landing, Split Lake, Nelson House and Brochet, 4 March 1974.

124 Minutes, Provincial-Hydro-Northern Representatives Meeting, Thompson, 23 April 1974.

125 *South Indian Lake Newsletter*, n.d.

126 Statement, Northern Flood Committee (NFC), Thompson, n.d.

127 Minutes, NFC Meeting, Thompson, 14 May 1974.

128 Letter, Tom Nepitabo, Vice-President, North Region, Manitoba Indian Brotherhood, to Schreyer, 17 May 1974.

129 Letter, Chrétien to Henry Spence, 29 May 1974.

130 The establishment of the federal Office of Native Claims in 1973 was one product of this change in attitude. However, at this time the federal government lacked a policy to deal with intervention on behalf of Indian claims that fell outside the domain of the office. Hence, while Indian Affairs had been sensitized to aboriginal rights issues as a result of the Calder case, it was unable to fully support the activities of bodies such as the Northern Flood Committee that did not fit the policy. See: Hickling-Johnston Management Consultants, *Interventions in Support of Indian and Inuit People* (Ottawa: DIAND, 1979), 30–31.

131 Letter, Chrétien to Schreyer, 29 May 1974.

132 Notes of Meeting, Thompson, 29 May 1974. At a meeting of the NFC on 7 June 1974, this problem was addressed. According to the minutes: "There may be a problem because funding is coming from Indian Affairs yet there are non-status representatives on the committee. It should be understood that there will have to be a greater number of status representatives since Indian Affairs is providing funds. This is the ONLY reason for this. What the committee does not want to happen is that in several months someone will try to break up the committee by saying that the status Indian members are running the whole show. There are more status members for the single reason that in this way the committee can be funded more easily" [emphasis original].

133 Letter, Schreyer to Chrétien, 4 June 1974.

134 Notes of NFC Meeting, Thompson, 29 May 1974.

135 Letter, NFC to C. Jaworski, Manitoba Hydro, 11 June 1974; Letter, Henry Spence, NFC, to all Chiefs of Manitoba, 12 June 1974; Letter, Henry Spence

to NFC members, 21 June 1974.

136 Letter, Leonard Courchene, for Henry Spence, to Charles Huband, 24 June 1974.

137 Letter, Huband to Schreyer, 5 July 1974.

138 Hickling-Johnston, *Interventions in Support of Indian and Inuit People*, 17.

139 Minutes, NFC Meeting, 7 June 1974.

140 *Manitoban*, Special Supplement, Nov. 1974, 3.

141 Letter, Schreyer to Prime Minister Pierre Trudeau, 31 July 1974. Reprinted in *Native Studies Review* 1, no. 2 (1985): 101–106. In contrast, the lawyers for South Indian Lake and the NFC argued that the 1966 agreement did not give Hydro a *carte blanche* to flood Indian lands.

142 Letter, W. Steward Martin to Huband, 31 July 1974.

143 Letter, Huband to Spence, 20 Aug. 1974.

144 Letter, Judd Buchanan, Minister, Indian and Northern Affairs, to Huband, 30 Sept. 1974.

145 Letter, Buchanan to Henry Spence, 30 Sept. 1974.

146 Letter, Huband to Martin, 16 Aug. 1974.

147 Ibid., 26 Sept. 1974, 15 Oct. 1974.

148 W. Steward Martin, Position Paper Regarding Strategy for Negotiations with Department of Indian and Northern Affairs, 1 Aug. 1975; cited in Tritschler, *Commission of Inquiry*, 215–216.

149 Minutes of NFC Meeting in Thompson, 23 Feb. 1975.

150 Tritschler, *Commission of Inquiry*, 213.

151 Letter, D'Arcy McCaffrey to Martin, 25 April 1975.

152 Letter, Schreyer to Residents of Northern Manitoba, 13 May 1975.

153 Ibid.

154 Ibid., 31 Jan. 1975. Paradoxically, these "benefits" actually served to increase the economic hardships experienced by the people. As one resident lamented, "Hydro promised us a new town, but they didn't say how much it was going to cost us" (interview with author, 5 July 1982).

155 Press Release. Interchurch Task Force on Northern Flooding, June 1974.

156 Report of the Panel of Public Enquiry into Northern Hydro Development. Appendix A. Transcript of Hearings, 22 Sept. 1975, 106–116.

157 Submission by the Sperling Citizens Group. Report of the Panel of Public Enquiry into Northern Hydro Development. Appendix A. Transcript of Hearings, 23 Sept. 1975, 131.

158 Report of the Panel of Public Enquiry into Northern Hydro Development. Appendix A. Transcript of Hearings, 23 Sept. 1975, 13.

159 Ibid., 59–60.

160 Tritschler, *Commission of Inquiry*, 216.

161 Hickling-Johnston, *Interventions in Support of Indian and Inuit People*, 18.

162 Memorandum, L.A. Bateman, Chairman and Chief Executive Officer, Manitoba Hydro, to J.J. Arnason, General Manager, Corporate Operations, Manitoba Hydro, 9 July 1976; cited in Tritschler, *Commission of Inquiry*, 216.

163 Hickling-Johnston, *Interventions in Support of Indian and Inuit People*, 19.

164 Ibid., 20.

165 Ibid.

166 Letter, Schreyer to Trudeau, 22 June 1977.

167 Hickling-Johnston, *Interventions in Support of Indian and Inuit People*, 21.

168 Warren Allmand, Minister of Indian Affairs and Northern Development, August 1977; from a testimonial plaque commemorating the signing of the Northern Flood Agreement which hangs in the NFC office in Winnipeg.
169 Northern Flood Agreement, 1976, 2.
170 Ibid., 72.
171 Ibid., 13–14.
172 Ibid., 40.
173 Ibid., 3.
174 Personal interview with Ken Young, Winnipeg, 13 Aug. 1986.
175 It is not my purpose in this book to examine in detail the mechanics of the Northern Flood Agreement. Such an undertaking, essential to our understanding of all aspects of hydro development as they relate to northern Native people, must wait.
176 Tritschler, *Commission of Inquiry*, 218.
177 Ibid.
178 Ibid.
179 Personal interview with Ken Young, Winnipeg, 13 Aug. 1986.
180 Tritschler, *Commission of Inquiry*, 209.
181 Ibid., 357.
182 Ibid., 220.
183 Ibid., 212.
184 Ibid., 219–220.
185 Ibid., 7.
186 Manitoba Hydro. Property Department. Registered Trapline Program, 1975.
187 Ibid. Commercial Fishermen's Assistance Program, 1978.
188 The author was involved in research on the commercial fishery for two summer seasons, 1981 and 1982, and had ample opportunity to discuss with the fishermen the issue of compensation negotiations. The description presented here is derived from these informal conversations.
189 Personal interview with Ken Young, Winnipeg, 13 Aug. 1986.
190 Claim no. 45. NFC, 8 March 1984.
191 Personal interview with Ken Young, Winnipeg, 13 Aug. 1986.
192 Agreement, between the Members of the South Indian Lake Trapper's Association Inc. and the Manitoba Hydro-Electric Board, and Her Majesty The Queen in Right of the Province of Manitoba, 1985.
193 Agreement, between the Southern Indian Lake Commercial Fishermen's Association Inc. and Manitoba Hydro, 21 Feb. 1984, 5.
194 South Indian Lake Community Council Resolution, 7 Jan. 1983.
195 Letter, Mayor Steve Ducharme to Andy Miles, Department of Northern Affairs, 5 March 1984.
196 *Winnipeg Free Press*, 8 Dec. 1984.
197 The author was a member of this board as a delegate representing South Indian Lake.
198 Personal interview with William Dysart, South Indian Lake, 18 Dec. 1986; personal interview with Donny Dysart, South Indian Lake, 17 Dec. 1986.
199 Shawinigan Consultants Inc., "Augmented Flows at Southern Indian Lake. An Analysis of the Water Regime and the Feasibility of an Environmental Impact Assessment." Final Report to Manitoba Department of Northern Affairs. Winnipeg, 1987, 3.

200 Press release issued by South Indian Lake. "South Indian Lake Augmented Flow Study Released," 28 Oct. 1987.
201 *Winnipeg Free Press*, 29 Oct. 1987.
202 Telephone interview with Colin Gillespie, NFC lawyer, 11 Aug. 1986; telephone interview with Leon Mitchell, 11 Aug. 1986.
203 Personal interview with Ken Young, Winnipeg, 13 Aug. 1986.

CHAPTER 6

1 Testimony by Walter Mink, in *Report of the Panel of Public Enquiry into Northern Hydro Development*. Appendix A. Transcript of Hearings, Winnipeg, 22 Sept. 1975.
2 See, for instance: James B. Waldram, "Relocation and Social Change among the Swampy Cree and Métis of Easterville, Manitoba" (Thesis, University of Manitoba, 1980); "The Impact of Hydroelectric Development upon a Northern Manitoba Native Community" (Dissertation, University of Connecticut, 1983).
3 J.E. Chamberlin, *The Harrowing of Eden: White Attitudes Toward North American Natives* (Toronto: Fitzhenry and Whiteside, 1975), 8.
4 Mel Watkins, "Dissenting Comment on Final Report," in *Report of the Panel of Public Enquiry into Northern Hydro Development* (Winnipeg: Interchurch Task Force on Northern Flooding, 1976), 86.
5 The Métis "colonies" of Alberta are an exception to this, although they were not formed until the early twentieth century. And, of course, many Métis never actually received scrip.
6 While the area around the Pinebluff Indian Reserve has been affected to some extent by the Squaw Rapids Dam, there is no indication that concern was ever expressed for the Indian people prior to the project's construction. In effect, the Indians were relocated from the fringe of the impact area into the core of the impact area just prior to the completion of the dam.
7 Thomas R. Berger, *Northern Frontier, Northern Homeland. The Report of the Mackenzie Valley Pipeline Inquiry*. 2 vols. (Ottawa: Supply and Services, 1977).
8 Robert Bourassa, *Power from the North* (New York: Simon and Schuster, 1986).
9 Mark Nichols, "Selling Canadian Power to the States," *Maclean's* 99, no. 7 (1986): 10–12
10 Ibid., 10.
11 *Saskatoon Star-Phoenix*, 7 April 1987.
12 Doug Smith, "The Shaping of Limestone," *Maclean's* 99, no. 32 (1986): 34.
13 Ian Mulgrew, "Land of Power and Glory," *Report on Business Magazine* (March 1986): 37.
14 Nichols, "Selling Canadian Power to the States," 10.
15 "Powerful Connections: Damning Our Rivers for Uncle Sam," *Business World*, written and produced by Catherine Holt, CBC Radio, 20 March 1986.
16 *Globe and Mail*, 6 Feb. 1986.

Index